THE
ROBERT MITCHUM
STORY

'It sure beats working'

THE
ROBERT MITCHUM
STORY

'It sure beats working'

MIKE TOMKIES

W. H. ALLEN · LONDON & NEW YORK
A division of Howard & Wyndham Ltd
1972

Printed in Great Britain by
The Northumberland Press Ltd, Gateshead on Tyne 8
for the publishers
W H Allen & Co. Ltd, 43 Essex Street, London WC2R 3JG
Bound by Richard Clay (The Chaucer Press) Ltd, Bungay.

ISBN 0 491 00962 3

To Vin and Bettie

Contents

	Acknowledgments	9
	Preface	11
1	Fatherless—the hard early years	17
2	The boy hobo. The chain gang and near starvation	29
3	Escape—to a lasting love. Years on the bum and boxing for meals	41
4	Professional stargazing, an odd wedding, and sudden blindness	53
5	Busting a vicious bronco—and into movies. 'A hundred bucks a week and all the horse manure I can take home'	67
6	Hollywood's newest star and biggest rebel. 'Paint my eyes on my eyelids man, and I'll walk through it'	79
7	Marijuana—police raid and arrest	89
8	Suspense, trial delays and final sentence	101
9	The prisoner	110
10	Aftermath and exoneration. Broke—but the world forgives. 'He never whined'	118
11	The reluctant brawler and the perverse non-conformist. 'If they treat me like an animal, I'll behave like an animal'	128
12	A proof of fine acting, a fallen bra on the Riviera, and 'just a bit of horseplay'	144
13	A rival to Harry Belafonte?	156

7

14 The husband and father. 'I'm not safe to be
   let loose!'   169
15 Quiet life on the farm—and a sock in the eye
   in Ireland   179
16 Critic bashing, with elephants and the Masai
   in Africa, and farm life begins to pall   192
17 'I don't care where I live as long as the roof
   doesn't leak'   202
18 'If you'll just do this wretched little film of
   ours, we'll pay your funeral expenses'   215
19 The Actor   226
20 On women and sex   236
21 The Man   242
   Appendix: Filmography   260
   Index   267

There are two eight-page sections of
photographs in the text.

Acknowledgments

Among the many sources from which he has drawn to help prepare this book, the author would like to acknowledge the help obtained from minor Robert Mitchum quotations recorded by journalists in various articles and news reports since the mid-Forties. Many such quotes coincide with or have been confirmed in the author's interviews with Mr Mitchum over the years, and several others have indeed been duplicated by other journalistic reports over the same period. As far as reasonably possible the initial sources have been acknowledged in the body of the book itself, but the author hopes the following acknowledgments will complete the formal list, names being arranged in alphabetical order: Susan Barnes (*Sunday Express*), Jack Bentley (*Sunday Pictorial*), Bill Davidson (*Saturday Evening Post*), Victor Davis (*Daily Express*), Joan Dew Schmitt (*You*), Hedda Hopper (Syndicated column), *Hollywood Reporter*, Helen Lawrenson (*Esquire*), David Lewin (*Daily Mail*), *Los Angeles Daily News*, *Los Angeles Herald Examiner*, *Los Angeles Herald Express*, *Los Angeles Times*, Roderick Mann (*Sunday Express*), Bernard McElwaine (*Sunday Pictorial*), Gerald McKnight (*Sunday Pictorial*), Robert Mitchum (his own written plea for probation in 1949), Aline Mosby (UPI), *Motion Picture Magazine*, Louella Parsons (Syndicated column), *Photoplay* magazine, Gene Ringold (his Filmography up until 1965), Fred Robbins (Syndicated column), Robert Robinson (*Sunday Graphic*), Lloyd Shearer (*Parade* magazine), Sidney Skolsky (Syndic-

9

ated column), *Time Magazine*, Tim Tyler (*Time and West Magazines*), *Variety*, Tony Wells (*To-day*), Dwight Whitney (*TV Guide* magazine), Earl Wilson (*Syndicated column*), Donald Zec (*Daily Mirror*). Particular thanks are due to Miss Bonnie Rothbart and staff of the Motion Picture Academy Library in Hollywood, the staff of the British Film Institute in London, and above all to Mr John Mitchum who, in a memorable day, gave generously of his time and whose early life anecdotes helped make the book more alive than it might possibly have been.

Preface

'The reason they're not developing characters like me in films any more,' drawls Robert Mitchum, denigrating himself as usual, 'is because it's against the law. I've survived because I work cheap and don't take up too much time.'

As he reluctantly turns to sign some business papers pushed under his nose by his secretary, I take a good look at this sardonic, complex man who despite a trouble-filled and tempestuous life still survives at the top of the Hollywood tree. 'A caged lion with a poet's soul,' he has been called.

Robert Mitchum is probably the only man in the world with a legitimate income of over a million dollars a year who has served three jail sentences: seven days on a chain gang in Georgia for vagrancy in 1933 when he was a mere boy, two days after a family squabble in 1945, and fifty days on a narcotics charge in 1949, when the mere word 'marijuana' seemed the very embodiment of evil.

Despite such obviously sensational milestones in his thirty year career, Mitchum is one of the few stars left whose name alone will pull audiences into a movie theatre. He has lasted through eighty-four films, the era of the powerful movie moguls, the panic years of selling out to TV and the fractured years of the trend-catching independents.

It still amazes him that people go to see his films. He never does himself. 'Movies bore me, especially my own,' he growls. An expert in self-disparagement, he can top

11

anyone else seeking to put him down.

'I know the secret of my appeal,' he once said. 'I bring a ray of hope to the great unwashed. The typical Mitchum fan is full of warts and dandruff. He sees me up there and he thinks, "If that bum can make it, I can be President of the United States." I've lasted because I trade on public amazement. People pay to see my films so they can marvel and say, "Is that old son of a bitch still there?" '

The finest minds in the film world aren't fooled by such devastating nonchalance—top men such as David Lean and Robert Bolt wanted him and no one else, and they waited for weeks to star him in *Ryan's Daughter*. Producers and directors know that Mitchum is one of the finest screen actors alive today.

He is an extraordinary man, the world's most enigmatic star, with a humor so ironically dry it frequently escapes the less subtle minds around him. Long before he broke into movies, at the age of twenty-five, his life was as indigenously early American as the fictitious adventures of Tom Sawyer or Huckleberry Finn. At fourteen, after a rebellious and poverty-stricken childhood, he became a rod-riding hobo during the Depression, a mine worker, tree planter, dishwasher, longshoreman, truck loader, professional boxer, song writer and, finally, sheet-metal worker.

Ever since Mitchum won his first job, in a Hopalong Cassidy movie in 1942, by mastering a vicious horse that threw him three times, he has had the most rumbustious career of any Hollywood star. Back in the early days his refusal to toe any studio policy line or to be part of the accepted Hollywood scene baffled many film chiefs. Frequently they rang his agents to complain, 'He acts like he doesn't want the job.' He's basically telling the truth when he says he never changed anything but his underwear since first arriving in Hollywood on a freight train.

Mitchum was, when needled, a doughty brawler in his youth. In 1951 he knocked out a champion boxer who picked on one of his friends in a bar. In 1956 three husky sailors went for him in a Tobago hotel; all three were soon thankful to be rescued by the U.S. Navy shore patrol. Despite his reputation, Mitchum never personally *liked* violence, and today, a more gentle, mature man, he wouldn't become involved in such physical disputes. 'Hitting a man never proves anything,' he says.

Despite his flamboyant, careless image, Mitchum is reliable. He has never been known to be late on a film set. And not only does he know his own dialogue pat, but usually everyone else's words, too. He has been known to drink all night and never fluff a line the next day.

It was shortly after his fifty-fourth birthday, in 1971, that I last met him. As he walked into his executive offices on Hollywood's Sunset Boulevard, I stared in disbelief— he was wearing a tailored silk shirt, tight pants, fashionable hairstyle, and trendy Le Mans sunglasses. When I'd met him a few years earlier, he had been paunchy, jowly, gray-bearded. He now looked impossibly fit, trimmed down to around a 190 pounds, the huge shoulders still taut and powerful, and except for the scars around his eyes, he looked like a man fifteen years younger.

Somehow we began talking about marijuana. 'I take it you're not still on pot?' I said.

He gave me a look, reached down suddenly and flipped me a hand-rolled cigarette.

'Oh, yeah? Try that.'

To my astonishment Mitchum had, just like that, 'laid a joint' on me. What made it more surprising was that he had not expected to see me. Having failed to see him in Pennsylvania, where he had been filming, I was in his office prising details from his secretary/manager when he just happened to walk in.

'Is this the real stuff?' I asked him.

'How would *you* know?'

I tried it. It was the real stuff. I asked him if he was going to have one. He held up the mug of ice-cold beer his secretary had handed him upon his entrance. 'Beer doesn't need a mix,' he said. He didn't smoke.

Since his being jailed on marijuana charges in 1949 had been one of the most sensational events in his controversial life, I asked Mitchum for his views about marijuana today. Is he for or against the legalization of pot?

It was a ticklish question, and he paused before answering. But when his answer came it was hardly that of a respectable millionaire, a pillar of the establishment.

'I don't see any reason for legalization,' he said. 'One problem is you can't organize it very well. It's very difficult to grade it. Alcohol consists of one pure basic spirit. The purer the alcohol, the more tax they put on it. But how do you do that with pot? Say you pay 50 cents a package; you don't know whether it's lemon seed or what it is. You can't control the strength, the quality, it's difficult.'

I expressed the opinion that marijuana only had the effect of a mild sedative. 'It's no worse than alcohol, which can rot your liver and kill you.' I suggested.

'Often does,' he replied.

'Certainly, but pot doesn't seem to have done you any harm.' He really did look healthy.

'It may have,' he said guardedly. 'Who's to say? But I'll tell you one thing. It can get you in jail! And if you use it, be damned careful selecting your companions.' He paused reflecting. 'When I was a kid hoboing around this country, it grew on every countryside track and railway. All the bums I moved with rolled it—not much sense in picking up cigarette butts when this stuff grew free all over the south.

'Through the Prohibition days it became the poor man's whiskey. He could buy a gunnysack full of it for 25 cents. Then came repeal of Prohibition. (Marijuana became illegal in America during the late 1930s.) Naturally, the big boys moved in on it. Then came the protection rackets, the undercover organizations, and it suddenly became big business with all kinds of cross-effects and illegal organizations, runners, fixers and so forth. The big setup. It's become big business, and of course the law had to step in.

'But today the Indians still use it just as they always did —west of the Mississippi and on across. Hell, they use it in their peace pipes.... It's like Louis Armstrong said: "The last time they passed the peace pipe around no one inhaled." And he was so right because all it does is make you relaxed and peaceful and love everybody.'

Even for Hollywood, Mitchum can be termed a hard case. A true hippie nearly thirty years before it was fashionable, he is the last of the original rebels, one who never became pretentious. This partly explains, apart from his appeal as an actor, why he is admired by both women *and* men. Another reason he has outlasted most top stars of his era is that he's the only one with whom the younger generation can really identify—and not only because he is a rebel or was busted for pot before any of them were born. When he threw me that cigarette, it was just Mitchum fooling around. He likes to put people on the spot, especially interviewers. And to bracket him with marijuana or the more sensational aspects of his life, though it is a natural and perhaps inevitable approach, is to miss much of Mitchum.

Behind those downward drooping eyebrows that seem to have been cleft by an axe, lurks a keen, wry intelligence, a sensitivity that has inspired him to write short stories, music (he once had an oratorio produced at the Hollywood Bowl), and poems. Some of his poetry is beautiful and intricate, though most of it is unfinished. Three times he has recorded songs in his soft baritone that have reached the top of the charts. One of them. 'Thunder Road', he wrote himself.

Another unusual fact about this highly contradictory man is that he's the only top star from his era who is still happily married to the girl he wed *before* he became an actor. He met dark-haired Dorothy Spence back home in Delaware when he was only sixteen, and he married her in 1940.

I worked in celebrity journalism for fifteen years, and during that time I met nearly every major star of the last twenty years. This book stems from the fact that of all the personalities I encountered, Mitchum was the only one who really baffled me. Indeed, his multifaceted character perplexes most who meet him.

Mitchum did not cooperate personally—although I've interviewed him journalistically several times over the years. On three occasions he's been asked about writing his life story. The first time he said, 'What for? The Los Angeles police have it all on file.' The second time he replied, 'No way. Everybody would have to leave town! Besides, I've had trouble enough.' And the third time he told me, 'I can't spell. Anyway, I think it would have little value.'

Robert Mitchum's story has considerable value, not only for its wealth of extraordinary experience or because it is intrinsically entertaining, but because of the humane wit, warmth and humor of the man himself.

The diametrically opposed tensions in Mitchum, always in conflict and yet overall strangely in harmony, have made up a character of unusual force. Robert Mitchum is a man who has won a uniquely personal triumph.

I

Fatherless—the hard early years

On a winter morning in the big railroad center of Charleston, South Carolina, a detachment of soldiers was busy with the task of keeping the trains moving. It was 1919, and the army had been detailed to keep as many normal services going as possible in the face of a wave of industrial strikes.

In the marshaling yard, soldier James Mitchum moved forward to perform his duties as brakeman. Stepping between the couplings, he unhooked the steam engine and its carriages from a set of boxcars and quickly gave the okay sign to a nearby colleague. The man immediately signaled the engineer-driver, another soldier, to go ahead.

But he gave the wrong signal. Instead of going ahead the driver backed up. James Mitchum was caught between the couplings. The huge iron buffers crashed together, completely crushing one side of his body.

As they heard Mitchum's cry and the shouts of his colleague, other soldiers dropped their tools and ran to help. Miraculously, Mitchum, a man of iron will, was still alive and conscious. Gasping with pain, he asked to be taken home to his wife, who was then seven months pregnant with their third child. Handling him as carefully as they could, the men hurried Mitchum back to the married quarters where, forty-five minutes after the accident, he died in his wife's arms.

At home with Mrs Ann Gundarson Mitchum on the day James was brought in mortally wounded, were her two children—daughter Julie and eighteen-month-old Robert

Charles, the man the world knows today as film star Robert Mitchum.

Shortly after the tragedy Mrs Mitchum returned with her children to her home town of Bridgeport, Connecticut, where she gave birth prematurely to her baby, a son she named John. Although the government paid her a compensation pension until each child was eighteen, it was a small one, hardly enough for rent and the barest food necessities. Mrs Mitchum had to provide for her children as best she could.

She obtained work, first as a photographer's assistant, later as a linotype operator on the local newspaper, the *Bridgeport Post-Telegram*. For the first few years she shared a house with her own mother, until young John was also established in school, at which time her mother moved to a farm that her seafaring husband had bought for her at Woodside, near Felton, Delaware.

The Mitchum children went to the McKinley Grammar school in Bridgeport and right from the start young Robert, an intelligent, nervous child, revealed a defiant nature, which frequently had him in trouble with his teachers. It is on record that he ran away from home at the age of seven and got as far as New Haven before he was found, brought back, and punished.

Some explanation of this early rebelliousness may lie in his unusual lineage, for Robert, who was born on 6 August 1917, certainly has a volatile mixture of blood in his veins. James Mitchum was of Scots-Irish descent on his father's side, and his mother was a full-blooded Blackfoot Indian. A short, wiry man, James had possessed a pugnacious temperament (although he only weighed 148 lbs he and his brother had a standing boast they could lick any *three* men in Bridgeport!) but this had always been offset by an exuberant good humor, plus an ability to play almost any musical instrument, which had made him a popular man.

Robert's mother was a Norwegian, born in Christiania (now Oslo). She had arrived with *her* mother, sister and brother in America at the age of nine, to join up with her father, a Norwegian steamer captain.

As a child Robert obviously suffered emotionally, as did the other children, from the loss of his father. Times were hard, and as his mother worked to better herself and to increase the family income, young Robert had long unsupervised hours during which he endured what he recalls as the 'psychic abrasions, broken windows and bloodied noses of boyhood'.

'I have no recollection of my father, except for a faded photograph memory of him,' he once said. 'My ideas about fathers came from other neighborhood kids. One old man used to whack his kids in the head if they got into a fight— and he'd whack 'em in the head again if they lost. Another made home-brew beer and elderberry wine. I was about eight then, and the kids used to sell us beer at two cents a glass and wine at three cents. Heck, we were drinking elderberry boilermakers at that age.

'I was always jealous of boys who talked about their dads taking them fishing or camping and teaching them how to play ball. We were pretty poor at times too. My brother and I had to share one suit, so we could never go out together.'

Brother John recalls those days too. 'Actually we didn't have a suit until we were quite older,' he says. 'But we shared all our other clothes frequently. I once had a pair of shoes someone gave me which were too long for my feet. They curled upwards like those Persian slippers with a bell on the end. Bob would point me out and say "Look out —there comes the Caliph!"'

The brothers shared many boyhood adventures, some of which ended in near disaster. Once in the dead of winter they went fishing from the Bridgeport docks. It was bitterly cold and they had no overcoats. 'We fished for a time, remembers John, 'but we got no bites at all, then Bob fell into the water. It was colder than hell, and Bob was yelling and he was in dire straits because the bank was sheer mud. I was too young and couldn't reach him, but finally a Portuguese fisherman came and pulled him out. We then had to walk all the way home. He was soaked to the skin, and his clothes were turning to ice on him. Just then the kid who'd been fishing with us, a guy called Harry Greenbaum, came up and said "Oh Bob, did you get vet?" This got Bob so goddamn mad it kept him warm all the way home. "Did I get vet!" he kept saying in fury.'

As a child Robert Mitchum was rather thin, not particularly strong, and acutely sensitive. For a time he felt somewhat overshadowed by sister Julie, who became a school monitor and first drew attention to the Mitchums' modest ménage by her excellence at dancing and the dramatic arts at local performances. At the time, mostly in an effort to please his mother, Robert began to write poetry. Some of his efforts, such as 'A Chreestmus Pome' and 'A War Poem,' were published in the local paper when he was nine. He was interviewed and photographed and, as he recalls, 'This small spotlight on our material impoverishment inspired in me an introspection ever at odds with my desire for expression.'

Despite being a bright pupil, he became more and more difficult to handle at school and was soon involved in a series of pranks that had the school authorities complaining to his mother. On one occasion, however, he was blamed for a disastrous fire which had not been his fault —as his brother John remembers:

'We lived half a block from a big ice cream factory, which was a thriving concern. At that time I was going to be a big explorer and hunter. One windy day I got some potatoes and built a big bonfire in the backyard. The idea was I'd roast the potatoes, pretending I was on safari. I lit the fire and the wind caught all my embers and carried them over to the ice cream factory, set fire to all the stacked up crates, and burned the whole four-story factory right down to the ground.

'As I was sitting on the pavement outside the house watching the fire, the police came up and asked me "Do you have any idea who started this fire?" I said "Yes, my brother. He's always doing things like this. That's the kind of boy he is." They finally traced and captured him but fortunately he could prove he was twelve blocks away at the time. And luckily they never came back to question me. I guess I lied pretty good at that age! But Bob came home and beat the hell out of me. I had thought that since neither of us was a suspect, we could let the whole thing drop, but he didn't look at it that way.'

Incidents like this were enough to give Mrs Mitchum premature gray hairs. Faced with the demands of her job, she occasionally sent the children to spend their holidays with Robert's grandparents on their farm in the quiet countryside of Delaware.

In 1927, by which time she had been promoted to proof reader, Mrs Mitchum married again. Her new husband was Hugh Cunningham-Morris, the feature editor of the *Post-Telegram*.

By any standards former Colonel Cunningham-Morris —known affectionately to the Mitchum family today as The Major—was an extraordinary man with an unusual background. A virile Englishman from a West Country family of high traditions, he volunteered for the Royal Navy before World War I but was rejected because he was only sixteen. He then signed aboard a merchant ship as an apprentice, but after two years he jumped ship in Australia and became a circus bareback rider under the name of St Elmo the Great. He was still there when the war broke out, so, like all true Englishmen of the day, he immediately sailed back and joined Winston Churchill's 'Wavy Navy' and was sent ashore in Belgium. In the battle he was wounded in the thigh by a machine gun bullet. He recovered and was sent back behind the German lines as a spy. Walking unchallenged through the German lines, he became a boot black in a small Belgian town. One day he was cleaning an officer's boots, and he discovered that the man was Baron von Richtofen, the great German ace pilot, whom he had once previously met in London. Richtofen recognized Cunningham-Morris, but being the gentleman that an officer was in those days, he refused to give him away. Cunningham-Morris escaped back through the German lines in a wicker basket covered with cabbages, on the flanks of a donkey.

Back in England once more, he helped to conceive the idea of towing dirigible observation balloons behind destroyers to detect German submarines in the English Channel. Shortly after this project was established, he joined the Camel Corps. One of the many stories with which 'The Major' regaled the Mitchum family in those early days concerned how, in the campaign against the Bedouins and the Turks, he charged into a Bedouin camp —and a one-pounder gun shell took his camel's head off. 'So I lay under the bloody beast and watched my men rout the enemy,' he told them.

Before the war ended, Cunningham-Morris, who was an immensely persuasive man with connections in high places, somehow contrived to join the Royal Air Force. But here his luck ran out. He was shot down while flying as an observer in a plane over North Africa. As he was parachuting to safety, a flak shell burst near him and blew a hole in his stomach. He landed in the desert and lay there until a medic found him. At first the doctor thought he was dead. As he bent down to push some protruding intestine back into place, Cunningham-Morris, despite the pain, managed to grin, and the astonished medic had him rushed back to the nearest hospital tent.

After the war Cunningham-Morris emigrated first to Canada, then to America in 1923. He went back into newspaper work.

'A totally fearless, indomitable man with a tremendous personality—and not a nerve in his entire body,' is how John Mitchum described his step-father.

At the time of his marriage to Mrs Mitchum, however, none of this fascinating background made any impression on young Robert, and as children often do, he resented this new man's presence in the home at first. He became increasingly difficult to handle and it was felt he would benefit by spending more time on his grandparents' farm. There, still shy, he scribbled essays and attended the local school.

In 1928 the new Mrs Cunningham-Morris moved the rest of the family to the farm, where she gave birth to her new husband's child, Robert's half sister Carol. This was when the first rumblings of the Depression of the early thirties were being felt, and Cunningham-Morris stayed at his newspaper desk in Bridgeport, sending his family all the money he could spare.

'He took on quite a task, marrying a woman with three children,' Robert said many years later. 'But you know how it is with step-parents. I'm afraid we kids didn't give this one much of a break for a long time. He had a box filled with medals from World War I, photos of himself on camels in Egypt, climbing out of old bi-planes in France, saluting the quarter deck on wind-jammers in Australia. When we were very small, we couldn't understand that he was full of shrapnel and couldn't work hard enough to keep us all together as a family unit. Of course, he was a very interesting man, but I couldn't see it at first.'*

Cunningham-Morris visited his family at the farm whenever he could. On one well-remembered occasion he brought his collie, Bosun, with him. A fox hunt was in progress, and Bosun decided to take part. He soon outstripped the other dogs, caught up to the fox, but instead of attacking it, he ran along with it as if to say 'Hi there, feller. Don't worry, I'll see you out of this.' And after dodging into a wood with the fox, Bosun turned off at a tangent —whereupon all the other hounds followed as he now had the smell of fox on him. This story is still a standard bar tale in Delaware.

All the Mitchums liked music and were, as Mitchum says, 'an around the piano type family for a while'. Of them all, Julie showed the most talent, and at fourteen she was a fully accomplished young entertainer. She obtained a permit to work as a juvenile, left high school, and called herself Miss Annette. When she was offered a good club job in New York, her mother and brothers moved there to be with her. Julie became an active source of family support through her dancing jobs in New York and around Philadelphia.

In New York City Robert was sent to Haaren High School on Tenth Avenue and 59th Street. From the peace of rural Delaware he suddenly found himself precipitated into a tough school in the 'Hell's Kitchen' area of the city. Hefty, belligerent kids of eighteen put their feet up on the desks in front of them, and when teachers said 'Remove them,' they would reply 'Make me.' One day Mitchum found the boy next to him had a bottle of gin in his briefcase.

Virtually in order to survive, Mitchum gradually be-

---

* Mitchum has more than made up for his juvenile omissions, actively supporting his parents since his career began to move, in the early forties.

came as aggressive as any of the youths around him and, when his natural leadership qualities began to emerge, he was soon in trouble. He was threatened once with expulsion for pelting his teacher with a pea shooter.

Through the intervention of his mother he found himself playing a 'G' melody saxophone in the school band instead. Considering his expulsion arbitrary and unfair, Mrs Cunningham-Morris demanded a 'trial' before the school board. During the trial the members of the board adjusted their spectacles and said Robert required 'adjustment'—surely there was *something* in which he was interested. Mrs Cunningham-Morris said there was—music. Robert quick-wittedly said he would like to play the sax, although he'd never played one before. The principal, who recognized young Mitchum's intelligence despite his rebelliousness, obtained a saxophone and gave it to him. To help Robert learn to play it Mrs Cunningham-Morris had to learn to play one herself.

Finally, however, Mitchum was expelled for getting into a fight and for dropping a firecracker into a brass horn in the middle of a quiet passage of the 'Poet and Peasant' overture. As the family continued to move around with Julie, this sort of thing happened in other schools as well.

It was during this transient period that Julie became engaged and married to a boy in the U.S. Navy, later moving with her husband to Long Beach, California. John Mitchum recalls his sister's romance for a rather odd reason:

'Julie's getting married was useful as well as romantic because her husband gave me a fine pair of navy pants with thirteen buttons. I was very proud of them because I could start going to school well dressed. At this time we were living on the fourth floor of a brownstone in New York. I got up one morning, and my pants had disappeared. My mother asked what happened. Bob said, 'I'll tell you what happened. He was careless, so completely careless that he threw them out of the window.' Later I walked down the street and there was this Italian guy, Joey Chickery, in them. I said "Where did you get those trousers?" He said "Your brother sold them to me for fifty cents." So then I had no pants fit to go to school in. My mother finally bought me a new pair for a buck.'

During the early Depression years the Major lost his job in Bridgeport. He stayed there for a while as a freelance writer but finally gave this up and rejoined his family, first in New York, where he also tried to freelance—without much success—and later when they all went back to Delaware.

John Mitchum says of this period: 'There was a long interval between 1932 and 1937 in which literally millions of people were very hard up. God bless the Major, he was really a soldier of fortune and was only truly happy during a war. But in peacetime he was a fish out of water. The first thing to go when times are rough is the arts, so he made very little from his writings.'

There was one occasion the younger Mitchum remembers when the Major broke a personal vow, went out mysteriously, and returned with what was then a large sum of money.

'He was always brilliant at cards, especially poker, but no one had ever seen him play it. There was a reason for this. When he was sailing on the old square riggers, the ship's crew once played a game of poker as they were going around Cape Horn. The idea was that whoever lost would take the watch. The boy who lost took the watch but was swept over the side in the storm and was never seen again.

'The only time we knew the Major to play poker after that was when we were really hard up in the Depression. One day when we were living in Delaware he scrounged fifteen cents together and walked into Dover, and got into a poker game. He came home with forty dollars.'

This was a unique occasion, however, and most of the time the family had trouble making ends meet. Robert, shy, defiant, and introverted throughout most of his adolescence, became restless; when he reached his teens, he began to leave home on lonely wanderings. His parents had a continual problem trying to stop him from playing hooky during the school terms, but during the vacations they became accustomed to his absences.

He didn't mind being on his own at all. From the age of ten he had been an avid reader, and by his teens he had read all of Shakespeare and Wordsworth along with the works of other poets, some of them as obscure as Nathalia Crane, child poet of the twenties, and Mary Austin, a forgotten Californian essayist. He particularly admired the novels of Joseph Conrad and later, of Thomas Wolfe. Like many basically introverted boys, Mitchum discovered that reading could provide an uplifting antidote to the boredom and petty irritations at home. At the age of fourteen he decided to cut out on his own.

'I was a thin ferrety-faced kid,' he once explained. 'What's more, the girls didn't want any part of me. They much preferred my brother John: I was always in trouble anyway, and there just didn't seem to be much to hang around home for, so I took off.'

John Mitchum remembers how Robert was with the local girls. 'I'm convinced that my brother was a dreamer,' he says. 'He put girls on pedestals and was very idealistic about them. He'd find out soon enough that they only had feet of clay after all, and it wounded him deeply. He liked to kiss them but didn't push it any further. I wasn't all that good looking maybe, but I was more relaxed with the girls than he was, more realistic and down to earth.'

Robert's first move was to go out to sea. Claiming to be eighteen, and with falsified seaman's papers to prove it, he talked his way into a job as a deckhand on a salvage boat plying from Fall River, Massachusetts. But the job didn't last long. After one short trip young Mitchum was left on board as nightwatchman when the boat was in harbor. He didn't stay aboard all night and the mate, arriving to find him absent from his post, reported him to his superior.

At the same time the captain learned from one of the seamen that Mitchum was in fact only fourteen years of age. Having Mitchum aboard put him in jeopardy with the child labor laws, and the captain was furious. He sent for Mitchum, verbally keel-hauled him in his cabin, and ordered him to leave the boat.

Mitchum did not know it at the time, but this was the prelude to more than five years of extrordinary adventure.

2

The boy hobo. The chain gang and near starvation

As young Robert Mitchum walked down the gangplank of the salvage boat and stepped onto the dirty dock of Fall River, the captain's rebuke still rang in his ears.

'What the hell,' he thought. 'Did the guy *have* to go on and on like that? So I left the boat for a couple of hours. So I lied about my age. But that was my crime, not his.' Sheepishly he realized that he still had his falsified papers in his hand. He stuffed them into the pocket of his windbreaker with an angry gesture.

Well, at least the captain had grinned a bit at the end —before thrusting his pay into his hands as a parting gift. Hardly a present, though. He'd done a full man's work on that trip. His first and last trip like that, no doubt. Well, it had been good to know he could work alongside full grown men and not be found lacking.

He sat down on a pile of fish boxes, wondering what to do next. Around him lay coils of rope, pools of oil and salty muck, the usual debris of the docks. The shouts of the stevedores unloading crates from the boats vied with the screams of gulls as they flopped into the brackish water looking for scraps.

As he sat there in the shadows of the dark hovering derricks, feeling suddenly alone, one of his favourite lines from his childhood reading came back to him, from Joseph Conrad's *Lord Jim*: 'Loneliness is a hard and absolute condition of existence.'

He smiled to himself, feeling much older than his four-

teen years. He rolled a cigarette and lit it. What now?
He knew one thing—he certainly didn't want to go home.
He didn't want to return to his parents or school or that
life in Woodside, Delaware.

It wasn't that he disliked Hugh Cunningham-Morris.
His stepfather was quite a character; he could tell some incredible stories, despite that odd British way of his. Robert's
was more a rebellious son's vague discontent, a restlessness
compounded from many sources. Mitchum felt he really
didn't fit in at home any more.

Of course, he realized he'd caused his mother some
anxious moments over the past few years—skipping school
the way he had, getting mixed up with the wrong crowd
at school in New York. Then there were the times he'd
got the local teenagers involved in mischievous pranks.

He recalled his mother's worried frown, her sadness as
she tried to understand what was bothering him and tried
to decide what to do with him. Well, he'd solved that by
getting the job on the boat.

And now he'd lost that job. He'd have to find some
work somewhere. He had a desperate desire to stay out
on his own, to prove to himself he could stand on his own
feet.

As he sat there, the hooting of a steam train rose above
the noises of the dock. Again and again the piercing
whistle sounded in his mind, savouring of far-away places,
of escape.

Here, it seemed, lay Mitchum's answer. He would travel
across America, getting whatever odd jobs were available
and gaining whatever experience of life he could. He
would do it the hard way because there was really no other
way open to him.

At first he toyed with the idea of leaving right away,
but he realized quickly that this would be most unfair to
his mother. So he paid a brief visit home to say goodbye.

Some days later he shouldered a pack of the possessions he'd need for survival and set off toward the local railway station.

When he reached it, he dumped his pack outside and inquired about the arrival time of the train that would take him on his way, three thousand miles to California— which to all eastern Americans in those days was still the proverbial land of milk and honey.

He didn't make the mistake of trying to board the train at the station itself. Instead he quietly went outside, retrieved his pack, and set off down the side streets until he reached a deserted part of the track east of the station. There, in the bushes, he waited.

In those days trains pulled freight cars as well as passenger cars, and Mitchum knew that the freights were usually at the back of the trains. There was less chance of discovery if he 'rode the rods' beneath the freights.

When the train hissed and clanked to a stop, Mitchum gave a quick look to make sure he hadn't been seen, then he climbed aboard a thick girder beneath a boxcar at the train's rear. Using his old raincoat to lie on, his pack as a pillow, he also took the precaution of strapping himself to the girder with one of the straps from his pack.

He knew he was in for a rough ride, but he had no idea just how tough it really was to be. As the train gathered momentum and screamed through the night, he thought the hellish din would drive him out of his mind. He tore pieces from a handkerchief, wet them with saliva and stuffed them in his ears to drown out the noise. When it rained, he was stung all over by the hissing dust and dirt.

After a few hours he had had enough. He left the train when it pulled in to a station and spent the night sleeping outdoors.

What he hadn't realized was that the real 'rod-riding'

31

days had ended a few years earlier; now the boxcars were constructed without the great interlacing of rods underneath that had harboured many a hobo in the twenties. From then on he tried to avoid riding the girders as often as possible. Other hobos told him later that they only rode the girders when the railway police, or 'shagmen', were working their way along the train roofs looking for them.

Sometimes Mitchum searched along the rear of the trains until he found a boxcar with an unlocked door, then he sneaked in with whatever freight it carried—often cattle—and bedded down on the floors. At other times, in fine weather, he climbed into the open gondola cars, which had slatted sides and were open to the skies. For short journeys he'd get behind the coal cars or stand on the couplings of the passenger trains.

Over most of the next five years Mitchum wandered across the length and breadth of America, stealing rides on trucks and trains. In those Depression years jobs were hard to obtain. It was a tough and dangerous life. Long before writer Jack Kerouac gave literary expression to the wandering, dissatisfied generation of the fifties, Mitchum experienced the rich, exhausting, and often humiliating life of the hobo. He found, as many other rebellious youngsters did years later, that a train or a truck hurtling along through the night on a lonely prairie road or track was a kind of magic lantern world for the poor man—isolated, detached, a place where he could come to terms with himself.

Altogether he made nine trips across the huge face of America. 'I rode underneath trains, inside the boxcars and, when I heard a guard coming, on the girders. All over!' Mitchum recalls. 'I made a lot of friends—tramps like myself or railroad cops, with whom guys like me had a running war.'

When he reached California after that first trip, he found even temporary work hard to get. But he eked out a living by hauling slop in run-down cafés, working his way up to become a counter hand. Often at nights, to save money, he slept outdoors. It's not difficult for a man in the warm climate of California to find protected spots to sleep. On the long beaches of Santa Monica and Malibu a man can make his bed in the many windless corners between the rocky sandstone cliffs.

During those traveling years the entire pattern of his life was dictated by the freight trains. Their destinations dictated his. The availability of food and jobs decided the length of his stay.

After the first few months in California he became homesick and he headed back east to visit his family again. On the way back he hopped off a slow freight and found himself in a small town in the Pennsylvanian coal fields. He was wandering around the streets, looking for a cheap rooming house to spend the cold night when an old lady, observing the lost look on his face, invited him in for a meal and gave him a room.

This woman's brother worked down in one of the local mines, and the next morning she gave him a note and sent him to get a job there. Mitchum, whose powerfully framed shoulders were now beginning to fill out with muscle, was hired. He was issued with a pickaxe and a sledgehammer and sent down into the mine with other pit workers.

He took one look at the hot, cramped and fetid tunnel and felt a sudden surge of panic. He did not know at the time that he suffered from acute claustrophobia. The thought of working in that narrow space, where it seemed any moment the walls could cave in on him, filled him with terror.

'The only thing that kept me down there,' he recalled years later to writer Bill Davidson, 'was a huge Polish foreman who weighed 250 lbs. He waved a twenty pound break-out hammer at my head and said "You no quit." Well, I didn't quit but I felt so sick I couldn't eat.'

So every day Mitchum handed the sandwiches the old lady had made for him to the foreman and worked at the coalface as best he could.

At nights there was little to do in the small town except play pool and drink—neither of which in those days was to Mitchum's taste. 'I just stood around on the streets and watched the miners making passes at the local girls.'

He stuck to the job long enough to pay back the woman who had befriended him and to give himself a little pocket money; then he left and paid a brief visit to his family.

After another sojourn in California, Mitchum headed due east across country. He had seen enough of the Salt Lake City-Denver-Kansas City-Indianapolis route, so he decided to ride the freight trains east through the southern states.

It was an even harder trip through Arizona, New Mexico, Texas, Louisiana, Mississippi, and Alabama into Georgia. At every station he had to dodge the more milit-ant railway police of those states. He had to find a place to sleep outdoors and somehow outwit the other, more experienced, hobos, who would have thought nothing of robbing the younger man of his roll if they had half a chance. Once Mitchum woke at dawn to find a traveling companion reaching under his pack for his money. Only a furious barrage of blows from Mitchum made the other man give up the attempt. Afterwards Mitchum gave the hobo five bucks he could ill afford because he felt sorry for the older man. But on that trip he learned never to stay more than a couple of nights in the same area and never sleep in the same spot twice.

'I seemed to be always moving on,' he remembers. 'In

those days motion itself seemed an adequate philosophy for me. I really had no other choice. Moving around like I did, though, I could be just any place, not high maybe but somehow alone and free.'

In Savannah, Georgia, just before his sixteenth birthday he had his first real trouble with the law. To this day Mitchum will occasionally refer to the police as the 'fuzz'. And his instinctive suspicion of many forms of authority, his hatred of hypocritical officials, spring directly from this experience in Georgia.

With about a dozen other youths of the road, Mitchum hopped aboard a freight train going south to Jacksonville and Miami. In his pocket he had some thirty-eight dollars —quite a princely sum during the Depression years.

When the train reached Savannah, he felt cold and hungry, so he jumped off to look for something to eat. He had barely had time to look around when a big policeman grabbed his arm and told him to come down to the station.

'What am I supposed to have done?' asked the bewildered Mitchum.

'Vagrancy,' said the cop with a grin that wasn't friendly. 'We don't like you Yankee bums around here.'

'I'm no vagrant,' protested Mitchum, producing a fistful of dollars from his pocket. 'I've got thirty-eight bucks, look.'

The policeman stared at him with dislike. 'Oh, a so-and-so wise guy, eh?' he said, clipping Mitchum with his club, then he ran him into the police station.

Without any preliminary court hearing, Mitchum was kept in a jail cell with eight other men for five days. On the sixth morning he was taken into a courtroom.

As the police brief against him was outlined, Mitchum realized he was listening to a burglary case. Two policemen gave evidence describing a burglar who had robbed a shoe shop—and the description fitted Mitchum exactly.

In a daze he sat and heard the policeman who had arrested him testify that forty dollars had been stolen from the shoe shop and that when he'd picked up Mitchum, he'd still had thirty-eight dollars on him.

He knew then that he was in real trouble. Burglary in Georgia in those days carried a jail sentence of anything from ten to twenty years. Fighting with all his wits to avoid such a sentence, furious at the lies and injustice, Mitchum shot to his feet and asked the judge on what day the burglary had occurred.

'You should know,' replied the judge looking quickly at his papers. 'It was on Wednesday.'

Said Mitchum. 'Your honour, do you know where I was on Wednesday? Heck, I was in *your* jail. I was arrested last Sunday.'

The judge coughed, shuffled his documents, then said 'Well, I guess I can't hold you on that charge, but a nice little indeterminate sentence for vagrancy should straighten you out.'

For a week Mitchum worked in the Chatham County Camp chain gang, repairing road surfaces in the Savannah area. Like the other prisoners, many of whom were Negroes, he was shackled at the ankles and chained to the men on either side of him. This was done whenever a work party was being moved from one job to another. The men were also chained to their beds at night. When they were actually working on the road, the chains were removed— but guards watched them with loaded rifles at the ready.

After the first day and night, Mitchum's ankles were blistered, inflamed and bleeding; just to walk at all was agony. He tried stuffing cloth and paper between his skin and the shackles but the guards soon stopped that. The pain of the shackles was an integral part of the punishment.

On the seventh day as the prisoners were being transported back to the farm, the guards removed their chains, so that the prisoners could do their hut chores more easily. Mitchum, now determined to escape, watched warily. The moment he thought the guards had relaxed their vigilance, he ran.

As he tore across the road and toward the fields and distant woods, he heard the guards start to shout. Then he heard the 'whuff' and thump of rifle bullets as they tore into the ground near his pumping legs—the cracking *sound* of the shots catching up to him later. Terrified that his last moment had come he zig-zagged desperately as he ran, praying that none of the bullets would hit him. Luckily none did.

After the first few shots there was silence. He reached the first clump of trees, oblivious now of the shackle pain in his legs, and poked his head round the trunk for a quick look. To his astonishment no one was chasing him.

'In those days they wouldn't spend fifty cents to catch you if they missed you with a rifle,' Mitchum explains. 'They just went out and rounded up someone else to take your place on the work gang. Probably by telling the same sort of lies they used to get me.' He does admit, in fairness to the Georgian authorities, that he falsified his age when arrested.

After a belly-crawling mile over flat fields, Mitchum ran through some more forest and by nightfall he found himself in a big swamp. It was now too dark to see where he was going so he lay down, covered himself with leaves and branches, and snatched a few hours' sleep.

Waking before dawn, he immediately started running into the swamp, trying desperately to see the firmest route. All day long he kept plunging through the mud and foul smelling ooze, sometimes only ankle deep, sometimes up to his waist. As he ran he saw dozens of dangerous water moccasin snakes, but terrified of being caught and punished, he kept on going.

Plunging through that daunting swamp as he did that second day, saved Mitchum from any possibility of re-arrest, which would have meant a much stiffer sentence, for by the time he came out on the other side he had crossed the border into South Carolina. He didn't realize this at the time, however, and he made his way north as quickly and as inconspicuously as he could.

The memory of that injustice died hard in Mitchum. Even today he bridles angrily at any story of official brutality and dishonesty.

As he worked and hitch-hiked his way up to Delaware, Mitchum experienced many arduous, lonely moments. The bruises and sores on his ankles didn't heal swiftly but he could neither afford expensive treatment nor go to a doctor without arousing suspicion. Instead, he treated his injuries himself with medicine from drugstores, washing them in creek water he *thought* was clean.

Most nights he slept in ditches outside the various towns.

'I tried to tell myself I was really living,' he remembers. 'But on one or two nights I cried myself to sleep, wondering what my mother was thinking.'

One night as he prepared to bed down in yet another roadside ditch, Mitchum wrote a small poem on the back of a postcard. It read:

Trouble lies in sullen pools along the road I've taken
Sightless windows stare the empty street
No love beckons me save that which I've forsaken
The anguish of my solitude is sweet.

For any man who knows what it is to wander alone in the wilds of a large country without a job and without money, and with a dwindling faith in himself, those few simple words strike a chord in the heart. For a mere boy they seem unusually apt and mature.

As he worked his way north during the leanest point of the Depression, reluctant to look for what little work there might be in the towns because his injuries might give his convict status away, Mitchum tasted the bitter fruit of the broke and friendless transient who survives, somehow, beyond the laws and confines of regulated society. Not even the bread lines or the Salvation Army soup kitchens were available to him. He spent his sixteenth birthday in the fields, trying to cook over a campfire the raw vegetables he had stolen from farmers' fields.

It wasn't the physical hardship that now bothered him so much as the sense of isolation, of loneliness. He resolved that when he got home he would stay a few weeks and then leave again—but this time he'd try and take his brother John with him.

It was on this journey that Mitchum had the first of two encounters with pellagra—a deficiency disease characterized by cracking of the skin and, if the malnutrition is continued, insanity and even death.

'I became acquainted with death, with the knowledge that I too would die, very very early,' Mitchum once said. 'I had pellagra twice when I was wandering the face of this continent alone. It was known locally as black tongue fever —from starvation. But I didn't get it too badly.' He paused, then added, 'But it was no one's fault but mine. It just took me longer to wake up than most kids, that's all. I must have been dumber than most to have bummed around the way I did.'

While Mitchum had been absent, his family had moved to a rented home several miles away, in a small hamlet called Rising Sun. Mitchum's grandfather had died suddenly. An uncle had come down from Canada to try running the farm for his widow, but had overreached himself, and the family had lost the place.

When Mitchum finally arrived at the new home, his

mother and brother John were shocked by his pinched and wasted appearance.

'He looked terrible,' remembers John. 'He was white-faced and really in bad shape. His left leg had swelled up huge, as big around as a tree stump, where the shackle marks had let in dirt and poisoned it. Mother rushed him to the doctors. They wanted to cut his leg off, but she said "There's no way you're going to cut his leg off." She went out and got herbs from the garden and made big hot poultices, put them round his leg and drew out literally quarts of pus. She bathed his leg and put these poultices on it day and night for a week and finally it drained completely and he got better. He has the scars there even now.'

Within ten days of such treatment, aided by his mother's good solid cooking, Mitchum had recovered his health. But his ankles took longer to recover, and for a while he hobbled round on an old pair of crutches.

As he told his fourteen-year-old brother of his adventures on the road, young John's eyes opened wide with fascination. Naturally at this point John worshipped his adventurous older brother, and as young brothers do, he wanted his approval.

Before Robert had left home, the two boys had gone by bus together from the farm at Woodside to Felton High School, but now John was going to Caesar Rodney High School, at nearby Camden. He was popular there and, although he was only fourteen, he was heavily built and played right guard on the football team.

One day John invited his brother down to visit his school and to meet some of his friends. Mitchum went, still hobbling on his crutches. Perhaps if he'd known of the momentous meeting due to take place that afternoon, he would have left the crutches at home.

3

*Escape—to a lasting love. Years on the bum
and boxing for meals*

Down at the school Mitchum found himself being treated
as the wounded hero. Among John's friends was a tall,
leggy, brown-haired girl of fourteen called Dorothy
Spence, who lived in Camden. Mitchum looked at her, instantly admiring her quiet beauty, and found himself
stricken with shyness.

When they were introduced, Dorothy asked Robert why
he was walking on crutches.

Mitchum, suddenly conscious of the theatricality of the
moment, pulled up his trouser-leg slightly and pointed
to the deep, half-healed scrape marks on his ankles.

'I've just done seven days on a chain gang down south,'
he told her. 'They picked me up for vagrancy. And heck,
those shackles when they cut into your flesh. Poison!
Worse than snake bite!'

Dorothy Spence should have had an inkling right then
of what she was getting herself into, but she just laughed.
This strange, slim boy with the haunted face captivated
her. He seemed completely different from the other boys
she knew. And this included brother John, whom she had
dated a few times.

John grins as he remembers the situation. 'I liked
Dorothy a lot, but I don't know whether I could call her
my girlfriend. There were four girls I kind of liked at that
point but my favourite was a girl called Theda, who used
to come with me behind the corn sheds and do a lot of kissing! But my brother immediately took a great shine to
Dorothy.'

Dorothy herself recalls that first meeting. 'To be perfectly honest I didn't really like him at first,' she once recalled. 'He never thought of paying a compliment like other boys. Instead, he teased. Yet every other boy I knew seemed dull by comparison. I was fourteen when I fell in love with him. We double-dated with his cousin one night and just spent the evening riding around in his cousin's car. And that was it. My family hoped I'd forget him when he left town again, yet somehow I couldn't.'

Within a few weeks, young Robert and Dorothy found themselves in the blissful agonies of teen-age love. 'It didn't really matter what I did or said,' Mitchum remembers, 'we both knew this was it.'

To young John, however, his older brother's romance was a minor tragedy. As he explains:

'As far as I was concerned, it was the worst thing that ever happened because we lived in Rising Sun, which was three miles from Camden. In the dead of winter I'd have to go and sit with him while he sat and courted her. They were very strict in those days in that area with their daughters! Sometimes they sat together half the night, like two dark bumps on a log, and I'd be twiddling my thumbs, bored to death. Then we had to walk the three miles back.

'When it was good weather we'd roller skate the whole distance. Right outside Camden there was a graveyard and a road ran near it. There were so many graves there that the tombstones made a hollow sound as we skated past them. And we skated faster when we got to that area because we felt all the ghouls were after us.

'Bob was a very shy young man in those days. He might be dying for a pee, but he'd never go or admit to wanting to when he was with Dorothy. He might have been absolutely bursting, but he'd doggedly sit there until it was time to leave. Then he'd crash into the bushes near the graves on the way home.'

At this time the United States government launched its New Deal to help cope with the effects of the Depression. Part of its plan was the newly formed Civilian Conservation Corps. It was a brave idea, a way of giving jobs to the unemployed and at the same time performing some essential jobs on the land. For a few months, until July, 1934, Mitchum toiled on a soil reclamation project, digging ditches and planting trees; but he finally grew tired of the regimented working schedules and the civil service mentality of the officials who were his bosses. When he had saved some money, he left with the idea of getting back to California.

Just before he hit the road again he told Dorothy, 'I'll be back for you. I don't know how long it will take, but I'll be back.'

And Dorothy replied simply, 'Okay, I'll be waiting.' She already knew that she was probably going to share her future with this unusual young man.

When he left Delaware, Mitchum took his younger brother with him. They decided to visit their sister Julie, who was living with her naval officer husband in Long Beach.

This time Mitchum devised a smart plan. He was through with taking silly and unnecessary chances—he thought. The two boys hitched from Delaware to the big Grand Central Market in New York City, where all the big trucks went to unload their produce. Finding a truck with Florida license plates, they persuaded the driver to let them ride back with him. In Florida they hitched with a pal of Mitchum's, who had also been in the Conservation Corps, to his home at Elmsley, a small town outside of Birmingham, Alabama. There the boys were treated royally by the family, given delicious meals of southern fried chicken. Young John felt the travelling life was all too good and easy to be true.

Two days later as the two boys were heading out toward California, they ran into trouble. They were hitching along the road when three young men in a 1929 Buick Sedan stopped and picked them up. It wasn't until they got into the car that they realized that all three were a little the worse for wear. The driver and his front seat companion were drunk, and so was the man in the back seat, who was playing a guitar. All three were from the Alabama hills, and no sooner had the Mitchums climbed into the car than the men began heading straight up into the mountains.

'Where you boys going?' they asked.

'We're going to California,' said Mitchum.

'Waal, we don't quite know where that is,' said the driver, 'but we're heading for Royal River, which is west.' The Mitchums said that would be fine. John takes up the story from this point:

'We were just kids really, and we certainly weren't going to argue with three full grown drunk men in a speeding car. We got high into the mountains and they pulled the car up by a sheer cliff. One of them said "This is just about where we hit them." The men then began digging about in the bushes and the weeds by the side of the road. One of them came out with a big jug of moonshine whiskey, and they all took big drinks. They offered it to Bob, who also took a very big swig. Then they offered me the jug. I said, very nobly at fourteen, "I don't drink." The men all laughed and said, "You drink boy or we're going to throw you offa the mountain." What could I do? I also took a big drink of the moonshine. I still remember a little of the next few days.

'They then took us down to Warrior River, to a cabin camp there, and suddenly a man ran out, "Ah don't want you guys here," he yelled. "Ah don't want no part of you. Ah'm gettin' mah shotgun." The driver said, "Ain't

no one goin' to run me outah no cabin camp. Ah'm gettin'
mah pistol." With that he reached into the car and pulled
out a German Luger.

'Next thing we know these guys are shooting it out! I
threw myself down on the floor of the car, and brother
Bob was right there with me. There was no way we were
going to get out with all that gunfighting going on. Finally
the shots die out and the driver climbs back into the car
with his pals and says, "Ain't no son of a bitch ever goin'
tell me what to do," and drove away. We never did find out
what actually happened. We figure he shot the other guy!'

The next thing the Mitchum brothers knew was that
they were in the middle of a noisy barn dance in a school
yard high up in the Alabama mountains. All they had
been trying to do was hitch-hike unobtrusively to California, and suddenly they were among the wildest bunch
of men they'd ever met. The men started fights at the dance,
whistles were blown, and when the sheriff's men arrived,
they high-tailed it out and took the two boys up to their
cabins.

'It was just like a scene from *L'il Abner*,' recalls John.
'All the girls wore dresses made from old cotton flour sacks,
still showing the "Gold Medal" sign right over their
breasts. Their old crone of a mother, who had no teeth,
came by and said "Heh, heh, looks like you boys had too
much tea!" Bob and I just passed out. We fell off the
porch drinking white lightning and went to sleep with all
these razor toothed hogs rooting round us, probably because we smelled so bad!'

The big mistake the Mitchum boys had made was to
disclose the fact that they could also play guitars and sing.
For several days they were virtually the captives of the
men who'd picked them up. Every time they tried to escape
down the dirt road, the men fetched them back in their
cars. Finally they did escape by persuading an old black

man in a café to drive them out while the men were all busy playing pinball.

As the Mitchums now felt hitching was dangerous in that area, they started riding the trains instead. First they stole a ride out to Houston. They soon discovered that riding trains together could be tricky, especially a moving train, because while one might make it, the other could fail to get aboard. Mitchum worked out a plan to cope if they ever lost each other.

'The idea was I'd set five or ten dollars care of general delivery at various places along the route,' he remembers, 'and when we got split up, John could pick up the money, buy sandwiches, go to a local movie, then hop on a train and join me wherever I was heading. The trouble was John didn't have a very good sense of geography in those days, and he'd wind up going somewhere in the opposite direction.'

In the end the brothers lost touch with each other completely. They were in Lake Charles, Louisiana, and were about to board a train due to pull out at any moment. John walked over to get a quick drink from the water tower. As he straightened up he found himself looking straight down the barrel of a .45 automatic held by a Creole railway detective. A town constable had a .38 pistol stuck into his ear. They said four words. 'Get out of town.'

John said, 'I want to get on that train,' which had just started to move slowly away. Robert, who was already aboard, yelled, 'Come on, they won't shoot you.'

'I'm not taking that chance,' shouted John, who had a feeling the policemen *might* just shoot him if he made a dash for it. He watched Mitchum sailing away round the bend before the two cops marched him out of town and told him to 'Git'.

'I had to catch another train at the water station way out of town,' he remembers. 'That one took me to Houston.

Then I got on the wrong train again and ended up in Little Rock, Arkansas. Then I went to Dallas, Texas, where I picked up ten bucks my mother had sent me, and from there I rode to Fort Worth. At that point the rails ended in a spur track so I had to go back to Dallas again. From there I got a cattle car all the way to El Paso. It was a slatted box car with straw on the bottom. That makes for really pleasant sleeping, I can tell you—all that dried up cow dung for 1,800 miles!'

The double brother act didn't stay on the road or the rails for long. Basically the Mitchum brothers are of different temperaments and, after joining John in California and visiting their sister Julie at Long Beach, Mitchum cut out on his own again for a short while. He was still searching for that intangible something, a way of life that would give him his own identity, even though he didn't know what it was. He explored the Pacific seaboard and slept in hobo camps, earning dollars as a dishwasher or casual laborer. He still got picked up for vagrancy sometimes, but in the northwestern states he found the police to be more lenient than they had been to him down in Georgia.

'After a while I began to regard jail as a kind of restful haven,' he recollects. 'At least for the occasional night anyway. I'd get taken in for various petty trespasses against the statutes. But really they were all fancy ways of saying vagrancy.'

In fact, he was beginning to look older; he was no longer in danger of being picked up on the more serious offense of *juvenile* vagrancy. He actually learned to use the police to his own advantage.

'Sometimes when I was cold and hungry I'd just check in at the local police station. Often they'd put me up in a cell overnight. In the morning I'd earn my meal by sweeping up the place.'

Mitchum has told many engaging tales of his traveling

days, but few are more amusing than the time he got mixed up in Washington state with an old Indian in a business called Dognapping. This is how Mitchum once explained it:

'This Indian was terribly fond of dogs, and they liked him too. In fact they liked him so much that everywhere he went they followed him home. So we started taking walks around all the rich residential districts. The dogs would leave their neat little gardens and follow my partner home. We'd wait a couple of days, until the reward notices went up or were put in the local paper; then we'd return the dogs to their grateful owners and collect the money. It was a lot of fun at the time!'

Returning to California, Mitchum moved in with Julie and her husband and brother John in Long Beach and got a job as a longshoreman. In September, 1934, the remainder of the family drove out from the east in a battered old jalopy, and the two families began to live in Julie's small three-room bungalow. Conditions were crowded to say the least. Young John was enrolled in Long Beach's Polytechnic High School, and over the next few months Mitchum went from his longshoreman's job to working as a truck loader and then as a building maintenance and repair man.

It was during this period, Mitchum once disclosed, that he really began to appreciate his stepfather's sterling qualities for the first time. He realized just why Hugh Cunningham-Morris had been a much decorated hero in World War I.

'We both learned to love him, just as we still do now,' John Mitchum says. 'Despite all his fantastic adventures and later hardships, he was always the complete gentleman. He gave us both something marvelous to to live up to —class, I guess. He left me with a total admiration for the British, although he never preached. Anyone who could be so accomplished, so courageous—he always had a

twinkling sense of humor and never lost his temper—
had to be one hell of a guy.'

Although the whole family had become closer than they
had been for some time the cramped conditions meant
that they were virtually living on top of each other.
After a year Mitchum felt he could relieve the situation by
working elsewhere and contributing to family finances. He
also felt frustrated because his wish to get a really good job
and build up a financial nest egg so that he could propose to
Dorothy didn't seem to be working out.

He had, of course, been courting her long distance by
letters all this time—in his own fashion. 'I would write
her threatening letters,' he once joked. 'And when I took
up boxing, I sent her pictures of me in fierce boxing poses
with my muscles flexed. But when I thought that wasn't
enough to keep my memory green with her, I hopped a
freight and went to Delaware to see her.'

In September, 1935, shortly after his eighteenth birthday, Mitchum hit the road again. This time he had two
main objectives. The first was to join up with a pal he'd
met in California, a youth called Frederick Fast, whose
father owned an auto factory in Toledo, Ohio. Fast had told
him if he arrived that winter his father might just give
him a good job in the factory. The second was to visit
Dorothy Spence, who by then was working as a secretary
for an insurance company. He planned to convince her
that he *was* courting her seriously.

Arriving in Toledo with a mere handful of dollars in his
pocket (having left some with his family), Mitchum was
picked up by the police and put into a Federal camp for
transients, from which he phoned his friend Frederick Fast.
'They were always locking you up for poverty in those
days,' explains Mitchum. 'It was a crime to be poor.'

Fast immediately drove down and took Mitchum home.
For the rest of the winter and early spring of 1936,

Mitchum stayed in Ohio, and for a while he was a house-guest in the Fast home.

Mr Fast did give him a job in his factory, operating a power punch press. But Fast was a rather conservative gentleman, and he soon found himself irritated by Mitchum's living habits. One idiosyncrasy that annoyed him was Mitchum's penchant for wearing shoes without socks.

'The temperature was frequently below zero,' Frederick Fast once recalled. 'But Bob was on a kick then where he didn't like socks and he just wouldn't wear them.'

Mitchum also hated his new job, and after a few months Mr Fast fired him.

It was in Toledo that Mitchum first smoked marijuana. Twelve years later, when he was a rising star and was convicted on a narcotics charge in Hollywood, Mitchum wrote in his plea for probation:

'My first use of marijuana was an isolated instance in 1936 when I was working in Toledo.'

When Mitchum lost the car factory job—but with his first objective achieved in that he had some money—he headed down to Delaware to resume his courtship of Dorothy. Persuading Mitchum to talk about his feeling for Dorothy Spence at that time is almost impossible. He hates anything smacking of sentiment, so he talks about it in his usual oblique style:

'I was clearly a young man of high purpose and noble intent, so I usually passed muster among the scallywags and ruffians with whom she had been associating!' The truth perhaps was that most of Dorothy's other male friends were perfectly ordinary, harmless, hard-working conventional—and boring—lads. If any one of them was a scallywag, it was Mitchum himself. But he told Dorothy he still loved her and that he'd be back for her when he had some more money behind him.

Having established that his girl was still very much interested, he once more hopped a freight train and headed west to rejoin his family. One night he stopped at a place called Sparks, Nevada.

He walked into a café and treated himself to a hamburger with all the trimmings. Then, his appetite appeased, he casually asked the café owner if he knew of any work going locally.

'Well, I need a good fry cook,' said the man, 'how'd that suit you?'

'No, thanks,' said Mitchum, who knew from his counter hand days that he was no fry cook. 'But I could do something a bit more physical.'

'More physical?' said the café owner. 'Like what more physical?'

'Actually,' said Mitchum for a joke, 'I'm a boxer.'

To his surprise the man immediately showed interest. 'A boxer, eh?' he repeated. 'Right. I got a little go for you Friday night. Fifty bucks, win or lose.'

Fifty bucks, thought Mitchum. Hell, that was a quick way to make fifty bucks. The guy probably wanted him to take on the local tough. So he'd probably get beaten. But fifty bucks was fifty bucks. And all for doing what he'd sometimes been forced to do on the road for nothing —fight. And this time he'd have those nice soft gloves on.

'Tell you what,' he said, 'fifty if I lose. Seventy-five if I win.'

'It's a deal,' said the café owner. 'You can sleep out back in the bunkhouse tonight. Come back in the morning and we'll talk.'

On the Friday night Mitchum had his bout and won. It launched him on a new career over the next few months —as a heavyweight boxer. He had a 47-inch chest, a 26-inch waist and really only one punch, a hard looping right.

Altogether he had twenty-seven fights, but Mitchum

doesn't like to talk about his fighting days. 'I want folks to know I was licked—thrashed!' he says. 'I hate fighting. It's too painful. It's not good for me. I much prefer the quiet life.'

Today Mitchum's face still bears the scars from the fights. He soon retracted his thoughts about the 'soft gloves', especially when he met dirty fighters, who smashed the inside lace part of the gloves across his face. Even now there is a deep livid scar running right across his left eyebrow, which makeup artists for his films struggle in vain to hide.

In Mitchum's final bout, his rugged, heavier and far more experienced opponent unwittingly helped set Mitchum on the road to movie stardom.

'That guy had my nose all over to one side, gave me the scar on my left eye, had me all messed up. So I quit.'

4

*Professional stargazing, an odd wedding, and
sudden blindness*

By the time Mitchum came back to his family in the overcrowded ménage in Long Beach in the summer of 1936, his
sister Julie had become involved as an actress, stage
manager, and general factotum with the Long Beach Civic
Theater. One day when he was complaining about the
frustrations of having to resume the same boring odd-job
existence he'd led before cutting out to Toledo, his mother
suggested he try to join Julie in the theater work.

Julie, who knew that her brother's stifled creative talents were at least part of his frustration, encouraged him.
He auditioned and was easily accepted. He didn't know it
at the time, but this act proved to be the turning point in
his life.

Mitchum worked first as a stage hand and then graduated to small acting roles. He had parts in plays such as
The Petrified Forest, The Day, and *Rebound,* and before
two years had gone by he was directing and writing one-
act plays. Two of his playlets for children, one of which
was called *Trumpet in the Dark,* met with considerable
local success. Later another won an award at the Pittsburgh
Festival of Arts for the best first play written by an
amateur.

For the first time Mitchum discovered a métier he really
enjoyed. He was working with a group of young people
who shared many of his ideas. But he talks about those days
in his usual diffident style :

'I'd never had so much fun before. The theater seemed

53

fine to me because you could dress yourself out of the wardrobe—so it was real easy on clothes. We used to dress up in harlequin outfits. Julie would come on with bells on her toes, and we wore long fur coats like Groucho Marx.

'I got sort of hooked on it right there and then. Well, there were a lot of amusing people backstage. It was real fun, and I figured ... one of the biggest movie stars at the time was Rin Tin Tin, a mother dog, and I reckoned if he could hack it maybe even a turtle could make out.'

Mitchum acted and wrote mostly at late-night sessions or in the early morning before going to work. He tried his hand at short stories and extended his boyhood interest in poetry. He had a few poems published in small literary magazines.

'I once wrote a story about a fashion photographer who fell in love with a bird on a drunken assignment in Florida,' he reminisces. 'I first sent it to Arnold Gingrich at *Esquire*. He said it didn't "hit hard enough". Then some quarterly published it and really screwed me up. I became the darling of the Beverly Hills writing set!'

He also began devising comedy material and song lyrics for Julie's nightclub act. They were so good that other entertainers began to buy his ideas. Some of Mitchum's risqué songs later became part of the repertoire of Nan Blackstone, Peggy Fears, and Ray Bourbon, the well known female impersonator. He also wrote and composed an oratorio that in 1939 was presented at the Hollywood Bowl at a fund-raising benefit for European Jewish Refugees, produced and directed by Orson Welles.

When asked about this achievement today, Mitchum speaks of it in deprecatory terms. 'Hell, it was a vaudeville black-out!' he says.

Nevertheless, his writing reputation grew, and he gave up his ideas about acting when Carroll Righter, the famous astrologer who was at the height of his fame and was a favourite of women's clubs and top resorts, heard about his work and hired him as a writer for what, to Mitchum, was a princely salary.

Mitchum's job consisted of writing all Righter's verbal pitches, ghost writing his syndicated newspaper column, and organizing his tours. The job appealed to Mitchum largely because it involved traveling through the midwest, New England, and other states, where he could visit old pals from his hoboing days. Not only would he be eating well and regularly, but he'd also be able to save that ever-elusive nest egg so that he could fulfill his promise to his girl back home.

Throughout the latter half of 1939 and the early part of 1940, Mitchum toured with Righter.

'It was really a vacation,' he once recalled. 'We operated around all the best summer resorts. I'd drum up interest among the guests at the hotels, and we charged a dollar admission for people wanting to find out what was giving with the stars. After the old guy gave his spiel, I'd pitch the women into having a horoscope reading. One day I asked the stargazer what the stars had in store for me. He said, "Plenty. According to my calculations you're going to buy a hotel." I never did get that hotel.'

In Palm Beach, Florida, in March, 1940, Mitchum took a leave of absence from the astrologer. He had managed to save up $2,300 and anyway, he was by then a little tired of being an assistant interpreter of what the stars foretell. He told Righter he was heading north to ask Dorothy Spence to be his wife.

Righter agreed to suspend their agreement for a few weeks, but before Mitchum left he insisted on comparing his horoscope with Dorothy's. What he found disturbed him, for Mitchum was a Leo and Dorothy, a Taurus. After examining the charts, Righter pronounced his verdict. 'Don't marry her,' he said. 'There will be great conflict.

Your horoscopes are completely incompatible.' This opinion, incidentally, was fully shared by Dorothy's family.

Such a pessimistic prophecy seems odd when one realizes that Mitchum has been married to Dorothy for well over thirty years and is today the only top star of his era still married to his childhood love.

Mitchum ignored the astrologer's warning, however, and set off back to Delaware to propose to his girl. And this is how he tells it:

'I left Florida, where it was ninety-five degrees in the shade, and I got off the Greyhound bus in Delaware in my thin ice cream suit and Panama hat—and promptly fell on my nose in four feet of snow. Dorothy picked me up, and I told her the whole sad story, and she said, "I don't think you're fit to be let loose any longer. I'd suggest we get married."'

Whereupon Mitchum flopped heavily into the nearest seat with a sigh and said, 'Dottie, that's just what I'd been planning all along!'

Dorothy had few doubts about becoming Mitchum's wife. 'I knew Bob's faults,' she once wrote in *Photoplay*. 'I don't care. When there is love, I concluded, who needs perfection?'

The couple went to Dover, the state capital, for some last-minute shopping for their wedding. Dorothy left to search for a white dress in which to be married. Mitchum and his pal Charlie Thompson, who was to be his best man, struck out to look for a ring. Mitchum found a fine plain gold band but had forgotten to measure Dorothy's finger. The two men solved this problem by borrowing the jeweler's sample scale and going out to look for the bride-to-be. They had forgotten the name of the store Dorothy had entered, so they simply wandered up and down the main street.

They were still doing this when Dorothy looked out

of the store window and saw them. Realizing they were looking for her, and being half in and half out of her gown, she just pulled it on and ran into the street. Mitchum measured her finger on the sidewalk, and Dorothy tore back into the store before they got the idea she'd run off with the dress.

If this prelude to the 16 March wedding had the elements of comedy, the wedding itself was sheer farce.

Mitchum, Dorothy and Charlie Thompson searched around town until they found a Methodist minister. They rang the doorbell, and an elderly man appeared. 'I bet I know what you folks want,' he chuckled. He led them into the living room, where the temperature was around zero. So the party then adjourned to the kitchen where there was warmth and a strong smell of cabbage.

The old man put on a frock coat. Then his wife came and sat down at the kitchen table. 'Do you want the old service or the new?' asked the minister.

'The old one,' said Dorothy because it sounded more romantic. So they had the old one.

After a weekend of celebration the couple caught a Greyhound bus heading for Los Angeles. By changing buses along the route and stopping off to enjoy themselves at various hotels, they turned the trip into a honeymoon. They arrived at Julie's bungalow exhausted and nearly broke.

Now, with nine people living in a three-room bungalow, congestion reached crisis stage. And Dorothy, who had never learned to cook, found herself learning the culinary arts not only from Mitchum's mother but from Robert himself.

Shortly after returning to California, Mitchum dissolved his agreement with Carroll Righter. For a year he returned to the haphazard pursuit of writing songs and special material for Sunset Strip nightclub acts and doing occasional acting stints in little theatre productions. At one time he had protracted half-hearted discussions with an agency who proposed a $500-a-week retainer if he'd sign exclusively with them as a writer, but it came to nothing. Finally, he quit this work when, after fulfilling a contract to write material for one particular show, he never received a cent of the $1,500 he'd been promised. Also, this kind of writing now rather embarrassed him. America was entering the war in Europe; the atmosphere on the home front was taut and serious; and Mitchum felt he'd be worse than a dilettante to write saucy nightclub material for his living at such a time.

For a while he debated with himself what he was going to do, but he didn't communicate his anxiety to his wife. Dorothy felt perplexed by his seeming inactivity.

'One day she turned to me, very embarrassed, and said, "What do you really *do*?"' Mitchum recalls. 'Well, that sort of question hadn't occurred to me before so I answered, "Hold on, we'll work something out." Things were a bit tenuous for me then.'

They became even more tenuous when Dorothy became pregnant, and imminent fatherhood suggested to Mitchum that he find a more tangible and reliable occupation.

'I finally figured if a feller was married and there was a war on, then he got himself a lunch box and really went to work. So I did that. I quit writing, got myself a lunch box, and went to work in the Lockheed aircraft plant—and almost wrecked the war effort.'

Mitchum was surprised when he went for the job at the factory in Burbank to find that the F.B.I. officials, who were checking every worker for security reasons, knew about his sentence on the chain gang in Georgia.

'They weren't too quarrelsome about it,' he says. 'But they came up and asked me, "Why were you on a chain gang in Georgia?" I said, "Who wasn't on a chain gang in

1933?" Hell, I met some charming people on that chain gang! But we soon sorted it out okay.'

Thus, in April, 1941, Mitchum started his job as a sheet-metal worker. He remembers his next year at Lockheed as being one of the most joyless of his life. 'That—and being in the army,' he says. 'But I preferred the army to working at Lockheed. I found myself working on a project in which I had no faith and no enthusiasm. We were building war planes that were really obsolete. When the war began someone had got up in Congress and said that America had all these planes lying out in Burbank so why not sell 'em to the Limeys? And they did. England had a contract for them and we were charging them plenty and still making them, but mostly they were rusting away in north Africa. Yet those old Lockheed Hudsons had one great selling point—once they were up in the air you couldn't knock 'em down. But they couldn't do anything of much use either. And the British were lumbered with the goddamned things.'

Mitchum became a shaper operator. Wearing a visor, a full rubber apron, and a lead skirt, he fed sheets and chunks of metal into a huge machine that ground, melted and shaped it. His booth was right next to that of James Dougherty, who was then married to a girl called Norma Jean Baker, who later became Marilyn Monroe. 'He used to bring me pin-up pictures of his wife and say, "Not bad, eh?"' Mitchum remembers. Despite such privileged interludes, however, the work turned out to be tedious for Mitchum.

When he was on day shifts, he counteracted this tedium by appearing in little theater productions at night. One such play was *The Lower Depths* by Maxim Gorky, and Mike Stanislavsky was its director. 'I spoke with a thick Russian accent, like Gregory Ratoff,' Mitchum remembers, 'and while we were on stage odd things would happen, like the lights would suddenly all go out. It would be somebody plugging in a hot plate to warm up some blintzes! We'd hear Mike arguing backstage, "To hell with the blintzes!" then he'd stick his head out through the curtain and ask the audience to bear with him.'

It was on the opening night of one such play, on 8 May, 1941, that Mitchum's first son Jim was born. Mitchum had taken Dorothy backstage to watch his début in a good role, but shortly before the curtain was due to go up, Dorothy told her husband she thought Jim was on his way. As Dorothy recalls: 'He borrowed a car, rushed me to hospital and then dashed back to concentrate on his part, or rather, try to concentrate. Then he returned to the hospital after the performance, with his makeup still on, to pace the floor with the other expectant fathers.'

At about this time Mr and Mrs Cunningham-Morris moved to their own house on Palm Avenue, together with young John and later, after her divorce, sister Julie. Robert and Dorothy moved into the converted back porch of the house. The 'chicken coop' Mitchum once called it. His small earnings began to help support the household, though living conditions were still uncomfortable and things were not made any easier by Mitchum's rapidly developing hatred for his work at the metal shaping machine.

'It was like something by Edgar Allan Poe out of *The Fall of the House of Usher*,' Mitchum recalls. 'It went at about 26,000 revolutions per minute and had great knives sticking out all over it. The Okies who came out there for jobs and were running similar machines, would write home and say "You ort to see this machine. It's bigger than Fred's tractor." They'd forget what they were doing for a minute and lose an arm. They were always getting banged up. If one of those knives came loose—look out! One did come loose one day, made a big hole in a guy, went right on through the building and landed some place in Glendale.

I was as nervous as hell about that machine and I figured that whatever I chose to do in later life, I couldn't do it with a hole in me.'

One day at work Mitchum was thinking about the man who'd been half killed by the flying knife blade when the foreman walked past. Mitchum had never liked the fore-man—he was the kind with a pocket of pencils and a sheaf of orders under his arm, a smug type who walked about with his hands flapping like wings from his lapels. He borrowed a pencil from Mitchum to check some things off his list—and kept the pencil. Mitchum flung a large wrench at him.

Hauled before his superiors to explain why he'd attacked the foreman, Mitchum offered so persuasive an explanation that they offered him a cent and a half an hour rise. Mitchum said no, that wouldn't do it. They offered him three cents an hour more. And Mitchum, who was in an essential 'frozen' war time job anyway, accepted this offer.

The end to his job at Lockheed came after he'd been put on the 'graveyard' midnight-to-morning shift. Not only did this mean he could no longer escape into the world of theater at night but with the overcrowded conditions at home—which the birth of his lusty, bawling son had done nothing to improve—he found it difficult to sleep during the day. He developed chronic insomnia and ultimately found himself going blind.

Mitchum remembers this period only too well. 'While on that midnight-to-morning shift I'd go to work, come home and go to sleep then wake up again and be sort of half awake, you know—that nightmare scene. Sometimes I couldn't move and I couldn't scream. I'd finally roll out of bed and that was it. Sometimes I'd wake up in the morning and see the morning shadows. I wasn't properly orientated. I'd think it was afternoon and believe I was fully refreshed. I'd get up, take a shower, go to the kitchen and discover I'd been asleep a solid twenty minutes. And that would have to do for the next three days. I got no real sleep for months, and it became a big problem.

'One morning in the street I couldn't see where I was going. That day I left the plant and tried to catch the usual streetcar down to Santa Monica Boulevard and Highland Avenue. It was about 7 A.M. I stood on the corner striking matches to light up the sign but I found I had to ask somebody what car it was as I couldn't read it. My sight got progressively worse and when I walked up the hill to get home I found I could barely see at all.'

In the house Mitchum told Dorothy there was something badly wrong with his vision. She immediately rushed him to a doctor who had just returned from a visit to Southeast Asia. The doctor made some preliminary tests on Mitchum's eyes, sat him down and started to tell him gently of the terrible diseases people suffered from in Asia —the mere *description* of which could send some delicate souls into a state of shock. And yet, he said, many of these people lived to be a hundred and twenty years old.

There was a good reason for that longevity, the doctor told Mitchum. 'They never *worry*. If a leg, an ear, a nose or a finger falls off from some disease out there, it's a fairly commonplace event. Above all they don't worry about it. That's what will kill you quicker than anything —worry.'

While Mitchum digested this seemingly irrelevant information, the doctor made some final tests. Then he said, 'I'm sorry to have to tell you ...'

Oh, my God, thought Mitchum. I'll never see again.

'There's nothing wrong with you,' concluded the doctor.

'What do you mean, there's nothing wrong with me?' said Mitchum indignantly. 'You don't go blind for nothing.'

The doctor replied, 'No, but let's say it's psychological. There's nothing organically wrong. It's to do with lack of sleep. You hate your job. You know when you wake up you'll have to do work you hate so you've been going without sleep so you won't have to wake up. You must quit that work.'

When Mitchum explained that he couldn't quit because he was in a frozen war-time job, the doctor said he could probably have him discharged on medical grounds. But as he thought of Dorothy and his new baby, Mitchum felt a brief moment of fear. 'I can't give up work,' he said. 'We've just had a baby. Hell, we'll starve to death.'

'Listen,' replied the doctor, 'the day has yet to come when a big oaf like you will starve to death. You give up that work and find expression in something you really enjoy. And that's an order.'

Torn now between a job he hated and the responsibility of providing for his family, Mitchum was in a quandary. Eventually it was his mother who helped him solve the situation. Over breakfast one morning she told her son, 'Why don't you try and get into the movies? You love acting, and if all those other idiots can get away with it, why not you? They're all being called up anyway. You've got a really good chance.'

Mitchum thought about it. He didn't really have much to lose. So he set about trying to find work in films. 'I had no burning ambitions to be an actor, and I wasn't much good at reading lines,' Mitchum once explained. 'But I was big and looked like I could handle myself in a brawl. I thought maybe I'd be good enough in professional movies to pick up some work as an extra.'

His work in little theater plays had already brought him to the attention of artists' manager Paul Wilkins, and when Mitchum went to see him, Wilkins also encouraged him to merchandize his talents. He agreed to try to find Mitchum work.

In the meantime, Dorothy came to the rescue. When baby Jim was old enough to be left a few hours during the day, she went back to work—as a part-time secretary to a local insurance firm for $80 a month. The Mitchums moved out to a small apartment of their own which cost $27 a month, and Mitchum drove his wife to work every morning and picked her up each evening in a battered 1927 Chrysler.

'The woman who rented us the apartment wanted to see the car first,' Mitchum recalls. 'If you had a big new car, you couldn't squeeze past it into the place! Things were tight. I used to borrow 17 cents from my mother, and with that I could buy a pound of hamburger and a gallon of gas.'

To keep some of his days free so that he could attend any auditions that might come up, Mitchum found a part-time job as a salesman at Chandler's shoe shop on Wilshire Boulevard.

'I wasn't much good at it,' he says. 'You got a bonus if you managed to sell the old dogs. One time a nurse came in and I sold her a pair of size nines. They were too big but I sold 'em. As they were wrapping them up I lost my nerve. I went up to her and said, "These aren't for you. Don't buy 'em." Then there was this hustler who kept coming into the store and trying on shoes, just wasting time. I was waiting on her one day and she got me mad and I yelled, "Beaver!" at her. The manager walked right over and fired me. Then he called me aside as soon as she was out of the store and said, "You *can* work okay, but you're just not cut out to be a shoe salesman."'

When Paul Wilkins began taking Mitchum around on interviews, the budding actor was handicapped by his poor wardrobe. He only had one suit. 'It was very theatrical—

a double-breasted blue pinstripe,' Mitchum recalls. 'It was so old it was falling apart. The seat of the pants was stitched across so many times that there was finally nothing left to hang the thread onto; so then I used two big strips of adhesive tape across the seat from the inside. It made sitting down in casting directors' offices a little difficult. I had to slide gracefully onto a chair in a horizontal position to keep myself from falling out!'

Wilkins wanted to know if Robert could ride horses. 'Sure,' said Mitchum. 'I used to work with horses on my grandparents' farm up in Delaware.' Wilkins then sent him along to see producer Harry 'Pop' Sherman at United Artists. Knowing Sherman to be an important producer who handled many westerns, Mitchum quickly borrowed a forty-dollar suit from his pal Jack Shay and went to the interview trying not to look as anxious as he felt.

'What can you do?' Pop Sherman asked him.

So Mitchum told him a little of his past, now he'd been a deck hand, a dish washer, a rod-riding hobo, a laborer, a longshoreman, a pro boxer and a sheet metal worker.

Sherman took another look at Mitchum's powerful shoulders, the slightly dented craggy face. This guy looked tough and he was honest. He had no great ambitions to be a star but would be happy as an extra, working props or even labouring on sets.

'I hear you also used to bust broncos for a living out Laredo way?'

'I've handled a few horses, sure,' replied Mitchum, realizing that the message about leading farm horses around in Delaware had become somewhat garbled en route to the producer's office.

'Okay,' said Sherman. 'Don't shave or cut your hair till you hear from us.'

Mitchum raced home, met Dorothy after work, and celebrated his impending employment in movies by buying her an ice cream soda at a drug store on Wilshire and La Brea. He then borrowed $55 from his grandmother's 'coffin' fund to pay his union dues and waited for the call.

Soon afterwards Paul Wilkins handed him a card and told him to take it up to the location where a William 'Hopalong Cassidy' Boyd western movie was being made. Mitchum caught a Greyhound bus to Bakersfield and took a local bus to Kernville, in the desert. Here his vision of playing a romantic cowhand who wins the hand of a lovely girl soon faded.

'I didn't know whether I was supposed to bring my own make-up or horse or what. I got off the bus smiling—I wanted to make a good impression. But they were all sitting around. It was a bright clear day. I figured by their attitude I had done something wrong. I took my cardboard suitcase into a tent, and somebody told me an actor called Charlie Murphy had been killed.' Mitchum had been hired to replace the actor quickly so as not to hold up production.

They told him he was playing a minor villain who gets killed by Boyd; then they dressed him for the part—giving him Murphy's hat—and took him over to a magnificent looking but ill-tempered horse that he was to ride.

What they didn't tell him was that this was the horse that had thrown his predecessor.

5

*Busting a vicious bronco—and into movies.
'A hundred bucks a week and all the horse
manure I can take home.'*

As he took the reins from the old wrangler who brought
the horse to him, Mitchum thought he detected a sly grin
on the man's face. He hadn't been on a horse since he was
a boy, and he knew the old timer knew him to be a green-
horn, but it was too late to turn back.

He climbed on the horse and before he could get set, the
animal reared, bucked and, threw him some twenty feet
into the dust. Mitchum slowly picked himself up,
grinning a little thinly to hide the pain in his back.
His eyes met those of the man who'd handed him the
horse.

'You don't get rid of me that easy,' he said. 'Bring that
goddamned nag back here!'

He climbed back on the horse and again it threw him.
When this happened a third time, Mitchum realized he
had to fight the horse to gain control. He slapped it around
the jaw hard, got back in the saddle and from then on had
no more trouble with it.

Such was Mitchum's inauspicious début in the movies.
He went on to make seven more Hopalong Cassidy
westerns—usually playing minor bad men. William Boyd
practiced such mayhem on him as knocking him off his
horse, slamming him against saloon walls, throwing him
over bars or filling him full of lead. But Mitchum didn't
mind any of that.

'I was working in movies. I was getting a hundred bucks

a week plus all the horse manure I could take home,' he once explained in his characteristic way. 'From then on my fortune was made. I had a deep baritone voice that was hard to mix, and the only concession I ever made to movies was to lighten it. I never went after a job. They just seemed to come after me. The bread kept getting better, and it sure as hell beat punching a time clock!'

Nevertheless, Mitchum is quick to pay tribute to the continuing faith and kindness of Pop Sherman, who, he said, 'illuminated my early path'. Mitchum worked really hard, and each of the many roles he had in the next eighteen months was slightly more significant than the last; in 1943 no fewer than seventeen of his films were released. In most of them he wore a beard, had a little dialogue, and played a villain. But he had other more interesting minor roles too. He played a soldier dating a small-town girl in *The Human Comedy*, with Mickey Rooney, a law-abiding rancher in *Bar 20*, an outlaw who turns honest in *Beyond the Last Frontier*, a soldier in Ireland during World War II in Columbia's musical *Doughboys in Ireland*, and a co-actor with Laurel and Hardy in a zany comedy about a dancing school called *Dancing Masters*.

'I was now a character actor, and I played just about everything,' Mitchum kids. 'Chinese laundrymen, midgets, Irish washerwomen, faggots. I even played a journalist once. I don't know what I was like. I never *saw* the pictures. But I got overtime, and I'd live on the overtime and save my basic salary.'

Early in his career it was obvious Mitchum had *something*, but quite *what* was not easy to define. Once, after being tested by Mervyn LeRoy, the director told him, 'You're either the lousiest actor in the world or the best. I can't make up my mind which.'

Mitchum, of course, was happy and proud that at last he had found a milieu in which he was accepted and welcomed. Encouraged by his progress, he, Dorothy, and Jim (nicknamed Josh) moved into a $50-a-month apartment, and on 16 October, 1943, their second son, Christopher, was born.

Dorothy once threw some light on what Mitchum was like as a husband during these early years.

'He taught me to cook after we were first married,' she admitted. 'And once he painted the living room three times to get the right colors. He refused to hire an interior decorator. "How can someone else tell me what I want to live in?" he said. He also made a dog kennel once. It took him six months to finish it, but his interest and good intentions were always there. "It's got to be done *right*," he said as our dog grew older and bigger in his place by the fire!'

Mitchum's first important role—in that it was mentioned by critics—was in William Castle's murder story *When Strangers Marry*. He played a salesman who helps a former girl friend (Kim Hunter) trace her husband, who is suspected of murder. Mervyn LeRoy then gave him a small role in *Thirty Seconds Over Tokyo*—as a crewman aboard the B25 that bombed Japan in World War II— and this performance impressed RKO sufficiently for the studio to offer Mitchum a long-term contract, in June 1944.

By this time Mitchum had received his draft papers, but a regulation exempting fathers led to his induction being indefinitely postponed. However, since he expected to be called up at any time, he signed the contract because it would give his family a secure income while he was away.

He looks back on his early RKO days this way: 'They were looking for a journeyman actor and like everyone else had a lot of attractive people on their books. But these actors didn't have, I suppose, enough versatility. They felt I could do a number of things, so by hiring me they'd be getting a lot for the same money. I was a sort of utility man there for ten years...I kept telling them I couldn't ride a horse or anything. But they went through all the old Hopalong Cassidy movies, then dressed everyone else up very badly and marched me out before the cameras in a tailor made outfit.'

'After that I was sort of on the hook. RKO opened the door for me—and I became their workhorse. Everyone had them. 20th Century-Fox had their workhorses. MGM had theirs. I was the workhorse of RKO. If I wanted the joint painted purple they'd paint it purple...I was teacher's pet.'

Mitchum's tough early life—when he'd had to scrape for every cent—soon made him realize that the Hollywood movie world of the day was full of phony values. His response was characteristic—if they wanted him, good enough, but he wasn't going to change. It would have to be on his own terms. In fact, by signing the contract Mitchum was at first losing money. He signed for $350 a week when he was earning an average of $1,000 a week as a freelance character actor. But clearly this income would end after he was called up. By signing with RKO he could guarantee a good regular salary going to his family while he was in the army, or a large sum if he lost his life.

He was under no illusions, and right from the start he summed up the situation with a very clear eye.

'They had forty stock actors under contract at the time,' he said. 'They were all six feet tall with lifts and padding. They all came in, chucked the producer's secretary under the chin and said, "Honey, did you get the script?" Then they drove their Cadillacs to the Mogambo. I figured—these cats were *working*? I should own the joint! The first thing they (RKO) wanted me to do was say, "Going up, sir?" as an elevator operator. I said, "No,

it ain't like that." They said, "You'll do it." I said, "No,
Dad. I won't." Of course he didn't.

Mitchum's first role for RKO was as the romantic male
lead opposite Frances Langford in the musical *The Girl
Rush*. Director Gordon Douglas wanted him for the role
and took him to the producer. Later, as Mitchum sat outside the room and heard the two men arguing in whispers,
he was startled to overhear the producer say, 'But he looks
like a monster.' Nevertheless, he got the part.

Mitchum did little to counteract such initial reactions
on the part of his superiors. Indeed, he occasionally, perhaps perversely, went the other way. Producers would ring
his agent after office interviews with him and complain,
'He acts like he doesn't *want* the job.'

When Frank Ross, then an RKO producer, was preparing to film *The Robe*, Mervyn LeRoy took Mitchum
along to see if Ross would consider him for the lead role of
Demetrius the gladiator. Ross was seated at his desk, and
Mitchum sat down before a large table on which reposed a
centrepiece containing a huge bowl of walnuts, oranges,
and avocado pears. During the interview Ross looked
Mitchum over carefully, then said, 'He looks like a clean-
cut all-American youth.' At that Mitchum cracked a wal-
nut and proceeded to eat the entire contents of the bowl.*

During his early days at RKO, before he was well
known, Mitchum had no dressing room, so he had to dress
and undress for his films on the set. 'Once I grabbed a
garden hose and took a shower outdoors,' he says. 'Soon
after that they found me a room.'

The studio next cast him in two Zane Grey stories—
Nevada and *West of the Pecos*—and in both he played a
sleepy-eyed self-confident cowboy who cares little for the
letter of the law but becomes an active crusader when his

---

* *The Robe* was shelved and when it was made, by Twentieth Century-Fox, in the fifties, Victor Mature played Demetrius.

own lackadaisical routine is disturbed by villains. Both films did well at the box office and Mitchum went on to play several variations of this tough but lazy cowpoke in later movies.

During the making of *Nevada* an amusing incident occurred. One of Mitchum's co-actors was Guinn 'Big Boy' Williams, a huge man reputed, along with ex-wrestler Mike Mazurki, to be one of the toughest hombres in Hollywood. Mitchum and Big Boy Williams were doing a fight scene and Mitchum, who was not too skilled at this point in the ballet-like movements of film fights, lashed out and socked Big Boy flush on the jaw. He expected Williams to crumple or at least wobble and certainly to get very angry. But Williams just stood there, blinked, and said, 'Kid, next time you throw a punch like that, move a little this way.' Mitchum was amazed. 'That was the best shot I ever threw!' he said later.

One day in 1944 Mitchum was walking along Sunset Boulevard when he was seen by director William Wellman, who was at that moment casting war correspondent Ernie Pyle's famous patriotic tale, *The Story of G.I. Joe.* Wellman was looking for a new actor to play the leading role of Lieutenant Walker, the humane, beloved infantry officer in Pyle's story. And this big guy walking in front of him looked just the part. He tapped Mitchum on the shoulder and asked his name.

'What's it to you?' said Mitchum.

'I'll tell you,' said Wellman. 'I'm a movie director and I'm filming *G.I. Joe* and I'm looking for a new leading man...'

'Aw, c'mon,' replied the suspicious Mitchum. 'Everyone's after that role—Gary Cooper, all the rest.'

But Wellman finally overcame Mitchum's initial hostility and talked him into going to the studio for a test. On the way down he asked Mitchum what parts he'd played. 'Well,' said Mitchum, 'I've played two support roles to a dog...'

Today Wellman still remembers that test as being the finest he ever made.

'I very foolishly made the test of one of the most important scenes in the picture—where he was the tired officer writing letters to the mothers of kids who'd been killed. It was my big mistake. Really, for I saw something so wonderful, so completely compelling, that I was mad at myself for not having built the set before so that I could have made the test the *actual* scene that came out in the picture. He was fantastic.'

Burgess Meredith, the distinguished actor who played Ernie Pyle in the film, also didn't realize how good Mitchum was at first. He says, 'Bob was a swinger—and I was a swinger in those days—we had a lot of funning around outside the set. But I didn't realize how good he was until after the first rough cut. A man came up to me and said, "I don't care what they say. I still think that you're good in this picture." I said, "Well, what else is good?' And the man said, "Well, there's a guy by the name of Mitchum that everyone's raving about." I realized then I was up against a real tough contender in the acting department.'

While those working on his film knew Mitchum had delivered an impressive performance, the rest of Hollywood knew nothing about it. And before G.I. Joe was released, Mitchum suffered his second major brush with the law and was also drafted into the US Army.

His encounter with the law in early 1945 appears to have had its roots in some trouble in Mitchum's family circle, and the only light shed upon it comes from Mitchum's own plea for probation in 1949 after his arrest on narcotics charges. He wrote, apropos of the incident just before his induction into the army:

'Five days prior to my induction I was jailed. Out to obtain a prescription for a sick child, I called my wife to discuss the prescription, and my sister answered the phone. She refused to allow me to talk to my wife and hung up the receiver. There followed several attempts, all of which had the same result, until finally, knowing my sister to be hostile to my wife (who was also ill and bedded), I told her that I would come to talk to Dorothy and demand an accounting before her.

'Upon arrival I was met by two sheriff's deputies and arrested. Pressed for complaint, my sister refused to sign, and at my own demand for justice, I was arrested, roundly beaten and booked at the Fairfax Avenue sheriff's substation.

'The next morning I was advised by the captain of detectives to plead guilty to a charge of being in an "intoxicated condition on private property" (over my objections) and pay a $10 fine and "forget about it". This I did and was sentenced by the late Cecil Holland to a term in the county jail, admitted Saturday, discharged on Sunday.'

On the following Tuesday Mitchum was inducted into the army and sent for infantry training at Camp Roberts, in California. When this was over, he was sent to Fort MacArthur, where he spent the remainder of his eight months of peaceful service functioning first as a drill instructor and later as medical assistant to the orthopedic examiner.

Mitchum naturally hated the idea of being in the army. 'When they took me away, I still had bits of the porch rails under my fingernails,' he jokes. But he served his time with docile efficiency. His service in the army followed the curious pattern of that meted out to many budding film stars whom the government had no wish to see killed. It was all spent on US soil. Mitchum refused all attempts to promote him, however. 'They wanted to make me a Ser-

geant but I told them I couldn't sew on the stripes! I met
a lot of the same type of guys I used to bum around with,
and we spent most of our time swapping lies,' he says.
'When they were mustering me out, someone said it would
be a bad reflection on the army if I came out as a private.
So some officer marked one chevron on my sleeve, and I
came out as a PFC.'

If Mitchum's war service was uneventful, his step-
father's most certainly was not. Hugh Cunningham-
Morris volunteered for service but was turned down.
Without saying a word to his family, he set the clock
back ten years, said he was in his early fifties, not his
sixties (which he was), and became a deck hand on a
freighter. Inside a year he was first officer on a ship making
ammunition runs down to the South Pacific. When that
job ended, he joined the crew of an army supply boat.
Within a few months its captain took sick and died at sea.
Hugh Cunningham-Morris was immediately commissioned
as captain. He took part in both the Philippines and
Okinawa invasions—where his ship was caught in a
typhoon and went high and dry on a coral reef. His
charmed life held out, however, and he was uninjured.
Later he returned to civilian life.

When Robert Mitchum left the army he found himself
being hailed as Hollywood's newest male star. *G. I. Joe* had
been released while he was still serving, and many critics
gave him rave reviews. The film had none of the false senti-
mental glamor of many war movies. Its battles were
realistic and Mitchum, as the young officer who united and
inspired the men under his command before being killed
at Casino, was brilliant.

Granted a hardship discharge in October, 1945—for by
then he was virtually the sole support of his mother, step-
father, half sister, wife and two sons—Mitchum was also
nominated for an Academy Award, the only Oscar nomin-

ation he has received. Characteristically, he didn't even show up for the ceremonies. 'The Academy hasn't messed with me since,' he smiles.

Despite the acclaim he received in Hollywood for his portrayal of Lieutenant Walker, Mitchum shrugged it off. 'I was lucky. No one could have missed in such a role. Coming down off a mountain strapped to a mule and having the camera panned right onto my kisser ... I was bound to click. But that doesn't mean I did any acting.'

Director Wellman, however, has different views. 'I think he should have won the Oscar,' he said some twenty-three years later. 'There are only a few stars left who I'd go out to see in a picture but I never fail to see Mitchum. There's something about Mitchum that just thrills me to death. I think he's one of the finest, most solid and real actors we have in the world.'

Hollywood's influential moguls evidently felt much the same way. As soon as Mitchum became a civilian again his new agent, Phil Berg, negotiated a unique contract which gave him no less than three 'owners'—RKO studios, tycoon Howard Hughes and independent producer David O. Selznick. He was given money for the first house he'd ever owned—which proved useful not only for his growing family but for temporarily accommodating army pals who took advantage of his generous nature and spent their nights with him when on leave. 'At least my pals no longer had to doss down on the floor,' he said.

Life was quite riotous at the new house, but Mitchum says, his two growing boys caused him no trouble. 'But they gave my wife a pretty awful time, running all over her. She was all tired out. But I'd come in from merely acting and lay down the law. They minded me too. When I'd been a drill instructor my voice could be heard a mile from the parade ground!'

His first film under the new contract was Dore Schary's

production, *Till the End of Time*. He played a former rodeo rider whose war injuries stop him returning to his old life. It wasn't a highly satisfactory part, and the film itself was an over-glamorized account of how three war veterans re-adjusted to civilian life.

'I was now a leading man,' Mitchum remembers. 'A cause for apprehension and embarrassment. It was much too late to start pursuing any particular design or direction. I knew I'd be a leading man until the string ran out.'

On his next film—when he was loaned out to MGM to play Robert Taylor's cryptic step-brother in *Undercurrent*, which also starred Katherine Hepburn—Mitchum indulged in a series of pranks and bawdy jokes. But his attempts to fool around and defrost Miss Hepburn were met with withering scorn. 'You know you can't act,' she said, 'and if you hadn't been good-looking you would never have gotten the picture. I'm tired of playing with people who have nothing to offer.'

Mitchum roared with laughter. For years he enjoyed quoting Miss Hepburn's remarks.

By this time Mitchum's brother John had also served a stint in the army and had fought his way to becoming a divisional heavyweight champion. In fact, he was never beaten in the ring, and after his discharge several leading promoters wanted him to turn professional. But John's heart was not in fighting—he was more interested in music. For a few years after his army service John was a leading choral director in Los Angeles, finally giving up this work to become an actor himself.

The only time that John and Robert ever came to blows personally was in 1946, shortly after John had left the army and was studying voice and music under the G.I. Bill as a prelude to his first career in music. Both brothers remember it as being a hard, tough fight, and neither wishes to repeat it. John tells the story this way:

'Bob hadn't actually boxed as much as I had, but that doesn't mean anything. I can tell you from first-hand experience that he's one hell of a fighter. That one time we fought was enough for me! The fight took place in his house, over a slight misunderstanding, one might say. We had both been drinking, of course. I was getting $90 a month from the government under the G.I. Bill, and it was a tight squeeze for me to live.

'Bob showed me a cheque for $5,000, out of which the government had taken $1,100 in tax. He was bitching like crazy about it and I said, "Why don't you shut up? You're whining like a child. There are people coming back from the war with one leg, no legs, half a leg, one arm gone, and here you are, bitching about losing a little money..." Whack! He hit me right in the head, and that started it.

'We fought so hard we did more than $2,000 worth of damage to his den—and he'd just fixed it all up with fresh paint and everything. It could have got a lot worse, but Dorothy finally stepped in and stopped us.'

Who won?

'Dorothy!' says John Mitchum diplomatically, adding with a smile, 'We were then and we still are very good friends, of course. It was just that we were both drinking. He hit me in the head, though, and I don't like that! It was funny really because just recently Dorothy said, "Isn't it nice that John and Bob have grown up at last? Now we can have some decent furniture around the house."'

6

Hollywood's newest star and biggest rebel.
'Paint my eyes on my eyelids man, and I'll
walk through it.'

In late October, 1946, Mitchum nearly lost his life in a plane crash. He and two companions were scouting for new movie locations around the countryside of his childhood near Bridgeport, Connecticut, when the small aircraft in which they were flying overshot a mountain airstrip. It tore through a barbed wire fence and finally came to rest a few feet short of a thick stone wall.

Mitchum and the others, Leonard Shannon, a publicity man, and Mel Sternlight, Mitchum's stand-in, were severely shaken and bruised. The plane itself was a total wreck.

However, this near brush with death, appears to have had little effect on Mitchum's boisterous nature. He showed as much ardor as ever for pranks and practical jokes on the sets of his next few films when work was not actually in progress.

But he acted well enough in the late forties for his career to gain considerable momentum. Although somewhat miscast as a suicidal song and dance man hopelessly in love with a thieving psychopath (Laraine Day) in *The Locket*, he won some critical plaudits. He was even better in *Pursued*, a rugged western filmed amid magnificent locations in Monument Valley, in which he played a rancher's son out to avenge his father's murder. In *Crossfire*, a well-received film, which told of the brutal murder of a Jew by an anti-Semitic soldier (Robert Ryan), Mitchum more than held his own against a cast of top Hollywood character actors. Its director, Edward Dmytryk, actually apologized to Mitchum for his role not being bigger, but Dmytryk said he'd asked for him because his name had considerable box office value.

When MGM borrowed Mitchum again to star opposite Greer Garson in *Desire Me*, Mitchum became impatient at the numerous script rewrites and the constant reshooting of scenes after the original director bowed out of the production. He began to clown it up with great exuberance. He incurred Miss Garson's temporary wrath by calling her 'Red'.

At the time he treated the film with irreverence. 'It's all being remade, and I think they're going to get a picture that will finally be entertaining,' he said. 'But it was so bad when they first ran it that after the first reel people walked out. So I put my collar up, sneaked out, and pretended I wasn't there. But I'm surprised with what Mervyn Le Roy has been able to do with it. You'd never know it was the same picture. In the original we were made to act like Shakespearean actors. Now there's some comedy in it.'

Mitchum hated what he called 'all the la-de-dah bull' that went with his new star career. Told by his studio once that he *had* to show up for a film promotion party, he arrived with his chest bare. And he didn't like press conferences either. 'Those things scare the hell out of me,' he once said. 'What am I supposed to say? If I tell them how I really feel, shoot straight, they can't print it anyhow.'

Columnists began to call him Hollywood's biggest rebel and during this period he did plenty to fan the flames. Writers such as Hollywood's Sidney Skolsky began giving him the big star treatment in papers and magazines. Skolsky duly recorded items such as:

'He is in awe of no one and still fools around with the pals he had before fame. He will often startle or amuse his leading lady. He is famed among friends for his impersonations. He is a good mimic and does, among others, Katherine Hepburn and Charles Laughton well. He has fooled Ronald Colman with his English accent. He is a good baritone ... He seldom gets angry and gets along well with everyone. He has no peeves or superstitions but will occasionally knock on wood. He drops clothes on the floor while undressing, sports tweeds, knitted ties and long pointed collars. He has a large lunch and a huge dinner. His favourites are porterhouse steaks and red wine. He dislikes fancy dressers. He can and does cook when necessary. He smokes any available, having no favourite brand. He even rolls his own expertly when he has to. Anyone he can't remember he calls "Peter" and that goes for females too ...' It was a familiar story.

Mitchum became known as one of film town's controversial outsiders. Yet it was precisely his nonconformist qualities—which he projected in his films too—that aroused curiosity. His original and often highly contentious personality intrigued men as well as women.

This defiant quality, which Mitchum established so firmly early in his career, has been carried through the present day. Fairly recently, when told that most people felt he just 'walked through' his films and thought 'Here-comes-the-Great-White-Trapper again,' Mitchum agreed with a grin.

'I don't take too much trouble, man,' he said. 'I came into being during the era of the ugly leading man started by Humphrey Bogart just after the war, and I always made the same film. They'd just keep moving new leading ladies in front of me. I'd close my eyes and when I opened them again there was a new leading lady. I woke up once and there was Marilyn Monroe.

'They said to me, "Look, we got all this rubbish to unload and we'll pay you a salary to help us unload it." Well, it was better than working. They could never decide to their satisfaction what type I was. One guy would say, "He's a broken-nosed Byronic." Another would say, "No, he ain't, he's an All-American boy." People started talking about Mitchum-type roles, but I still don't know what they mean. They'd paint the eyes on my eyelids man, and I'd walk through it. The least work for the most reward.'

Many were fooled by this apparent unconcern, but Edward Dmytryk was not. He said, 'On the surface he is irresponsible and vague and, yes, wacky. But underneath he knows the score as few men in Hollywood do.'

Mitchum became a top 'beefcake' star in the days when screen men were expected to look like men. Mitchum's lazy eyes, laconic acting style, and his naturally powerful torso became his main trademarks to the uninitiated. One woman fan told a reporter that Mitchum had 'the most immoral face I've ever seen'. The remark was widely quoted around the world. Back in those days—long before the days of unisex—when the *difference* between the sexes was what was emphasized, Mitchum became the prototype of the screen hero.

He accepted it with reluctance, however. Asked by a woman reporter how he kept so fit, he replied, 'I don't play golf, tennis or do anything remotely resembling exercise. I like to take my exercise by lying in the grass and looking up at the sky. Sometimes just *thinking* about exercise will get me in shape.'

Through films such as *Out of the Past* (released in Britain as *Build My Gallows High*), *Rachel and the Stranger* (in which he had an interesting role as a vagabond hunter who helps farmer William Holden realize he loves his bond servant Loretta Young) and *Blood on the Moon*, Mitchum's stock among his peers increased. But many of

82

those who now met him for the first time mistook his rebellious independence for conceit.

'People say I've changed,' he told Hedda Hopper at the time. 'But I haven't. *They* have. The other day I went into a store to buy a present for my wife and got the brush-off until one of the sales girls recognized me. Then they all but handed me the store. Now if, for example, I fail to speak to a doorman, people say, "See Mitchum? He's gone high hat since he hit pay dirt in movies. Won't speak to a doorman, eh?" Well, five years ago I wouldn't have spoken to him either, and what's more, he wouldn't have spoken to me. He wouldn't have let me in the joint.

'I used to have an acute social conscience—probably from the way I was knocked about in life—but then I discovered just how boring people could be. And that did it. I just don't like these get-togethers where a lot of people spout off on subjects, such as politics, about which they know nothing. I don't mind a good argument, but questions brought up at these times are usually too dull.

'But there is one good thing about this business—you're privileged to meet some great people. There is a bond of sincere commiseration. The stuffed shirts form a fence out front and you can get behind it with a few you like and smoke corn silk.'

In *The Red Pony*, the film based on John Steinbeck's novella, Mitchum delivered his most sincere performance of the period. Despite a script by Steinbeck himself and the direction of Lewis Milestone, the movie did not match the quality of the story, but Mitchum, as a tough-tender ranch hand who helps his employer's son to train a wild pony, was excellent.

He was now working so hard he began to feel the strain. 'I'm tired,' he told Hedda Hopper. 'I haven't had a vacation now in seven years and I'm going to take one. My wife told me to go away by myself if I wanted to. The idea sounded good till I started thinking about it. Who would keep me out of trouble? Naturally, my wife. So we'll go together—New Orleans, Miami, maybe Nassau or someplace where people haven't heard of Bob Mitchum.

'No, movie success, if you can call it that, hasn't changed me. One big difference is this: I used to have to apologize for some of my acquaintances, but I don't have to do that any more. They're accepted. We used to need friends when we first got here, but now we've got so many we lock the door at night!'

By 1948 Mitchum was earning almost a quarter of a million dollars a year and if he felt misgivings about his way of life—he undoubtedly still felt acting was something less than masculine—he found some compensation in mixing with former army buddies and other hangers-on in a tough, basic, boisterous social life—a far call from the conventional star's life.

In the circumstances, it was perhaps inevitable that something had to snap. On 31 August, 1948, it did. Mitchum was arrested on narcotics charges. He was subsequently sentenced to sixty days in jail and the circumstances behind the arrest and the trial provided Hollywood with one of the most sensational scandals it has ever known.

The background to the story is complicated and is best understood with the help of Mitchum's own explanation, which he wrote in his long and unsuccessful plea for probation.

'Mitchum was psychologically ill-equipped for his sudden rise to fame,' the official probation report stated. And in the light of his own statement this appears to have been true. Among the large entourage of back-slapping hangers-on he had attracted round him in the three years since his Oscar nomination for *G.I. Joe*, Mitchum was a lavish entertainer. Naturally, Dorothy didn't take to every member of this sycophantic, wild-living group, some of whom smoked marijuana, and there were arguments between them.

Mitchum wrote: 'The new popularity brought new faces with endless requests for assistance—requests which were always met. I suppose I honestly believed that it was helping erase a moral debt by granting aid to others of the same social-financial background who had remained less fortunate than I.

'At any rate the rumor spread that I was a "soft touch" and an additional and more disquieting rumor that I was associating with people who indulged in the use of marijuana.

'This last gossip brought a swelling stream of acquaintances who appeared to accept me as one of their number, although their curious jargon was foreign to me, and their pressing social invitations hinted at a social pattern of some mystery.

'Although progressing famously in my profession, I was constantly obsessed with the phantom of failure, and in the next two years I several times answered entreaty by sharing a cigarette with one or more of these sycophants.

'In late 1947, endowed with a new contract, and facing a future which promised relief from my financial obligations to my family, the picture faded when my best friend and trusted manager [Paul Behrmann] admitted the complete disappearance of my funds and refused an accounting. More hurt than angry, I declined to prosecute, although I was eventually subpoenaed by the state as a witness for his prosecution on another matter . . .'

This 'other matter' occurred in February, 1948, when Behrmann was brought to court in Los Angeles charged with obtaining $10,000 from Wanda S. Schoemann, a

Burbank housewife, on the pretext it was to be used as a loan to Anne Nicholls, author of *Abie's Irish Rose*, another of Behrmann's clients.

Mitchum, who had refused to prosecute his manager on discovering the loss of his own funds, was subpoenaed with his wife Dorothy to give evidence against Behrmann in the Schoemann-Nicholls case. On 4 February Mitchum told Judge Clement D. Nye that he had been forced to struggle along on a cash spending allowance of $20 a week doled out by Behrmann. But for Dorothy it had been even worse, Mitchum said. She had received only $10 a week from his RKO studio salary.

Questioned by Prosecutor Herbert Grossman, Mitchum testified that Behrmann once withdrew $8,000 from his bank account while he and Dorothy were on a personal appearance tour in Oregon. 'I knew nothing about these withdrawals until I got back home,' Mitchum told the court. 'I have only $20 a week for my personal use. Behrmann, as my agent, got everything else.' Dorothy Mitchum gave evidence that she had checked one of her husband's bank accounts on their return home and discovered it had shrunk to $58.

Richard Ellis, who was then Mitchum's secretary, also gave evidence. He testified that Behrmann once called him and blamed Mrs Mitchum for having instigated the prosecution against him. 'He said if Mrs Mitchum did not stop making trouble for him, he would do something violent,' Ellis told the court. 'He said he would do away with her.'

Mrs Anne Nicholls was also called to the stand, where she denied she had authorized Behrmann to negotiate a loan for her. Behrmann, who denied guilt, was released on bail after the hearing but later served a prison sentence on the embezzlement charges.

In his plea for probation after his own arrest on narcotics

charges later in the year, Mitchum went on to explain the subsequent events:

'His [Behrmann's] reaction to my involuntary appearance [in the Schoemann-Nicholls case] was an avowal of vengeance which assumed form in a campaign of careful slander, and a confidential cultivation of my mother and sister, instilling in them the belief that I had maneuvered his failure and in reality was myself the thief. Records prove the monstrous falsity of this concept.

'My mother and sister, doubting my sanity, implored the cooperation of my wife in suggesting my visit to a psychiatrist, which suggestion I accepted. Dr Frederick Hacker, whom I visited, adjudged me rational, but suffering a state of overamiability in which failure to please everyone created a condition of self-reproach. He told me that I was addicted to nothing but the good will of people, and suggested that I risk their displeasure by learning to say no and following my own judgment.

'Soon after these visits my wife and I, with the children, traveled to Delaware to visit, and I remained there until June [1948] when, following a quarrel concerning the continuation of my career, I left to return here, expecting to begin work on the fifteenth of that month.'

Before the Mitchums traveled east, it had been no secret that Dorothy was dissatisfied with the sort of life Mitchum's screen prominence had helped to create for her. 'While it's not true that we are separated,' Mitchum said on his return alone, 'it's nevertheless true that she prefers New York to Hollywood and wants to live there. But I work and live in Hollywood and can't find it possible to do as she seeks—move to the east.'

Before she had left Hollywood, Dorothy Mitchum had told friends: 'Bob has gone Hollywood and I can't take it or the people he associates with.'

Back in Hollywood in June, Mitchum in fact did *not*

87

start the film he'd been due to make. After weeks of tests and fittings, the picture was canceled. Then, still hoping for a reconciliation with Dorothy, Mitchum started to look around for a new house with more rooms. While doing this he also started painting and remodeling their present home. Busying himself with saws and hammers he spent several weeks helping workmen to turn the place into two rental units.

Even then it began to appear his reconciliation might not take place as soon as he'd hoped, and as Mitchum wrote in his probation plea: 'I was somewhat depressed over the lack of communication from my wife, who was adamant in her refusal to melt, and I began drinking a great deal more than was good for me. However, I spent much time in the sunshine and at the beach, and my secretary was most solicitous of my welfare and comfort.'

Depressed at the turn his life seemed to be taking, Mitchum turned more and more to the company of his friends.

This then was the discontented and turbulent background of his life when on the night of 31 August, 1948, in the company of a friend Mitchum was arrested at 8443 Ridpath Drive in the Laurel Canyon hills, which was then the rented house of an actress named Lila Leeds. Miss Leeds, age twenty, who had not achieved any important screen prominence while under contract to both MGM and Warner Brothers, and her friend, a twenty-five-year-old dancer from Philadelphia, who was staying with her at the time, were also arrested.

7

Marijuana—police raid and arrest

The police raid and Mitchum's subsequent jail sentence on marijuana charges provided Hollywood with its biggest controversy for many years. The circumstances and background of events that led up to the raid have never yet been satisfactorily explained.

The raid at 8443 Ridpath Drive, was initially staged by Detective Sergeant Alva M. Barr of the Los Angeles police, who was assisted by Sergeant J. B. McKinnon. Cooperating in the case was William Craig, head of the federal narcotics office in Los Angeles.

The police report of the raid stated that Mitchum had been under observation since the previous December, following reports that he had been smoking marijuana. Officers who had followed and shadowed him had gained information that had led them to the 31 August rendezvous. They had not necessarily expected Mitchum to appear at the cottage that night. 'We just got a break,' disclosed Barr.

The night of 31 August was warm, and when the two officers arrived to take up their positions, they found that some of the cottage windows had been left open. First they heard Miss Leeds talking over the phone, they reported. Then they overheard her put the phone down and tell her friend, 'The boys are at the bottom of the hills, and they're lost. But they're loaded.'

A few minutes later the officers heard a car stop and then two men walked up the rough steps and path to the door of the cottage. One was Mitchum, alleged Barr, adding that he recognized him 'immediately'. The detectives allowed the two men to enter the house but kept watch. They saw Mitchum and his friend sit down. Mitchum wore a red, black and white lumber jacket and tan slacks. He wore no hat but his hair was awry. The first thing the officers alleged they heard Mitchum say to Lila Leeds was, 'Let's turn these lights down. They hurt my eyes.' The lights were dimmed. Then a girl's voice said, 'Oh, but you've got brown ones and white ones too. I want some of the white ones.'

Barr said he then saw Miss Leeds take some cigarettes from the packet Mitchum offered. She lit one and passed it to Mitchum. Then she took one herself. Miss Leeds' friend said, 'Gee, what will it do to me? And what happens if it knocks me out?'

Mitchum's answer was 'Oh, Daddy,' the detective added.

'We went to a side door,' Barr went on. 'We found the screen door open and we were greeted by two big dogs. We played with them, and the dogs went out. We then tried to get into the kitchen door, which was hooked.' Barr said Miss Leeds' friend evidently mistook their noise for dogs' scratching and opened the door. Barr flashed his badge at the surprised girl and backed her into the front room, where the other three stood.

Both men had cigarettes in their mouths, the report continued. Mitchum's friend laid his down on the couch, and Barr seized it. Mitchum took the cigarette from his mouth, the end of which was aglow. He then crumpled it and threw it down. Barr said he burned his fingers picking it up, and he then picked up a standard brand cigarette package, which Mitchum tried to brush aside. There were fifteen marijuana cigarettes in it, Barr alleged. Barr put the two partially burned cigarettes into the package, then went over to where Miss Leeds stood and took two fresh and two partially burned marijuana cigarettes from her hand. One, said Barr, had lipstick on it. Miss Leeds said, 'I may as well give you the rest of them,' Barr alleged. She then reached into her bathrobe pocket, drew out a packet wrapped in newspaper and put it into Barr's hands. He unwrapped it and found what he said were three marijuana cigarettes and eight benzedrine tablets. The detectives then called headquarters. Policewoman Eleanor Whitney arrived and took the two women into custody. The two officers took Mitchum and his friend into custody. While the men were taken to the County Jail, the women went to Lincoln Heights Jail. All four were booked on felony charges of narcotics possession.

Mitchum's own version of the events that led up to his arrest differs from the police story but throws considerably more light on the surrounding circumstances. In the words of his own written plea for probation:

'I had met Robin Ford some years before when he was engaged in the promotion of a resort development, and had befriended him on several occasions, granting him the use of my car, etc., and he has always appeared to be trustworthy and well balanced.

'Learning that he was active as a real estate agent, and hoping to help, I suggested he help me find a house. He introduced me to Miss Leeds, with whom I went to the beach, in Ford's company, on one occasion, and with whom, on another occasion, I dined. Ford had relayed to me her declared interest, and I thought it best not to see her again.

'On the 31st of August, Ford and I had made an extensive house-hunting tour, and returning home he stopped to call Miss Leeds at approximately six o'clock, at which time I also called my agent [Phil Berg] to discuss a new script.

'We proceeded to my house where my secretary reported the day's business and relayed the list of telephone messages, one of which reported at 7:05 P.M., was from Miss Leeds. Ford called her and asked me if I would speak to her, which I did. Miss Leeds told me she had a new house and invited us up to see it. She suggested that we arrive after ten o'clock as the house wouldn't be ready until then. I said we might, although I rather felt that we wouldn't, being quite tired, and having a script to read. Ford and I went to the kitchen where we drank a fifth of Scotch while talking. My secretary reminded me to get something to eat, and left for her home. The secretary's name is Reva Fredrick.

'At 11 o'clock I decided to go out and eat before retiring, intending to drive into the valley from my house above Ventura Boulevard, and Ford, reminding me that he had no coat, requested that I drive him to Melrose Avenue, where he resided, to get one.

'En route to the Melrose Avenue apartment, he asked me to stop at Fountain Avenue and Havenhurst, which I did and he got out of the car, returning in a few minutes. I recall that the dashboard clock, which was correct, read 11:20. We proceeded to the Melrose partment, and he disappeared, returning in about five minutes to tell me that he had forgotten his key.

'As it was most logical to proceed to the valley through Laurel Canyon I started up that way, and again Ford asked me to stop. He said he wanted to call Miss Leeds, which apparently he did, and told me that she wanted us to come up. I was hungry by then but I reluctantly consented to stop in for a minute. After climbing the long stairway, we were met at the door by Miss Leeds and two affectionate boxer puppies which Miss Leeds described as "ferocious", to the general amusement. Another girl entered the room, and Miss Leeds introduced her as Vicki Evans. I remarked that I thought someone was outside the house and I went to the front windows to look out. Seeing nothing, I crossed the room and sat down on the couch. Miss Leeds crossed over and handed me a cigarette and upon accepting it, I looked up and saw what I believed to be a face at the window. I said, "There's a face at the window." Miss Evans said, "It's those damn dogs," and ran into the kitchen.

'At that moment there was a loud crash and two men burst into the room, holding Miss Evans as a shield. Without bothering to drop the cigarette, I crouched to throw one small table before me at the men, thinking it was a hold-up, and at the same time one of them shouted, "Police officers!" and moved toward me. Realizing that I had burned my fingers, I released the cigarette and rubbed my sore fingers on the couch. Sergeant Barr retrieved the cigarette and moved across the room to Miss Leeds.

'Not wishing any further moves misinterpreted, I offered my wrist to Officer McKinnon, who had already handcuffed Ford. I observed cigarettes in a crumpled Philip Morris wrapper on the table, and pushed them over towards Barr. He attempted to thrust the packet into my hand, and said, "These are yours." I replied they were not, and he said, "Look, don't give me any business, and we'll get along fine."'

When Mitchum and Ford were being charged at the County Jail, the booking officer formally asked the star his occupation.

'*Former* actor,' replied Mitchum.

'Who's going to bail you out?'

'Who knows?' said Mitchum dejectedly. 'I've got two bosses, David O. Selznick and RKO pictures.'

'Any tattoos?' asked the policeman.

Mitchum rolled up his shirt sleeve and pointed to a tiny blue spot and said 'It's an obscene word, too small to read.'

Within moments Hollywood's reporters were swarming

in, and Mitchum told them, 'I'm ruined. I'm all washed up in pictures now, I guess. This is the living end.'

One ironic facet of his arrest was that next day Mitchum had been due to make a speech on the steps of City Hall in a National Youth Month program. His appearance was hastily called off.

But the worst part of it all to Mitchum was that it would probably mean the end of his hopes for reconciliation with Dorothy. At the very moment of his arrest she was in a car heading toward Hollywood from the east with their two sons.

When the newsmen heard Dorothy was on her way back, they asked Mitchum if it *was* for a reconciliation.

'What *now?*' snapped Mitchum. 'I'd like to believe it *might* mean reconciliation. But my wife is a very resolute woman.'

After being formally booked, Mitchum, Robin Ford, Lila Leeds, and Vicki Evans were all released on bail of $1,000 each, pending a habeas corpus hearing on 8 September. Police told the press at this point that Mitchum and Miss Leeds had both partially admitted that they had been using marijuana for a long time.

Next day top Hollywood columnist Louella Parsons wrote that Mitchum was in a state of mental collapse at his home in Oak Glen Drive following his release. She said he had been ordered to bed and to sleep and not to talk to anyone until he had had a rest. But later that day Mitchum bitterly denied making any sort of confession and intimated that he believed he was being 'framed'.

The police were proud of their coup. For some months rumors had been circulating that a dope scandal was hovering dangerously over the film colony. Luncheon groups had discussed the growing incidence of drug use quite freely wherever movie people of the day gathered, and clearly the police were expected to make some move to counter increasing public concern. This must have been known by the heads of the studios, yet little was done by the top executives to bring their employed stars under control.

On 2 September Detective Sergeant Alva Barr told newsmen:

'We are going to clean the dope and the narcotics sellers out of Hollywood. And we don't care *whom* we have to arrest. This raid is only the beginning of the clean up. There is a lot of "stuff" being used in Hollywood. We have, besides Mitchum, a number of other important and prominent Hollywood screen personalities under surveillance, not only actors and actresses but others prominent in pictures.

'We have been watching Mitchum and Miss Leeds for eight months. We have had others under surveillance for that long, others are facing arrest. Hollywood can let this serve as a warning. Evidence is hard to get, but we're getting it and we are out to get not only the "users" but the "inside ring" who are supplying the big people in Hollywood with marijuana and other narcotics.

'Many of the big shots—stars and other top names,' continued Barr, 'do not patronize the small street or corner peddlers for fear of a shakedown and other dangers. However, we have reason to believe there is an "inside ring", perhaps of not more than three persons, right inside the film industry, who are supplying a large number of narcotics users. The most prevalent use is of marijuana, but we know that other drugs are being used.'

None of the top executives at his studio believed that Mitchum was a serious user of marijuana. They told newsmen he never gave any signs of being 'doped' and that he had turned in some fine performances. Indeed, David O. Selznick was charging $175,000 a picture to hire Mitchum out. RKO stood to be hit heavily by the scandal, it seemed. Films such as *Rachel and the Stranger*, *Blood on the Moon* and *The Red Pony*, which Mitchum made on loan-out to Republic, were still not yet on general release.

But both RKO and Selznick stood staunchly by Mitchum and said they would see him through his troubles. They immediately hired a brilliant lawyer, Jerry Giesler, who had successfully defended many famous stars in sensational cases, and an able advocate, Norman Tyre. They also issued a joint statement to the press:

'All the facts of the case are not yet known. We urgently request members of the industry and the public to withhold its judgment until these facts are known. Both studios feel confident the American people will not permit Mr Mitchum's prominence in the motion picture industry to deprive him of the rights and privileges of every American citizen to receive fair play.'

Jerry Giesler and Norman Tyre also issued a statement: 'There are a number of unexplained facts and peculiar circumstances surrounding the raid made yesterday in which Robert Mitchum was involved. His many friends have expressed their opinion that when all the facts are known he will be cleared. We therefore ask the public to withhold its judgment on the matter.'

As matters turned out, after a reinvestigation into the case nearly two and a half years later, this statement from the two lawyers reveals an unusual perspicacity.

As soon as news of Mitchum's arrest broke into print, the small three-room frame bungalow on Ridpath Drive became a sightseeing center for the curious. Landscape gardener Walter Caldwell lived next door with his wife and three small daughters at the time. On 2 September he said, 'I don't mind anyone having fun—but I hate to have to listen to it at four o'clock in the morning. Since Saturday it's been like one continuous party. That night expensive

The Depression years ... Mitchum at eight years old.
Miss Reva Frederick and the Mitchum family album.

Miss Reva Frederick and the Mitchum family album.

Mitchum (16) with friend and brother John (15) (far right).

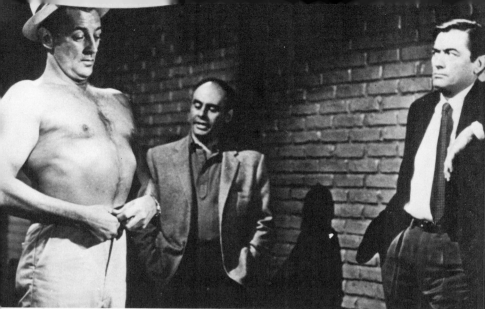

Universal International Films.

20th Century Fox.

A confrontation—Mitchum a psychopath intimidates attorney
Gregory Peck, the man responsible for him being jailed—in
Cape Fear (1962).

A skinny Mitchum in *Dancing Masters* (1943) with Laurel and
Hardy. One of Mitchum's too few comedy parts.

Mitch, a grizzled drunken sheriff and John Wayne, a hired gun who helps recover his manhood, in a scene from *Eldorado* (1967).

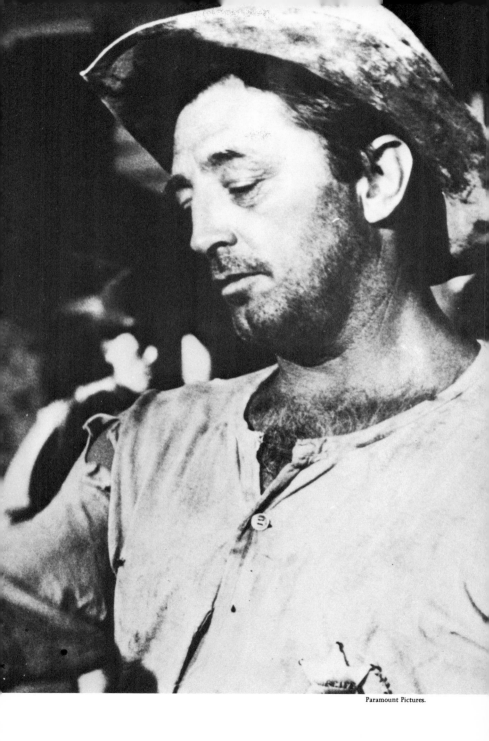

Paramount Pictures.

Mitchum—playing a murderous preacher—in threatening pose.
The Night of the Hunter (1955).

Mitch and Bill Boyd in *Hoppy Serves a Writ* (1943). 'I was always being slammed against bar-room walls by Hoppy.'

Mitch as Lieut. Walker in *GI Joe* (1945). The film that gave him his only Oscar nomination.

Warner–Seven Arts Pictures.

20th Century Fox.

In *The Good Guys and the Bad Guys* (1969) Mitch momentarily gets the worst of a fight with George Kennedy.

Mitch and Monroe in the famous kissing sequence in *River of no Return* (1954).

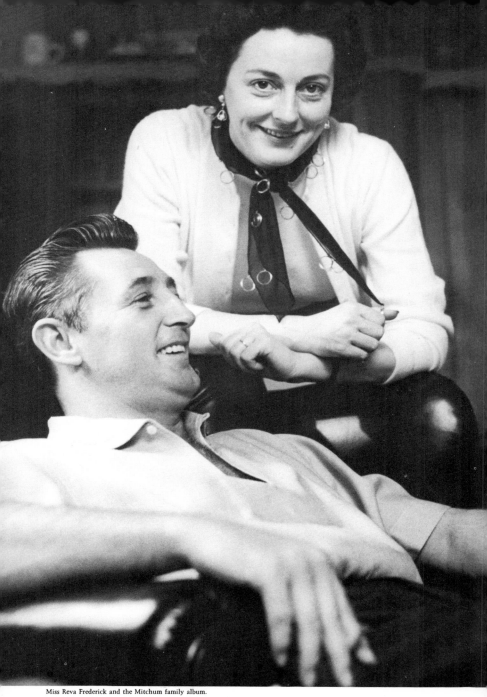

Miss Reva Frederick and the Mitchum family album.

Bob relaxes with his wife (1955).

Los Angeles Times and RKO Productions.

RKO Productions.

Family party. Left to right, Jim, Trina, Chris and Dorothy.
Mitch threads fishing line watched by his sons Jim and Chris before
their wilderness trip in the camper he designed (1952).

The famous Mitchum look ... An early portrait.

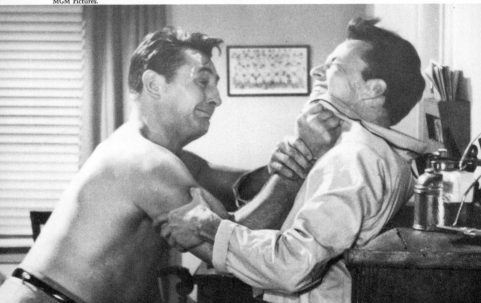

A match for Mitchum ... he confronts Hepburn in *Undercurrent* (1946).
Mitchum and Sinatra fight in *Not as a Stranger* (1955). 'I wouldn't want to tangle with Frank Sinatra.'

Mitchum smiles cynically as he watches a shipmate show a young lady how to land a big fish. *Fire Down Below* (1957).

At 54, Mitchum's fighting image is still intact. *Going Home* (1972). A near-exhausted Mitchum shears a sheep in *The Sundowners* (1960)—one of his finest roles.

A tender tableau—Mitchum and Deborah Kerr in a scene from
Heaven Knows, Mr Allison (1957).
Elsa Martinelli is Mitchum's leading lady in *Rampage* (1963).

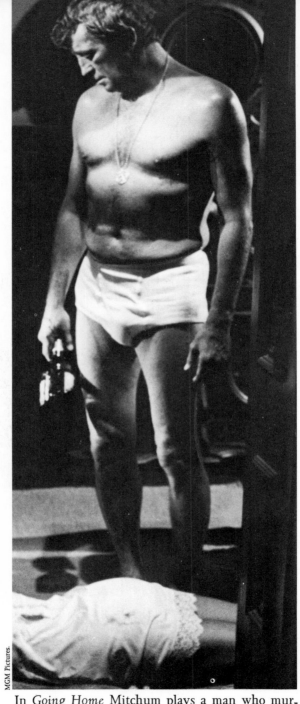

In *Going Home* Mitchum plays a man who murders his wife: the corpse is Sally Kirkland (1972).

cars were parking a block each way from the girls' place.
There must have been a hundred people there. They came
and went in batches. One group would be going up as
another group came down the steps. Auto horns were
blowing after 4:00 A.M. I don't know what marijuana does
to people ... but it sounded like everyone who went up
there grabbed a hammer and immediately started pounding. And the music never stopped. Nobody could sleep.'
Caldwell then took his family up into the mountains—
'to catch up on our sleep.'

As Mitchum stayed behind drawn curtains at his home
in Oak Glen Drive, preparing himself for the court battles
ahead, the only uplifting aspect was that his arrest *did*
help him to effect a true reconciliation with his wife.
Dorothy read the news in the middle of her transcontinen-
tal car journey with her two sons from New York, and she
decided to stand by her husband in his crisis.

At 6:30 A.M. on 3 September newsmen and photographers began to gather outside Mitchum's house, to await
Dorothy's arrival from the last lap of her journey—a ten-
hour drive from Los Vegas.

At 10:00 A.M. Dorothy arrived, parked her gray sedan
with its New York license plates, dashed up the steps with
her sons, seven-year-old Jim and five-year-old Chris, cried
to reporters, 'I am awfully tired,' and unlocked the front
door. As the boys ran inside, some newsmen saw Mitchum
and heard him call the boys' names: 'Josh! Chris!'

Later, a moving van delivered an upright piano, rented
from a local store, to the house. The mailman brought a
huge box of letters from all over the country. Mitchum's
secretary, Reva Fredrick, arrived next with two bunches of
chrysanthemums. Then two men came to fix the window
screens securely and to water the lawn. Shortly before
noon, Reva Fredrick left, taking the two Mitchum boys
with her. Jim and Chris were later left with Mitchum's

mother so that they would be shielded from all the fuss and publicity.

Six hours after Dorothy's arrival the first batch of newsmen were admitted into the house to talk to and take pictures of the reunited couple. Dorothy, obviously under strain, wore a ballerina gown, the reporters noted. She looked as if she had been crying.

She and Robert kissed each other on the steps of their house for the benefit of the insistent photographers; then Dorothy spoke to the press, staunchly defending her husband:

'Everybody ought to be able to see that Bob is a sick man; otherwise he'd never be mixed up in a situation like this. Our differences were the same all married couples get into. We have now made them up. I love my husband and am back now to stay with him. I'm indignant, though, that not only Bob but our whole family should have to suffer simply because he is a motion picture star. Otherwise I don't think all this fuss would have been made just because a man may have got mixed up with bad company. I'm sorry I cannot answer questions today. I have driven all day and all night to get to my sick husband as fast as I could, and I have had no sleep at all.

'I have only one favor to ask. That is that nobody bothers our children. They are very young, they love their father, and do not understand what it is all about.'

Mitchum said, 'I'm awfully happy that my wife feels the way she does. It's a great comfort to me.' Then he went back inside on the orders of Jerry Giesler.

Later, as more and more reporters and photographers lined up for access and were finally admitted to the house, Mitchum showed he had lost none of his wry sense of humor, despite his serious predicament.

'Was your marriage ever really in jeopardy?' asked one newsman.

'Every time I went to the studio in the morning,' Mitchum bantered.

'And every time he didn't shave,' Dorothy added, trying to be cheerful.

'What are your immediate plans?'

'Lunch!' replied Mitchum.

As studio officials arrived and supervised the picture sessions, one of them told a photographer, 'Don't get him looking up so high.' The asinine publicity machine of the Hollywood of those days was still busily at work.

Mitchum's gratitude for Dorothy's intensely loyal support at this time was real. As he wrote in his probation plea later: 'She had suffered the pitiless avalanche of publicity with enormous courage, and my gratitude for her forbearance is borne in deepest humility.'

Some newspapers became quite prim and indignant after the arrest and reminded Hollywood that it was a narcotics sensation that had first threatened the film industry with obliteration back in 1920—when handsome young Wally Reid, a public idol created by *The Birth of a Nation*, ran afoul of the federal authorities.

On the day of Dorothy's return home, the Selznick studio issued a further statement: 'We wish to thank all the individuals, groups, publishers, and newspaper men and women who have deluged us with telegrams and telephone calls volunteering advice and assistance to the end that Robert Mitchum's career may not be damaged through any public misunderstanding of his present plight.

'We are confident that the press will continue to give to its reporting of developments in the Mitchum case the fair and full and just treatment which distinguishes it from the press of some other countries.

'We are further confident that when the facts are fully understood and reported, there will be an end to the mental anguish that is being suffered by Mr Mitchum and his family, and that his place in the affections of the country's millions of theatergoers will be untouched.'

Two days later Jerry Giesler announced that Mitchum would not go before a Grand Jury hearing because the normal machinery of the lower courts had adequately dealt with many similar offences in the past. However, since the authorities clearly wanted justice to be *seen* to be done, on 8 September the County Grand Jury hearing was held.

The police evidence of the raid was presented. Then Sergeant Jay Allen, police chemist, produced twenty-five cigarettes allegedly seized by the raid officers which, he said, tests proved to be of 'the flowering leaves of *cannabis sativa*', or marijuana. Six of the cigarettes had been partially smoked, he reported.

'It was not a very good grade of marijuana,' Allen maintained. 'I would call it a medium mixture.' Mitchum and Lila Leeds declined to give evidence, as was their right, until a private investigation set up by Mitchum's attorneys had been completed. The Grand Jury returned indictments on Mitchum, Leeds, Evans, and Ford.

On the following day the four surrendered to Superior Court Judge Thomas L. Ambrose on the indictment, which charged them on two counts—possession of marijuana and conspiracy to possess marijuana, both in violation of the state narcotics laws.

8

Suspense, trial delays and final sentence

As Mitchum walked into the Los Angeles Hall Of Justice with his lawyers, it seemed the strain of the past nine days was beginning to tell. He looked haggard. But when a mob of loyal fans outside shouted encouragement and beseeched him for his autograph, he smilingly signed their books. This hearing proved to be merely a formal legality—held so the date of the actual trial could be assigned. Judge Ambrose confirmed the indictments and arraigned all four for trial on 21 September.

By then thousands of letters had been received by Mitchum's studio from all over the world, most of them expressing sympathy for the star. These letters, together with the sentiments expressed by the multitudes outside the court, implied that getting high on marijuana was no more in collision with mass mores than the more popular and financially rewarding method of teasing the electrons of one's physiology into a higher frequency with alcohol.

Indeed, while Mitchum was awaiting trial, a trailer of one of his films was roundly applauded in some local movie houses. Further proof that his stock with the public had not deteriorated came when both *Rachel and the Stranger* and *Blood on the Moon* began to show excellent returns at the box office. RKO showed no hesitation in casting Mitchum as the star of *The Big Steal* while he was still on bail, but they delayed the start of shooting in the belief that his immediate future would be decided by trial within a few weeks.

Despite all such popular support from outside, however, Mitchum and the others had to endure nearly five more months of suspense before knowing their fate. There were complications, adjournments, new suits and countersuits, and even a car accident, which delayed the day of final sentence until February, 1949.

On 21 September the four entered court again, only to be instructed to return in eight days to plead guilty or not guilty to the charges.

Before the next hearing Giesler made Mitchum, Leeds, and Ford file demurs to the charges, citing six instances in which the indictments returned by the Grand Jury were faulty. One demur was that the description of the offense was in language which could not be understood by 'ordinary persons', some of the charge being worded in Latin. Judge Ambrose denied the demurs, however, and after receiving 'not guilty' pleas, set the case for trial on 22 November before Superior Court Judge Clement D. Nye.

On 1 October, columnist Irv Kupcinet claimed that Mitchum was already paying the price for his arrest. 'His seven-year-old son returned home from school the other day and exclaimed that his schoolmates were teasing him by saying, "Is your old man out of jail yet?"' wrote Kupcinet. On another occasion, he added, Mitchum encountered a group of police officers who had told him they were keeping a special jail bunk warm for him.

On 8 October a plea by Vicki Evans that she was not responsible in the case was rejected by Judge Ambrose, who directed she should face trial with Mitchum and the other two.

The next complication came on 27 October when actress Nanette Bordeaux, who owned the cottage in Ridpath Drive, filed charges accusing the four of being trespassers in her home for a period of several weeks. She claimed that during this time they 'destroyed and removed furniture and burned the walls and furnishings through the careless and negligent handling of cigarettes'. She asked for $2,500 damages. She claimed she had rented the place to an actress who had illegally sublet it to Lila Leeds and thus to the other three also. When filing this suit, Nanette Bordeaux said that she resented references to her property as a 'shack' and a 'marijuana den'. She maintained the place was a small but attractive cottage, furnished in modest good taste.

On 13 November the trial date was again delayed because Jerry Giesler had been injured in an accident on 2 October when his car had gone out of control near his Beverly Hills home and had crashed into a palm tree. Attorney Grant D. Cooper, for the defense, said Giesler would be ready for the trial during the latter part of December. But both Judge Clement D. Nye and Deputy District Attorney Adolph Alexander said they would be on holiday at that time. The trial was then held over until 10 January, 1949.

Nine days before this date Mitchum's mother was ordered by the prosecution to be ready to appear at his trial. She was handed a subpoena at her home in North Palm Drive, Beverly Hills, but Deputy District Attorney Alexander said he was not sure she would, in fact, be called to testify. (She was not.)

On 10 January the trial was finally held. But the case that the world's newsmen had anticipated would be one of the most sensational in Hollywood's history proved, for them at least, to be something of an anticlimax. Detective Sergeant Alva Barr's testimony of the raid was heard again, but no witnesses took the stand for either the prosecution or the defense.

The reason was simply that Giesler had waived his clients' rights to a jury trial and had asked for trial on only the charge of conspiracy to possess marijuana—with the charge of actual possession to be held in abeyance. Exercising this option was a sagacious move on Giesler's part, for the conspiracy charge carried the possibility of probation, while the possession charge carried a mandatory sentence of ninety days in jail. His ploy of offering no evidence for the defense also meant that Mitchum, Leeds, and Ford would not be subjected to merciless cross-examination, and had the effect of throwing them upon the mercy of the court. Vicki Evans, who now only had the lesser charge of *visiting* a place where marijuana was used proffered against her, did not attend this hearing. Her attorney told the court that she was in New York and didn't have enough money to pay her fare to Hollywood, but that she would appear as soon as possible to face trial.

Judge Nye pronounced the trio 'guilty as charged', told the court that he would rule later on probation reports and pleas entered by the three, and set the date for final sentence as 9 February. Mitchum took the guilty verdict with a deadpan expression. All three were once more released on $1,000 bail each. The case against Miss Evans was postponed by the judge to an indefinite later date.

After the trial, Deputy District Attorney Alexander said that his department would probably drop the heavier charge of actual possession of marijuana on the day Mitchum, Leeds, and Ford were sentenced. 'We would be saving the public's money,' he said. 'Besides, we don't like persecuting people.'

Even in the brief respite before final sentence, Mitchum's troubles were not over. On 19 January he sued for $10,000 damages in a cross-complaint to the suit for $2,500 damages brought by actress Nanette Bordeaux. He claimed an advertisement had appeared in the *Canyon Crier* on 6 January at Nanette Bordeaux's request and that its purpose was to sell furniture belonging to her through the unauthorized use of his name. His complaint said the ad read

'Robert Mitchum sat here. Charming sofa and arm chair. New slip covers hide cigarette burns, $15. Souvenir hunters have taken everything else.' Mitchum asserted that Bordeaux sold her furniture from the advertising at a great profit without ever receiving permission to use his name.

Twelve days later he also filed a deposition in direct answer to her claim. His statement said, in essence: he had only been in her home once and thus couldn't have damaged her furniture in the way alleged; and he not only couldn't have but didn't. Mitchum had a sneaking suspicion that Bordeaux's interest lay partly in attracting publicity for herself. 'If the kid's looking for a screen job, I hope this will get it for her,' he said laconically.

Nanette Bordeaux's attorney told reporters that the newspaper in question and not Bordeaux had caused her ad to be printed as it had appeared. He also disclosed that Lila Leeds was suing Nanette Bordeaux for $100 for the loss of two lamps she claimed were hers. His client's answer to this, he said, was that Lila Leeds could have her lamps back any time she wanted to pick them up.

On the appointed date, Mitchum and Leeds appeared before Judge Nye for sentence. Mitchum looked pale but composed. Leeds had spent the previous eight days ill in bed. Robin Ford and Vicki Evans did not appear. The prosecution revealed that Ford had been involved in a new arrest and that Evans had been detained in New York and was being returned to Hollywood by the District Attorney's office. Judge Nye then postponed sentence on Ford and Evans until early March.

The Judge, who had been studying the probation reports on both Mitchum and Leeds since the last hearing, was told that the defense was completely in accord with them. (The recommendations of the Probation Department were never made public.) Judge Nye also duly considered the long written plea for probation prepared by Mitchum, which the star had ended with the following observations:

'Millions of pages of ugly black newsprint have shocked me into the realization of my true position, and the enormity of my transgression. I consider myself neither maladjusted or misused, and I shall regard without malice any further payment to society as merely a delay in the constructive pursuit of my new-born citizenry.

'It is not true that I helped Lila Leeds move into that place on the Sunday before my arrest. I had never before been to 8443 Ridpath Drive. I did not have any marijuana when I entered the house, nor did I know or believe that anyone else there would have any marijuana available.

'I have no quarrel with the testimony of the officers at my trial, except for the perhaps unavoidable fact that almost the entire emphasis was placed on me and on the name of Robert Mitchum instead of giving each person and each fact its normal relationship to the others.

'This, of course, arises out of the fact that I am a motion picture actor, and I am, therefore, the conscious or unconscious subject of overemphasis.

'My first use of marijuana was an isolated instance in 1936 while I was working in Toledo. I had no further contact with it until about 1947, at a time when I was working very hard. During 1947 and 1948, I occasionally used marijuana when in the company of people who used it. I was never a confirmed smoker of marijuana and never purchased marijuana for use by myself. The only explanation I have for the use of marijuana is the fact that when you are in the company of people who use it it was easier to go along with them than not to.

'The only effect that I ever noticed from smoking marijuana was a sort of mild sedative, a release of tension when I was overworking. It never made me boisterous or quarrelsome. If anything, it calmed me down and reduced my activity.

'I have never used any other drug. My attitude with respect to the future use of marijuana is that I will not use marijuana at any time whatsoever.

'I am asking for probation in the hope that it may be granted. If I did not think it should be granted, I would not ask for it.

'It is my feeling that a transgression of the law should be punished. It is my belief that I have already received, both before and after my conviction, far more punishment than the law itself would have envisaged for a first offense of this kind.

'Time in jail would add nothing to the subjective feeling I already have about what I have done. It could only penalize my family by reducing their income. (Creditably, he did not mention *The Big Steal*.) It could only subject me to the possibility of termination of my employment. It might even make it impossible for me to secure work in the motion picture industry.

'It is my earnest hope that the attitude with reference to probation shown by the probation officers, who treated me as just another human being, will be that evidenced by others who have to make this decision, which is most important to me,' the plea ended.

Before he passed sentence on Mitchum and Leeds, Judge Nye addressed the star: 'I cannot overlook the responsibility that you, Mr Mitchum, have to hundreds of thousands of young Americans who idolize you,' he said. 'You have worked yourself up to a position of prominence in the motion picture industry. Up to now this has meant nothing but glory for you. But you may have overlooked the responsibility which goes with this prominence.

'You have failed to set an example of good citizenship. I am sorry for both of these defendants, but respect for law and order must be taken into consideration. This case has attracted attention not only locally, but throughout the world, and I'm treating it the same as I would any other case of a similar nature.'

He then sentenced both Mitchum and Leeds to serve a year in the County Jail. This sentence was suspended, and both the defendants were placed on probation for two years, with an order that the first sixty days of the probation be spent in the County Jail with all good time earned while in confinement to be taken off the sentence. Under this ruling, Mitchum and Leeds, if they behaved suitably in jail, would gain their freedom in fifty days.

Judge Nye then ordered the second charge of actually possessing marijuana 'Off Calendar', which meant it would be dismissed after the legal time for an appeal had expired. This legal time was ten days after sentence was passed.

After pronouncing sentence Judge Nye declared a recess, and the courtroom became a minor bedlam. Photographers rushed in and took pictures of the principals. Spectators crowded to the rails and shouted encouragement to Mitchum and the actress. Studio officials went into a quick huddle. Mitchum's sentence would clearly mean an abrupt halt on *The Big Steal*.

Mitchum was then handcuffed by Deputy Sheriff Walter Horta, while Deputy Sheriff Marjorie Kellog took Leeds into custody. The four then walked up from the eighth to the ninth floor of the Hall Of Justice, rode the elevators to the twelfth floor, and disappeared behind the iron bars of the jail.

As he went through the jail doors, Mitchum smiled and told newsmen that he was satisfied with Judge Nye's verdict.

'This is the last time anything like this will ever happen to me,' he vowed. 'It has been a sad lesson. I hope it will save other people from a similar fate.' He was in fact unprepared to go to jail, for he had even forgotten his tooth brush.

'I always travel light, but I guess this is a little too light!' he quipped.

9

The prisoner

Robert Mitchum, now Prisoner No. 91234, hadn't been in jail twenty-four hours before his attorneys filed a motion for stay of sentence until 1 April, to allow him to complete *The Big Steal*.

Jerry Giesler's motion claimed that a stay of sentence would save many persons being thrown abruptly out of work. 'There are more than a hundred and fifty studio employees working on *The Big Steal*, which is about half finished, and this is at a time when *all* picture employment is at a low ebb,' Giesler claimed. 'The cost of laying off this company, the loss of time and pay for all these people, will be staggering.'

At the brief hearing which Mitchum attended next day, Giesler told Judge Nye: 'I'm not speaking for Mr Mitchum as an individual but rather for all these people who face a lay-off on the studio lot because of his enforced absence. I should have made the request at the time he was sentenced, but in the confusion I overlooked it.'

The plea didn't work. Judge Nye told Giesler: 'I can't make an exception in this case. I realize that someone is being hurt, but such is the case with practically every other prisoner in the County jail. If I tried to aid every innocent person who suffers with every convicted person I would have to empty the jail. The studio officials should have realized there was a hazard about Mr Mitchum's appearance from the time he was arrested last September.'

After this hearing, both Mitchum and Leeds, who had spent only one night in jail, were seen again by reporters.

'I have no kick coming,' said Mitchum. 'I don't like jail, naturally, but they treat us okay.'

Leeds, now Prisoner 91233, said 'The thing that bothers me is the clanging of the cell doors.'

Both were again interviewed as they worked at their respective chores of mopping and cleaning up their cells. Both wore jail issue denim blues, though Mitchum was allowed to keep his expensive dark brown Cordovas and brown socks. Under jail rules, prisoners could wear their own footwear except when shoes were high-heeled—thus providing a possible weapon. Mitchum said he had slept 'fine' on his two inch-thick mattress on one of the steel bunks. He also liked his jail breakfast of oatmeal, applesauce, coffee and bread, served at 6:30 A.M.

Prisoners were allowed to buy some foods plus candy, tobacco, and newspapers from a prison concessionaire, and Mitchum took advantage of this to stock up with four quarts of milk and two cartons of cigarettes. Supplies were not permitted from outside sources, for obvious reasons.

Mitchum, who was at this time earning $3,250 a week as an actor, was allowed to keep only 'a couple of bucks' in his pocket. Visitors other than attorneys were restricted to two a week, and each visit lasted only fifteen minutes. All prisoners' letters were censored, but they could write as many as they wished. Their 6:30 A.M. breakfast was followed by a bowl of soup at 10:00 A.M. and dinner at 3:00 P.M. Each man had his own cup and spoon, which he had to keep scrupulously clean.

From the start, Mitchum took easily to the others. He didn't try to act the big star but was highly sociable. He engaged in card games and conversations with his cell mates. When newsmen asked him how he spent his spare time, he replied, 'Oh, we just talk over our lives of crime! Mostly the other fellows don't bother with me too much, they have their own troubles.' But his popularity was undeniable.

Four days after his incarceration, many sections of the world's press were still clamoring for more news and pictures of the star, and reporters were once more admitted to the jail. They found Mitchum had already been elected cell 'trusty'.

'I'm really proud the men in the tank recommended me to the jailers to be the tank trusty,' he smiled. 'That's considered quite an honor, you know. The men and I get along well.'

When he was told that Chief Jailer Charles Fitzgerald might transfer him to work at the County Honor Farm at Castaic, Mitchum was none too pleased. 'I kind of like it *here*,' he said. 'I don't get into trouble here, and I might if they send me someplace else. I'm due to take over my new job as trusty on Saturday. No, I'm not so happy at the thought of leaving.'

Both Jerry Giesler and RKO told Mitchum they thought he would be happier with the outdoor work at the Honor Farm. They also reasoned the bobby soxer's idol of the day would keep in better shape by working hard in the bright sunlight than doing his time in a prison cell.

When he was taken out for a physical examination to insure that he was capable of working on the farm, Mitchum disclosed a further fear about his transfer. He thought the other prisoners out there—some seven hundred—might resent the fact that he was a movie star. 'In the tank, in jail, we have plenty of supervision,' he said. 'I felt as if I were in church.' But Fitzgerald allayed his fears and said he would have nothing to fear at Castaic. 'Actually there is a closer supervision of the prisoners there than in jail,' he said.

On 16 February Mitchum was taken along with other prisoners to the Castaic Honor Farm in the Sheriff Department's shiny new bus. As he boarded it, he said, 'I don't know if I'll like it up there, but I'm going to do the best I can. I hope it's something constructive.' As newsmen and photographers watched, the bus pulled out with seven other prisoners. Mitchum sat on the last seat by himself, his hat pulled down over his eyes. The heavily barred vehicle was followed all the way by a motorcade of press cars. It arrived late, and Mitchum missed his lunch.

He was taken with the others to the storeroom and issued overalls instead of the jail denims; then he heard a lecture on the rules of the farm. He was told he had to rise at 5:30 A.M., clean his bed area, etc., have breakfast at 6:30 A.M. and report for work at 8:00 A.M. Then, as the press cameras clicked around him, he was taken to the dairy yard to see if he could persuade a cow called Bossy to yield some milk. His early experience with farm life proved useful, for he expertly filled a pail. Then he answered reporters' quips by shooting a stream of milk over them from Bossy's teat.

For the first few days he was schooled in the where, what, why, and how of his new home, under the direction of Chief A. W. Willey of the Rehabilitation Division. He had to fulfill various probationary chores before earning the right to one of the better jobs. Finally, he became one of twenty-five men who toiled eight hours a day in the cement block factory to turn out a daily quota of a thousand blocks.

He arrived at the cement plant at 8:00 A.M., worked until 11:30 A.M., and returned to the mess hall for lunch. Then he worked on the twelve-pound blocks until 4:30 P.M., when he returned for supper. After this he could amuse himself in whatever way he wished until the lights went out, at 10:00 P.M. He could watch movies, get books from the library, play cards, indulge in such sports as boxing or wrestling, or attend educational sessions at the farm school.

When reporters visited him again, he told them, 'I had chronic insomnia, just like a lot of other people on the Hollywood merry-go-round, before I came here. Now I'm sleeping like a baby. I haven't had so much sleep in years.'

By then RKO had moved filming of *The Big Steal* out to Mexico. Mitchum's stand-in was handling the star's role in the long shots, the idea being that Mitchum would complete the close-ups later, after his release from jail.

On 3 March, 1949, Mitchum's suit for $10,000 against Nanette Bordeaux, in which he claimed she had no right to advertise her sofa for sale with the line 'Robert Mitchum sat here', was dismissed in court by Judge William K. McKesson, who said:

'Movie stars are not in a position to claim the right of privacy because their faces and names are sold to the public, and they aid in selling.' In his sixteen-page opinion, the judge took judicial notice of the public reputation of Mitchum and maintained: 'Justice does not require that the courts profess to be more ignorant than the rest of mankind. Justice is represented as blind, but not necessarily as ignorant ...

'The public has acquired an interest in the name and actions of Robert Mitchum, and he has lost his right to exclusive use of his name, if indeed he ever had such right.'

The ruling also sustained a demur to Mitchum's suit, presented by Bordeaux's attorney, who stated he was ready to present evidence that his client had not written the advert nor authorized use of the actor's name.

On 8 March both Mitchum and Lila Leeds were taken from their respective prisons to attend the trial of Vicki Evans, but after standing about nearly all day they did not give evidence. Miss Evans' attorney, Jerry Webber, withdrew subpoenas on Mitchum, Miss Leeds and Robin Ford when he learned they had been counselled to stand pat on their constitutional rights and refuse to tell about the alleged marijuana party at Miss Leeds' rented home last 31 August. Mitchum and Miss Leeds left before the case ended. In fact Miss Evans was never convicted.

Before Mitchum went back to Castaic, the ubiquitous press corps descended upon him again. He told them: 'My job up there has been making cement blocks. In fact the boys have named me, "Mr Cement Block of 1949".' He said his free day off in court did *not* please him. 'I missed the big game with the road camp team,' he complained.

On 17 March Robin Ford received the same sentence as Mitchum and Miss Leeds but he had already spent forty-seven days in jail while awaiting sentence—on another charge.

On 24 March Mitchum arrived back at the County Jail to put in the last week of his sentence. He had a newly acquired moustache, sported a heavy tan and looked extremely fit after losing some seven or eight pounds. He said he was glad to be in the home stretch of his jail term and he was not griping about his stay at the Honor Farm.

'It was a relief to get away for a while. It's been the finest vacation I've had in seven years,' he said. 'I feel wonderful. I worked hard, slept well and batted to an .800 average on the Rancho softball team, playing second base. We won seven out of eight games. I have never felt better in my life. That farm was just like a weekend in Palm Springs—great for getting into shape.'

Chief Jailer Charles Fitzgerald and other officials described Mitchum as a model prisoner. 'He was a hard, energetic worker,' they said. 'He asked no favors; he cheerfully took any assignment handed to him.' Fitzgerald also said that Mitchum had been transferred back to the County Jail partly because a constant stream of important business visitors had interrupted his work schedule at the farm. One of these visitors, who were mostly agents, writers and studio officials, was tycoon Howard Hughes, who gave Mitchum candy and nut bars, bottles of vitamins and instructed the actor to keep up his strength.

This was at the time when Hughes was taking over complete control of RKO and also buying out Mitchum's contract from David O. Selznick. Hughes personally liked Mitchum and it was perhaps lucky for the star that he did, because after Mitchum's 1948 arrest Hughes could easily have canceled Mitchum's contract under the morals clause and put him among the unemployed.

Mitchum was pleased when Hughes bought the remainder of his contract. 'Selznick was always loaning me out,' he once said. 'Maybe he thought I wasn't good enough to be in his own pictures! Sometimes I was loaned for roles I didn't want to do, but I was too new in this business to be temperamental, so I did what I was told.'

On Wednesday, 30 March, Mitchum and Leeds were released from jail, having served fifty of their sixty-day sentences. Both had earned the maximum ten days remission for good behavior. They didn't meet afterward because they had been instructed not to associate under the terms of their two years' probation.

Looking fit as he emerged from prison, Mitchum said, 'I'm traveling light. Light in possessions and light in my heart. I came here with four handkerchiefs and $12.60 in cash. I guess I gave some dough away to help fellows transferred to the Folsom Penitentiary, but I did make thirty cents in a poker game!' He thought he was still solvent, however. 'I've got an extension until May to file my income tax return. Until then I'm solvent anyway! I have to be back before the cameras next Monday. Heck, I've got to work to pay my taxes.'

Reflecting on his weeks in jail, he added, 'I've been

happy because I've had privacy here. Nobody envied me. Nobody wanted anything from me. Nobody wanted my bars or the bowl of pudding they shoved at me through the slot. I did my work, and they let me alone.'

He said he had developed a new taste for privacy and planned to have more of it. 'I'm through with my so-called pals. I'll see only my wife, my two children, and a couple of close friends. Parties? I'd stand out like a monster at them. I'm typed now—a character—and I guess I'll have to bear that the rest of my life.' He told the newsmen he was sorry that his case had involved the film industry, but it obviously hadn't been possible to treat him merely as an ordinary human being.

'I wanted to serve the time and now I've served it,' he added. 'Now I'm in the clear and I intend to remain that way. And now, if you'll excuse me, I'm heading for home.'

Mitchum's experiences in jail enabled him to reflect objectively about the penal methods of the day. His ideas, based on observation of his fellow prisoners rather than on himself—for he had received a great deal of attention—revolved round the theme that the prison system was archaic. He said he felt newcomers should first receive a special classification by a psychiatrist. Then the prisoner's treatment and remedial conditions of sentence should be tailored to help his or her rehabilitation to the utmost. Considering this is very much in line with the views of to-day's pioneering penologists, Mitchum proved to be unusually advanced in his social thinking at the time.

He added, with characteristic color: 'You get a new chimpanzee and put him in Griffith Park Zoo and everybody rushes to look him over. And if the keepers don't feed him well and take the best care of him, the public raises hell. But you put a person in a cage and nobody seems to care how he gets along.

'And it doesn't even amuse the children.'

10

Aftermath and exoneration. Broke—but the world forgives. 'He never whined.'

After leaving jail Robert Mitchum headed straight home to Dorothy and young Jim and Chris. After a few days with his family he was sent on to Mexico to complete *The Big Steal*. For the next year he worked quietly and diligently to reestablish his career. It wasn't too hard a task, for clearly the public was on his side. While he had certainly lost all resemblance to being a model for American youth—'I'm sure through with playing scout-masters!' he said—the world's moviegoers seemed to be fascinated by his Bad Boy image and certainly respected him for taking his medicine without whining.

But this was by no means the end of the marijuana affair. There were persistent rumors around Hollywood that Mitchum had been 'framed'. In 1949 and again in early 1951 there came two extraordinary sequels.

On 22 September, 1949, District Attorney William E. Simpson's office disclosed that every phase of Mitchum's narcotics arrest would be reinvestigated to determine whether extortionists had engineered the case.

This investigation was part of a larger inquiry into organized crime in Los Angeles, and it followed charges before the Grand Jury by Mitchum's former manager Paul Behrmann that a Hollywood blackmail syndicate headed by gambler Mickey Cohen used party girls to entrap wealthy men.

Chief Investigator H. Leo Stanley told reporters that while he did not question the legitimacy of the arrest that

118

resulted in Mitchum's conviction for conspiracy to possess marijuana, he was interested in 'reports that the case was engineered'. He said Leeds and Evans would be questioned to determine whether they themselves were victims of extortionists. Behrmann, who had refused to answer some of District Attorney Simpson's questions before the Grand Jury, had told the court that he had evidence that Cohen headed a blackmail ring from which Cohen collected sixty percent and the party girls kept the balance, from the blackmail 'shakedowns' with rich men. As various businessmen gave evidence of shakedowns and blackmail to the investigators, the D.A's office issued an order for Leeds, Evans, and five party girls to be brought in for questioning. The two girls, and one of the other girls named, vigorously denied being implicated, but they gave helpful evidence to the D.A's office.

The possibility that all this might have had something to do with Mitchum's arrest arose from the fact that Mitchum had testified against Behrmann in the latter's grand theft trial involving the $10,000 allegedly obtained on behalf of Anne Nicholls, the *Abie's Irish Rose* playwright. District Attorney Simpson revealed at this point that both Mitchum and Leeds, who had also been on Behrmann's books, may have earned Behrmann's enmity by dispensing with his services. Furthermore, he added, besides discharging Behrmann as his manager, Mitchum had ignored reported threats of reprisal if he testified during Behrmann's theft trial. Mitchum's testimony in that trial had strengthened the state's case, at the end of which Behrmann had been convicted. Another figure in the Behrmann = Mitchum difficulty had been Mitchum's former secretary, Richard Ellis, who was also named by Behrmann before the Grand Jury as being involved in the extortion racket.

For several days the investigation continued, and on 27

September, 1949, witness after witness trod a path to Leo Stanley's door. Lila Leeds, dressed in a black tweed suit with a blue mink scarf, gave Stanley a detailed account of her business relationship with Behrmann, as well as a hitherto untold story of the events leading up to the marijuana arrests.

Lila Leeds told Stanley that out of all the girls mentioned she knew only Vicki Evans and a girl named Betty Doss. In her new version of the marijuana party incidents, she said she first met Vicki Evans shortly before the raid and that Evans moved into her rented home four days before it took place.

She told Stanley that two days before the raid she was with Evans in a Vine Street café when she saw a girl named Betty Rice in the company of a 'pock-marked fellow named Rudy'. After she and Vicki Evans went home, Betty Doss phoned her and said that Betty Rice and Rudy wanted to come up to the house. She refused to invite them, however, and Betty Doss showed up alone.

Referring to the actual day of the raid, Leeds told of how Ford called her to ask permission to visit her new quarters. A little while later he called again and wanted permission to bring Mitchum with him. Soon afterward, she told Stanley, a man representing himself as a film reporter phoned her for an interview and she gave him her new address. Early in the evening Ford phoned that he'd be delayed but would be up later.

'I was putting up Vicki's hair, and I was smoking a marijuana cigarette,' she told Stanley. 'Why didn't the cops who were outside watching, as I found out later, pinch me then? But they didn't. They waited till Mitchum got there. Vicki wasn't smoking that night, and I noticed when Ford and Mitchum came up and were smoking, Vicki kept away from them. I checked all the doors and windows and locked them all before Mitchum arrived.' Leeds added that while she, Mitchum, and Ford were smoking mari-juana the dogs barked and that Evans opened the back door. It was then that the police came in. Among the police raiders who arrived subsequently, she said, she recognized the 'pock-marked Rudy', whom she later iden-tified as Officer Rudy Diaz of the Vice Squad. Leeds told Stanley as she finished giving him evidence: 'I'm not accusing anyone of entrapment or of being a stool pigeon.'

Mitchum himself gave no evidence at this investigation and made no accusations. But some years later, when it was all over, he did express his doubts to writer Bill Davidson:

'I'd still like to know the answers to some pertinent ques-tions. Why were the newspapers tipped off, before I even arrived at the Leeds house, that a big-name movie star was going to be picked up on marijuana charges that night? Why did Robin Ford stop off to make so many phone calls that night? Why didn't the police raid the Leeds house earlier, since they testified they had seen Leeds smoking long before I arrived? Why did Vicki Evans go to the kitchen door just as the police broke in, and why was she the only one of us who never was convicted? Why did a half dozen other movie stars come up to me later and thank me, saying *they* had been invited to a party at that house that night, but when they arrived it was already surrounded by police cars, lights flashing, so they took off?'

The results of the District Attorney's investigation were not publicly announced. But on 31 January, 1951, the Los Angeles court quietly reviewed Mitchum's marijuana conviction and declared: 'After an exhaustive investiga-tion of the evidence and testimony presented at the trial, the court orders that the verdict of guilty be set aside and that a plea of not guilty be entered and that the informa-tion or complaint be dismissed.'

The court's action had also been prompted by Mitchum's own request for a review of his case after he had completed his period of probation.

The astonishing part of it all was that Mitchum never tried to publicize the court's belated exoneration. His silence was all the more exceptional because he had a powerful studio behind him and some of the best press agents in Hollywood at his disposal. In later years he has, in response to questions, referred to the exoneration, but only *en passant*—as if it no longer mattered.

If Mitchum had had any doubts about his status as a star before going to jail, he certainly had none after his release. As Dorothy once said 'He never really looked upon himself as a movie star, although he soon started getting big parts and the money got better. I don't think he really knew he was a star until the trouble in 1948 and there was all that fuss when he went to prison. He sort of discovered he was a star by the way the other prisoners talked inside. He made friends with some of them, and for years they still came to see him.'

Mitchum also resisted all tempting offers from media to put out 'I've learned my lesson' stories the public might have expected. 'I hope I don't get into any more trouble,' he said. 'But who can say what he might do tomorrow? If I put out some phony reform story and then fall from grace, I'd look like a liar.'

To Hedda Hopper Mitchum expanded this theme a little further: 'I think everyone ought to enjoy himself as much as possible so long as it doesn't cause pain to others. I'm firmly convinced that of the people who manage to achieve anything, the worthy ones are those who use their position to help *others* improve their shining hour.

'It's a sad thing that nobody learns except through experience, so sometimes the desire to do good backfires.'

It appears that Mitchum must have suddenly felt he

was beginning to sound like he was in a pulpit for he suddenly changed tack slightly. 'John Barrymore, for instance, fathered a whole school of crazy actors. They tried to be like him [Barrymore was a heavy drinker], but none had his constitution or ability. So they all fell dead! As for myself, well, there was a time when I thought I might have something on the ball but I've practically given up. I think I'll be a journeyman all my life. You see, I can't act like an actor's evidently supposed to. These other birds do all the right things; wear clothes that fit, know all the other stars, talk professionally. They even convince *me* they're good actors. So when I go to see their pictures, I think they're good. But to me, all my own pictures look like clumsy old sandwiches.'

The world's movie audiences, though, clearly liked Mitchum's old sandwiches and flocked to his films after his release more than ever before. As his popularity increased, it was clear the public personally admired a man who took his punishment without complaint and who never once lost his sense of humor.

Mitchum doesn't think his jail term helped his career or that people liked him because he was Hollywood's hell raiser. He thought it was probably more because they knew he genuinely didn't really care about being a star. His nonchalant attitude certainly endeared him to his boss, Howard Hughes, who once said to him, 'The truth is, Bob, you *really* don't care, do you?'

Hughes himself did care. He realized that Mitchum was probably the best horse in his stable and he was prepared to back him to the hilt. On a four hour visit to Mitchum at the Honor Farm, Hughes had asked the star if there was anything he needed? Mitchum, who now owed his defense attorney Jerry Giesler some $50,000 in legal fees, had replied, 'Yes, sir. I need something all right—about fifty thousand bucks.' Hughes hadn't batted an eye but had told Mitchum to remind him of that little matter upon his release.

Mitchum did so and Hughes loaned him a large sum of money at six percent, to be deducted from his future pay. He also instructed the studio to hire a private detective to help keep Mitchum out of further trouble. (The 'shamus' Mitchum called him.) It took Mitchum until well into 1951 before he was back on his feet again financially.

But money itself has never been a matter of prime concern to Mitchum. As he said at the time, 'I'm not interested in accumulating a fortune. I figure if I can give my boys ten thousand each when they turn twenty-one, they ought to be able to make the grade. I wish somebody had handed me ten grand when I was twenty-one.' He smiled then added, 'My kids see me around home so much they think the picture business is a great racket. They figure all you have to do to earn your check is ride horses and kiss pretty girls!'

In *The Big Steal* Mitchum played an army finance officer who pursued a man suspected of stealing a government money shipment. He was joined in the chase by the suspect's girl friend (Jane Greer) with whom he exchanged wry cracks and amorous clinches en route. As soon as shooting was finished, Mitchum took his family on a fishing trip off the coast of Mexico.

When the picture was released, it did well at the box office and Mitchum was announced as the star of half a dozen new films.

'But do you think I'll get a good script?' he asked. 'The answer's no. I didn't like *The Big Steal* but it's making a barrel of money, so I'll be doing *The Big Steal* from now on. When a studio comes up with a musty old script that brings in the shekels, the actor hasn't got much of an argument.

'So I don't bother the studio, and it doesn't bother me.

Somebody hands me a script, I look at it and ask, "When do I start?" If there is a good story on the lot, you've got to smuggle it out to read it. And I do mean smuggle. The other day I was sneaking a script through the gate and "the shamus" caught me. He wanted to know what I had in the bundle. I told him it was none of his business and got by with it.'

RKO hurried his next two films into production and release. They were obvious popular entertainments. The first was *Holiday Affair*, with Janet Leigh, and the second was a fast-moving drama called *Where Danger Lives*, in which he played a San Francisco intern involved with an insane beauty (Faith Domergue) who murders her husband and shifts the blame onto Mitchum.

Of *Holiday Affair*, Mitchum said airily, 'It's a cutie. I play a clerk in a toy department. And Janet, who's a buyer for a rival store, gets me fired. We wind up with her seven-year-old son and an electric train on our hands. So you take it from there.'

Despite his apparent disregard, Mitchum wasn't going to let Hughes or RKO turn him into a doormat. Asked how he got along with Hughes, Mitchum replied, 'The phantom, you mean? We get along fine. I told him I'd discuss his problems if he'd discuss mine. The studio wanted to put me in one picture that would have had me playing a fourth-rate Pat Novak. That was too much. I took the matter to Howard. He said, "Okay, you don't have to play it." And that was that.'

In 1949 Mitchum was awarded the Least Cooperative Actor 'sour apple' award by the Hollywood Women's Press Club. Naturally, after all the publicity about his jail sentence, Mitchum had been trying to cut down his exposure in the mass media and had given few interviews. He wired the women at their annual luncheon: 'Your gracious award becomes a treasured addition to a collection of inverse citations. These include prominent mention in several Ten Worst Dressed Americans lists and a society column-ist's Ten Most Undesirable Male Guests list, which happily was published on the date I was made welcome at the County Jail.'

Olivia de Havilland, who had been voted the Least Cooperative Actress, did not acknowledge her award. Loretta Young and Alan Ladd were given 'gold apple' awards that year for being the Most Cooperative Actress and Actor.

In the summer of 1950 Mitchum starred opposite Ava Gardner in a nineteenth-century period drama, *My Forbidden Past*. He played a Yankee doctor married to a feckless girl (Janis Carter) who becomes involved romantically with a scheming beauty, played by Ava Gardner. Mitchum didn't like the script, so he made his own suggestions.

'I was at first penciled in as a real square John,' he said. 'We didn't have much of a script to start with, so I suggested that the first scene should be about like the climactic one in *Ecstasy*. I figured that if we were going to give the public a shock treatment, we might as well do it up brown.'

He next played a gambler opposite Jane Russell in *His Kind of Woman*. This sexy melodrama had him involved with Raymond Burr as a gangster who wants to impersonate him, Jane Russell as a nightclub singer who wants to marry him, and Vincent Price, as a way-out ham actor who wants to rescue him from Burr. The film displayed Jane Russell's large and beautiful bust to advantage, had her singing some excellent songs, revealed Price's great comedy talent, and made a fortune at the box office.

Mitchum then played an incorruptible police captain in a slow-moving drama called *The Racket*. Determined to smash a crime syndicate, headed by Robert Ryan, he survives attempts at a frame-up, temptations of bribery and the machinations of Lizabeth Scott. In the end justice triumphs.

Nineteen-fifty-one was a good working year for Mitchum. And the smoldering embers of the aftermath of the marijuana affair finally died out when he and actress Nanette Bordeaux settled her $2,500 house damages suit. At the hearing in early May, Bordeaux gave evidence of how she alleged Mitchum and the other three had damaged her property. Then Detective Sergeant Alva Barr took the stand. His testimony was interrupted by Mitchum's attorney Milton Rudin, who asked for a recess. It was granted. At the end of his conference with Nanette Bordeaux's attorney Rudin anounced they had agreed on a settlement. Mitchum would pay an unspecified sum to 'cover actual damage'. Thus ended the case.

II

The reluctant brawler and the perverse non-conformist. 'If they treat me like an animal, I'll behave like an animal.'

By the middle of 1951 Mitchum was in the clear financially. He paid off his debt to Howard Hughes, and from then on became his own boss, hiring himself out from the aegis of his own production company. This had many advantages, the most obvious being that legally chargeable company expenses enabled him to reduce the government's bite on his movie income.

From that time to the present day Mitchum has never owed a penny to anyone, and he has paid all his taxes promptly. His finances are more stable than those of most stars.

From 1949 to 1956 Mitchum made more than twenty films, and his position as one of the world's leading stars became firmly entrenched. Yet throughout the early fifties it seemed that Mitchum the great screen success had not quite outgrown the former two-fisted hobo, for he still managed to get involved in some newsworthy scrapes.

In early November, 1951, while on location filming in Colorado Springs, Mitchum floored a soldier called Bernard B. Reynolds, a professional heavyweight boxer, in the Red Fox Bar of the Alamo Hotel. It was a hard, tough fight, in which a piano was knocked over and a table smashed. Mitchum emerged unscathed, but Reynolds, who was twenty-seven and a football player, was taken to the hospital with a suspected skull fracture.

This was no ordinary brawl. Reynolds had been a top-class fighter. He beat Caesar Brion of Argentina in the semifinals of a series of elimination contests to find a challenger to the winner of the clash between Joe Louis and Jersey Joe Walcott in 1947. In his career Reynolds had lost only two bouts, in 1946 and 1947, and had knocked out nineteen of his twenty-eight opponents.

'I was the aggressor,' Mitchum admitted afterward, 'but I was aggressive like a policeman.' One witness said the fight started when Mitchum stepped in to protect his friend Charles McGraw, who was playing his driver in the film he was making, One Minute to Zero.

Mitchum himself has never disclosed how the fight began, but two witnesses claimed they saw Mitchum kick Reynolds in the head. Sergeant First Class Lee. E. Haynes of the Camp Carson Military Police and George N. Right of Denver, who were in the bar at the time, said that they saw the star kick the soldier. Mitchum denied this and said they fell to the floor during the scuffle.

'I grabbed him by the lapels,' Mitchum later explained. 'He kept yelling and swinging his arms about. I put my arms around his. He shook his right arm loose and swung at me. I ducked the punch and we fell to the floor. It was pure self-defense ... If I hadn't decked him, he'd have decked me —might have been real painful.' Then he added, 'An actor is always a target for the belligerent type of guy who thinks he's tough and movie he-men are softies. I never start a fight, but I assure you I can always finish one if there's no way out. This one was unavoidable and I'm sorry it happened.'

Later, police said no complaint had been lodged against Mitchum.

One Minute to Zero put Mitchum back into uniform, as an infantry colonel fighting in Korea during the 1950 'police action' when thousands of the North Korean soldiers filtered through American lines disguised as refugees. The film did little for Mitchum's career, but it did re-unite him with his younger brother John, a character actor by now, who played a captain relaying Mitchum's messages to an artillery outfit.

If his brawl with Private Reynolds had left a rather bad taste in Mitchum's mouth, John remembers the filming for more romantic reasons. Just as he had helped Robert meet his wife Dorothy when they were both teenage boys in Delaware, so did Mitchum, in a fashion, help John meet *his* wife Nancy.

'Nancy was working with the Farmers' Insurance Company in Colorado Springs as an underwriter,' John recalls. 'And I was with Bob when I first met her. I fell in love with her at first sight, just as Bob did with Dorothy.'

John Mitchum and Nancy were married on 31 August, 1952, a date which had been somewhat unfortunate for elder brother Robert four years earlier.

At least one person on the film perceived that behind Mitchum's tough exterior lay a kind heart. Actress Margaret Sheridan remembers: 'He was always helping the little fellow. When I started on the picture, I was terribly nervous because my first dialogue scene was with Bob. I knew well that I was going to blow my first line. Bob sensed it too, and before I could fluff he blew his line with a very amusing ad lib that eased the tension, particularly mine.'

While he was making *The Lusty Men*, in February, 1952, Mitchum's image as a wry nonconformist was really set. A natural rebel, his defiance always seemed to spring up when he was around authority in any shape. It was this impulse that had made him call Greer Garson 'Red' the first time he played opposite her; no one else on the MGM lot would have dared address Queen Garson with such irreverence. He had also been something less than submissive with other top stars, but it was exactly this rebelliousness that had made him so good in *G.I. Joe*. Always on the side of the underdog, Mitchum delivered some more of his defiant views to Aline Mosby of the United Press while making *The Lusty Men*.

'This is a ridiculous and humiliating profession,' he yawned. 'I make faces for the silver screen because I just don't have anything better to do at the moment. The silliest part is that most movie stars play it straight. They're so serious. Why doesn't everyone have fun working? What else is there? You don't get to keep much of what you make anyway.'

Between scenes Mitchum put his words into practice. He sang loudly, fired a deadly water pistol at fifty paces. 'Tomorrow I'm going to bring in some real pistols,' he joked. 'We gotta shoot things up a bit. It's getting a little too dignified around here.' He also livened up his working hours by eating garlic before his love scenes with Susan Hayward.

He said one strange part of the film world was its social life. 'I don't know many stars socially. They don't seek me out either. They've all got Cadillacs and buy their suits at Eddie Schmidt's and they've got time to play. I guess I don't. In fact, I don't know anybody socially. I have a sign on my gate—no peddlers, actors or agents allowed. I don't go to parties because I don't like the effort of leaving or getting there. I think it must be a lot more fun to run a country store than be a film star. I wouldn't give a darn if I lost my acting job tomorrow. This movie business is such nonsense.'

At this point Miss Hayward walked by on her way to the set and Mitchum hollered, 'There goes the old gray mare!' Miss Hayward just smiled and waved. She, at least, was a match for Mitchum.

The Lusty Men proved to be a good film—a fast-paced story about rodeos in which Mitchum played a washed-up bronco buster forced to bathe in the reflected glory of a rising champion (Arthur Kennedy), whom he is helping to train. The two men competed for the affection of Susan Hayward. The excellent acting plus the exciting action sequences made the film a great success.

On 3 March, 1952, Dorothy Mitchum gave birth to a baby daughter weighing 7 lbs 10 oz at Hollywood's Good Samaritan Hospital. The child was named Petrina (nicknamed Trina) after Mitchum's grandmother. Mitchum naturally was delighted at having a daughter, and gossip writers wrote gushing stories of how Trina became a softening influence in his life.

Certainly Mitchum was a much finer father than his public image might have led some people to suspect. Dorothy once told of the time when young Jim went back east to visit her family.

'The day after he left Bob began eyeing the mail box,' she said. '" Why doesn't he write?" he wanted to know. Three days later Bob was still watching for the mailman. "Why don't your folks write and let us know how he is?" he asked about twenty-five times. He finally made a long distance call to make sure Jim had arrived safely.' Mitchum had apparently forgotten the tribulations he'd caused his own mother and step-father at Jim's age.

In the late summer of 1952 Mitchum began to take his children into the wilds of the High Sierras on hunting and fishing trips—to try to give them the kind of childhood they couldn't have in Hollywood. His hunger for the outdoors was real and he didn't allow his treks into the wild to be publicized. For them he built a special cabin on the back of a big Ford truck. It contained two bunks, the lower a studio couch that pulled out into a double bed and the upper one slung in chains from the roof. The cabin could be removed to the ground and then pulled back up by an ingenious winch device. It was fitted with a refrigerator, a butane stove, a clothes closet, a sink and a water tank.

Mitchum devised it for travelling through rough country which a car and trailer could not penetrate.

Once the camper was finished, Mitchum took off into the High Sierras and later into Idaho for some salmon fishing, with his two boys and his stand-in, Tim Wallace. The group combined business with pleasure for Mitchum had made a deal with RKO that he would make personal appearances for *One Minute to Zero* at Denver and Colorado Springs—provided he could have a vacation after the theatre stints. He went a long route round, heading through Arkansas and Mississippi, and he hunted animals (to observe but not shoot) and fished on the way. One highlight of the whole tour was salmon fishing in Idaho. Gar fishing also intrigued Mitchum because the fish were caught by the uncommon skill of throwing spears.

When he passed through the towns he was often recognized. 'The word gets around very fast,' he said. 'You buy gas or order a hamburger and the grapevine telegraph starts. There are two things you can do—insulate yourself in the best hotel or find out where the boys are and join 'em. These cowboys are no cream puffs. If they take a dislike to you, they can make things pretty tough. If they find you speak their language and can take care of yourself with your fists or at the bar, then you're in.'

Mitchum finally attended the publicity junkets, clad in a blue suit, shook hands, said witty thing to female fans and signed autographs along with other stars of the film and then took off again.

After playing an ambulance driver cum chauffeur in *Angel Face*, a film in which Jean Simmons was cast as a deranged murderess, Mitchum flew out to Africa to be reteamed with Susan Hayward in *White Witch Doctor* for Twentieth Century-Fox. The director of this film was the redoubtable Henry Hathaway, a tough veteran who tolerated no nonsense from his actors.

It was Mitchum's first film for Fox since becoming a star and he insisted on taking his friend and stand-in Tim Wallace with him—at $175 a week which was good pay in those days. The studio wouldn't agree at first but gave in when Mitchum announced that Wallace was *also* his drama coach!

One day on location Tim Wallace was standing quietly reading a paper. Nothing annoys Hank Hathaway more than people apparently standing round idle when he's working, especially if they're reading the trade papers. He went up to Wallace and said 'For the money you're getting, can't you even be a good stand-in?'

'I'm reading,' said Wallace in his Brooklyn accent. 'I'm reading the paper. It's not me they're lighting—it's her. What is it—you don't want me to read the paper?' Hathaway's reply has not been recorded, but he met his match when he came up against Mitchum himself.

'Hathaway and I got along fine—in the end,' remembers Mitchum diplomatically. 'He screams at people on the set. So I'd sit by him and say, "That's right, Henry. Give 'em hell, Henry."'

On the last day, Mitchum and Susan Hayward had a long, complicated scene to shoot, in which they leaned up against a rock in the jungle and went through six pages of dialogue. Mitchum decided to send Hathaway up.

He walked onto the set, turned to the director and said, 'What am I supposed to say?'

Hathaway was furious and shouted at him 'We've got six pages to shoot and you don't even know your lines?'

Mitchum said, 'Just tell me what I'm supposed to say and I'll say it.'

In the suddenly tense atmosphere no one dared to bring Mitchum's lines to him. Hathaway shook his head in disbelief. 'You must be kidding,' he said.

Mitchum said 'Will *somebody* please bring me the script so I can find out *which* scene by the rock this is?' Finally he got a script. He glanced briefly over the lines then said, 'I'm ready.'

Hathaway glared at him, then said, 'All right, you smart son of a bitch. Action!'

Mitchum went through the whole scene absolutely letter perfect.

It was the last scene shot in the film and after it was over there was a silence on the set. Then Hathaway turned to Mitchum and said, 'Bob, you're the most wonderful guy I ever worked with in my life.'

To which Mitchum replied, 'What do you want for these prices? Bums?'

Later Henry Hathaway was overheard speaking on the phone to Darryl F. Zanuck, then the powerful head of the Fox studio, and he was saying, 'This sonofabitch is the most phenomenal actor I've ever seen. He glanced through the script and did six pages of dialogue—four in solid African—letter perfect, with every nuance.'

Such moments, however, did not save the film from being a banal yarn about a wild game hunter in the Belgian Congo in the early 1900s who guides a nurse to a missionary. Only exciting animal sequences offset an implausible script.

But it had been a tough location, and on his return to Hollywood Mitchum began to unwind in rather boisterous style in 'nights out with the boys'.

This was also around the time that the star had a small problem at his studio. One day Mitchum, who disliked ringing telephones and occasionally stuffed chewing gum into their works to prevent them from ringing, tried to get a line from the operator to make an outside call. When the dial tone was not forthcoming after a slight argument, Mitchum lost his temper and half destroyed his dressing room. The *Los Angeles Herald-Express* reported:

'Robert definitely made a partial wreck out of the room. He is said to have jerked two phones from the wall, to have broken a glass on his neon-lighted dressing table and to have kicked a hole in a big ceramic pot holding a plant. After that he proceeded to the set and is said to have told assembled fellow workers, "If they treat me like an animal, I'll behave like an animal."'

In March, 1953, Mitchum's carousing was blamed when Dorothy and Robert separated for a short while and Mitchum moved from the family home into an apartment. An RKO spokesman stated that it was only a trial separation. It didn't last long, though, and two weeks later the Mitchums revealed they had reconciled. Robert took Dorothy out to dinner on their thirteenth wedding anniversary on 16 March, and the problems between them were resolved. The Mitchums have never separated since.

Shortly after this Dorothy visited her husband when he went down to Mexico to star with Jack Palance in a melodrama called *Second Chance*. Mitchum played an aging boxer on a fast tour of South America who becomes involved with a gangster's moll (Linda Darnell) who is being pursued by Palance, a professional killer. It was filmed in color with the new 3-D method, and it contained several exciting sequences, the chief of which was a fight to the death between Mitchum and Palance in a disabled cable car suspended some 7,000 feet above an isolated valley in the Andes.

As usual, Mitchum was in a devil-may-care mood when talking about his role. 'I'm playing a fighter barnstorming South America and he tells the girl, "No more running for you and me. Why do you think I'm down here picking these second-raters? Because in the ring my legs go all rubber on me." He's a professional boxer who will soon be thirty-two and he's afraid to go back to the States.

So right off you're playing a chicken shit fighter. Now get that, dad. I've seen a lot of boxers in my time but never one that was afraid to take a fall. I boxed and I wasn't afraid of being hit. Man, that's easy. You get tired, you just stick your chin out and let a guy hit you, take it and then you settle down for a little rest.'

He talked about the difficulties of screen fights. 'If one of the fighters varies his timing by a fraction, you can get a real wallop. This happened with Jack Palance. He miscounted during one of our fight routines and laid me flat for a full count. During other scenes one boxer was so backward in his arithmetic I got knocked out three times.' He added the director was not pleased because real punches didn't look as authentic on screen as false, well-rehearsed ones given a good thud.

Mitchum and Dorothy were sitting together when Hollywood columnist Hedda Hopper visited the location. She asked Mitchum what Hollywood had given him that he couldn't have got anywhere else.

But it was Dorothy who replied: 'Well, I've got three kids, but I suppose I could have got them anywhere.'

Mitchum thought this was hilarious, and he laughed loud. 'Sure you could have got them anywhere!' he said.

'You're always fighting for good stories, though,' said Hedda Hopper to Mitchum.

'I've never fought about a story,' he replied. 'It's a dead cinch you're a loser.'

'Why don't they give you good stories?'

'Why doesn't Woolworth go into Tiffany's?' he replied.

'Tiffany's make money too.'

'Sure, but they attract a better clientele. Have you ever seen a typical Mitchum fan? Glazed eyes, hasn't shaved —who needs it?'

'Tell us about Second Chance—is it your own project?'

Mitchum groaned. 'I hate to say this but I honestly

don't care. I make no suggestions. Of course, if every-body's bumping into each other, I might make a slight suggestion. But I said to RKO, "This is your baby. I'm gonna read the lines like they're written." That is my job. I've got one year left with RKO.'

'Will you sign with them again?' asked Hedda Hopper. Mitchum laughed sarcastically. 'I don't think so.'

Hopper asked him what kind of roles he liked to play.

'I'd like to do wonderfully important parts, difficult parts that require three days' work with a ten-week guar-antee. I'd go in, do my bit, pack up my makeup and go back to the farm. I'd be brilliant in a three-day part. When I'm interested, I know my lines and everybody else's. When I'm not, I go on the set and say, "Tell me what to say." No fret, no strain, no pain. If you want my interest, in-terest me. If you just want my presence, pay me.

'I do feel uncomfortable,' Mitchum went on, 'when people I meet in the commissary who could be telephone tappers, FBI men, grips, turn out to be the producer or writer or a combination of both. It embarrasses me. I'll listen to their story but I'm like the guy in the carnival. I'll give anyone thirty cents to listen to their story but if it's a bad story I'll give them thirty cents and tell them to go away. But often they embarrass me by saying, "We think it's fine." If they said to me, "It stinks but let's make it," *then* I'm with them. I ain't here because I'm displaying any facility or versatility.'

This conversation took place at a time when Hollywood films were beginning to be hit by television, when box office receipts were dwindling and the brief panic venture into 3-D movies—when audiences had to be issued with special glasses—had begun.

Hopper asked Mitchum what he thought of the future of the film business?

'It's like a country privy,' he replied. 'When you get

enough shit in there, especially in the summer and not in the winter when it's frozen, it topples over of its own strain. Shit is shit. Now they've got these trick glasses and you can see the pile from both sides. Some factory bum had some glasses over he couldn't sell, I guess. You know, when business is bad in Hollywood everyone starts fleeing in panic. During the Depression the auto business was in a bad way. But what did they do? Instead of fleeing in panic they retooled, turned out completely new models. They forced people to buy them with their innovations. It was a solid development. But if they run short here everyone runs around marooned. I think we're now at the enough-rope stage. Venal nepotism has reached a new high. Okay, let 'em have their home in Florida and four million shares of stock and fourteen purple Rolls-Royces, but let *somebody* get to work. All these trick glasses—somebody will end up with rabbit fever. We really must re-establish the motion picture theater as an institution. Imagine a thousand years from now—people will wander through our ruins and find a picture theater. All the seats are facing the same way but there are no religious symbols. They'll say, "Why did people congregate? There can't have been *that* many politicians!" '

While they were in Mexico City during a brief hiatus from filming, Mitchum and Jack Palance found themselves in a dangerous situation with a Mexican army general in a nightclub. Various versions of this incident circulate around the movie world. One is that Mitchum saved the day, the other that Palance did.

This is the story as Palance told it to British columnist Roderick Mann:

'I'd had a couple of drinks with him at a party and because of the altitude I was feeling pretty awful. [Mexico City is 8,000 feet above sea level.]

'Mitchum and I had already escaped one near brawl, so

we went to a club somewhere and as we came in a big
Mexican general got up and embraced Bob. He tried to do
the same with me but I wasn't feeling like it, so I pushed
him away. And he fell, right there on the floor.

'Well, you know what a general is in Mexico? God—
right? The next thing you know he'd drawn a gun on me
and someone in the band had a machine gun out. So I
did the only thing I could: I hurled a table at them.

'Suddenly there was this big drama going on. It was
only stopped by an American expatriate who happened to
be in the club and drew a gun on the general while I escaped. Of course, when I got back to the States, I found
old Mitchum had taken all the credit for my rescue.'

Anyone who has traveled in Mexico at length can find
unlikely elements in this story, but getting Mitchum to
elaborate further on it is almost impossible. Ask him about
it and he shakes his head, looks irritated for a moment, then
says: 'Ah, let the Palance version stand. He still has to go
down there to work! Look, he's still alive, isn't he? And
that's owing to one or two things, mostly the generosity
of the Mexican general.'

Mitchum's last film under his RKO contract was a rather
unsuccessful attempt to resurrect screwball comedy in *She
couldn't say no* (released in Britain as *Beautiful but Dangerous*) with Jean Simmons. In it he played a doctor in a
little town in Arkansas who tries to pour oil on troubled
waters when heiress Simmons disrupts local life by spread-
ing big money around.

In the summer of 1953 there came Mitchum's famous encounter with Marilyn Monroe, who was then the world's
top female star. Twentieth Century-Fox made casting history when they put Mitchum and Monroe together in
River of no Return, filmed partly in Canada.

Mitchum, however, remained distinctly unimpressed.
During one scene while he was romancing Monroe in a

backwoods barn, Mitchum put his arms round her beautiful body, then, as her lips parted slightly in anticipation of his kiss, he suddenly stepped back and said, 'How in hell can I take aim when she's undulating like that?'

Such moments apart, Mitchum and Monroe became quite good friends, and Mitchum regaled her and crew members with his stories about working on the shaping machine at the Lockheed aircraft plant, when his partner had been the husband of the then unknown Marilyn.

In *River of no Return* Mitchum played a laconic backwoodsman who helps his son and dance hall girl Monroe escape from treacherous Indian attacks and get back to civilization, by poling away on a raft in dangerous rapids. The film was photographed in the new widescreen Cinemascope technique, and Mitchum expressed his views about it thus:

'This new medium is going to turn a lot of actors gray overnight,' he said. 'The new lens brings you so close to the audience it's impossible to use doubles or stunt men. I've done things in this picture which would give some stuntmen the shivers. The amazing thing is how Marilyn and Tommy Rettig, who plays my son, have done them. We've dodged arrows in mountain streams and poled an awkward wooden raft over fast stretches of rough water. I was so struck with admiration for my two companions, I almost forgot to be frightened for myself. But there's no question that close views of actors struggling against danger will make action movies more entertaining.'

The film's director was Otto Preminger, another martinet who brooks no temperament from his actors. Mitchum admits the closest he ever came to a real fight on a film was with this director.

One day Preminger saw an actor crossing the set with a glass full of vodka. He was furious and he shouted, 'There'll be no drinking on my set!'

The actor paused and said, 'I'm just taking this to Mitchum.'

Preminger thought for a moment, then said, 'Oh, that's different.' And that was the end of that confrontation.

Many years later when Preminger was asked on television in Hollywood for his views on Mitchum, he replied with extraordinary generosity: 'Unfortunately I only made two pictures with him—*Angel Face* in 1952 and *River of no Return* in 1953. In spite of the fact that working conditions on both these pictures were not ideal I remember Bob Mitchum as a man of professional integrity, and I would like to work with him again whenever it's possible. But beyond that, during the fourteen or fifteen years that have ensued, while I see him much too rarely, when I do it's as if we had parted only yesterday. Bob has a warmth, a feeling apart from his intelligence that makes him a friend for life even if you've only had a fleeting experience of work or of personal contact with him.' Coming from Preminger, this was praise indeed.

On 3 December, 1953, back in Hollywood, Mitchum ran into some more trouble with the Los Angeles Police Department. A triple charge against him alleged that he escaped lawful custody, delayed a police officer in the performance of his duty, and speeded at 70 miles per hour in a 35 miles per hour zone in his Jaguar on San Vicente Boulevard near the intersection with Bundy Drive. He was alleged to have driven off at high speed, leaving traffic officer J. N. Ryan standing agape with his ticket book out after he'd stopped the actor for speeding. Officer Ryan reported that Mitchum had asked him, 'You got a witness, bud?' And that when Ryan said, 'No,' Mitchum had grinned and said, 'Well, neither have I. See you in court.'

A warrant was issued for Mitchum's apprehension but before officers could actually serve it, Mitchum's attorney appeared at West Los Angeles police station and posted

$250 bail. A short time after this the desk sergeant said he had received a call from Mitchum protesting that he didn't know anything about the bail posting and that he'd said, 'What are you guys trying to do, make a big thing out of this? Why, a hundred people a day do the same thing.' Mitchum was also alleged to have said he didn't realize Ryan was a policeman so he went on home. He further claimed the officer had taken his driving licence.

When Mitchum appeared in court next day, Judge Leo Freund granted him a delay until the following Tuesday to enter pleas to the charges. Five days later the Judge ordered him to pay a $50 fine or serve five days for speeding and to pay a $150 fine or serve ten days for delaying an officer in the performance of his duties. The star pleaded guilty to the two charges. The third charge of escaping lawful custody was dismissed.

Mitchum told the court he now fully realized he had made a mistake. He paid his fines and later retrieved his licence from the police. When fining him the judge added the comment: 'It was a stupid but not too serious act.'

12

*A proof of fine acting, a fallen bra on the
Riviera, and 'just a bit of horseplay'*

During 1954 Robert Mitchum made three films which,
although not the biggest box office hits of his life, were extremely interesting cinematically and proved he was now
maturing into an actor of considerable depth and ability:
Track of the Cat, directed by William Wellman whose film
G.I. Joe had helped Mitchum to his only Oscar nomination,
Not as a Stranger, directed by Stanley Kramer, and *Night
of the Hunter*, directed by Charles Laughton.

Track of the Cat was a brave attempt at something new,
an allegorical tale about the conflict between good and evil.
Although this film was shot in color, a black and white
effect was deliberately created by having the sets, clothes
and trees devoid of natural color. Mitchum played a strong-
willed but selfish and bitter son who has endured battles
with Indians and privation in the rugged north Californian
mountains to help make the family's isolated homestead
viable. Having thus sacrificed himself, he changes and
wants everything for himself, including the affections of
his younger brother's fiancée, and control of the family
farm. His alcoholic father, older brother and spinster sister
are unable to stop him but his younger brother (Tab
Hunter) opposes him. Mitchum, representing evil, is finally
killed by evil in the shape of a marauding black
cougar—which in turn is slain by the 'good' younger
brother.

Before making the two other films—certainly two of his
best—Mitchum was involved in a couple of imbroglios

which proved he was losing none of his ability to attract trouble.

In early 1954 he had a row with his studio over a film called *Cattle Queen of Montana*. Before his contract expired, in August, RKO wanted him to make the film. Shooting had already started at Glacier National Park, but Mitchum claimed he wasn't notified until a few days before they wanted him at work. In his casual way, he said, 'I glanced through the script but I'd rather go fishing—and that's what I'm going to do.' He was put on suspension and didn't work again for RKO before his contract expired.

In April the same year Mitchum won some questionable publicity at the Cannes Film Festival, but through no fault of his own. While standing with his broad back to the Mediterranean, a shapely starlet, Simone Silva, who was wearing a swimming suit topped by a pink veil, suddenly leaped and clinched with him after first removing her bra. In the ensuing scramble as some fifty photographers struggled to record this—for those days—daring scene, six fell into the sea, one broke his ankle and another suffered a fractured elbow. But the survivors managed to take dozens of shots and their pictures made front page news around the world.

'Simone must have been lowered from a helicopter because I never saw her coming,' Mitchum later protested. 'I had my back to the sea and I could either stay put or leap into the sea to get out of her way. I just didn't jump, that's all. At first I didn't realize what was going on. I was having a good time, but when I saw the photographic evidence afterward I got quite mad.' Later he shrugged it off. 'If a girl wants to have her picture taken like that, it's none of my affair.'

Dorothy Mitchum, who was accompanying her husband and was standing nearby at the time, was furious.

That same night she and Robert were in a harborside café when Miss Silva walked in. Dorothy turned to Mitchum and in a voice like a cut diamond, said, 'This is where we leave.' And Mitchum followed her out quietly.

Next day Dorothy brandished one of the pictures as she packed to leave with Robert. 'How would you like a picture of your husband showing him with such a girl being printed all over the world?' she asked. She also tried to have the local American consul prevent release of the photographs but it was beyond the man's control.

Festival officials were also scandalized and asked Simone Silva to leave Cannes. Back home in London the actress, whose parts in the past had been mainly supporting roles, said she had engineered the pose because she needed the publicity and wanted to get to Hollywood.

'Look what that nude calendar pose did for Marilyn Monroe,' she told reporters. 'I'm always cast as the bad girl anyway. The photographers got down on their knees to plead with me to take the top off. As long as sex is box office and I keep my figure, I'm out to be the sexiest thing on two legs. So I took it off.

'I want to go to Hollywood,' she added earnestly. 'I thought a startling photo with Bob Mitchum would enhance my chances. After all he's a top star out there.'

Although in the summer of 1954 Mitchum faced the prospect of being off a regular studio salary when his RKO contract expired, his future career seemed set fair. He was already signed to make Not as a Stranger and Night of the Hunter and had made a deal to co-produce Bandido for United Artists. Then in June he was in Mexico looking for locations for that film.

He returned from Mexico to shoot Not as a Stranger, a film which he himself grudgingly described as 'all right'. But with volatile talents such as Frank Sinatra, Lee Marvin and Broderick Crawford also heading the cast, it seemed inevitable that some shenanigans would erupt. 'It wasn't a cast so much as a brewery,' Mitchum remembers. Once during shooting, the stars staged a mock barroom knife fight in the dressing rooms, which resulted in shattered doors, uprooted telephones and a smashed balustrade, through which the hefty 240 pound Broderick Crawford hurtled to the ground, miraculously surviving his fall without injury. Director Stanley Kramer once said he remembered the picture as 'ten weeks of hell'.

In spite of such donnybrooks the film was considerably more successful than *Track of the Cat* and was one of the best movies released in 1955. In *Not as a Stranger* Mitchum played a dedicated young intern whose ambitions make him marry an older nurse for monetary reasons. Although Olivia de Havilland was somewhat miscast as the nurse, all performances were credible.

Then on 12 January, 1955, Mitchum again found himself in the headlines. American newspapers carried stories that, after less than a week's shooting on a film called *Blood Alley* at San Rafael, California, Mitchum had been fired from the cast at the request of director William Wellman, ironically the same man who'd given Mitchum his first big chance in *G.I. Joe*. Wellman accused Mitchum of indulging in a series of pranks that were 'detrimental to the making of our film which is too expensive for this sort of disruption'. One of the pranks, it was alleged, included Mitchum's shoving the film company's transportation manager George Coleman into the chilly waters of San Francisco Bay.

Witnesses said that Mitchum was at the top of the gangplank to the ferry used by the crew to get to Angel Island from the mainland, and that he started jumping on it so the gangplank shot up like the end of a seesaw. One of his jumps jarred Coleman into the water.

'It was just a bit of horseplay,' claimed Mitchum, who

had hoped hands could be shaken and the incident forgotten. He added that he and Coleman were the best of friends but had disagreed over a transport problem. 'There were about fifty of us on Angel Island, which is about twelve miles from San Rafael,' he said. 'We couldn't get back to town even to buy a toothbrush. I told Coleman I'd like to get a bus to take us into San Francisco. He asked who'd pay for it, since it would cost twenty dollars. I told him I'd pay for it. Coleman went to the production manager and snitched on me and I was told to mind my own business. But I wasn't sore. We've been the best of friends for a long time. I love the guy. I didn't push him into the water. It was just horseplay and besides, he weighs 278 pounds and I weigh only 190.'

Wellman, who said he wasn't going to have any such horseplay on his movie, complained to producer Bob Fellows and to John Wayne, whose company, Batjac, was making the film. At first Wayne laughed. 'Oh, Mitchum will be all right,' he said. 'He's just been vacationing too long.'

But the differences were apparently irreconcilable. Fellows flew north to confer with Mitchum and Wellman, a mutual agreement was reached, and at Sausalito Fellows announced to reporters that Mitchum would withdraw from the film. He said shooting on the $2,500,000 movie would continue; they'd shoot around Mitchum and a new star would be named in a few days. The role, in a cast including Lauren Bacall and Anita Ekberg, was one of the most sought after among the current crop of films. Fellows said he wanted either Humphrey Bogart or Gregory Peck to replace Mitchum—and that rumors that John Wayne himself would take the role were wrong.

Before Mitchum left he announced, 'I am going back to Hollywood and am withdrawing from the picture. There are no hard feelings but we didn't see eye to eye. It's just as well it happened at the outset instead of later in the film.'

Within a few days of arriving home Mitchum found his wife involved in a minor domestic drama. On 19 January Dorothy was fined $25 in West Los Angeles Court after testifying that their family dog was able to run at large because 'he outwits me'. The Mitchum dog, a valuable Weimaraner, had been impounded by the dog catchers four times during the past year for roaming loose in violation of the city's leash laws, the court was told. Dorothy told Judge Leo Freund that she tried to keep the dog within the fenced yard at their Mandeville Canyon Road home but that it was difficult to confine the large animal because 'he has learned to open gates in the fence'.

'Has he learned to answer the telephone yet?' asked the judge as he levied the fine.

By 26 January the *Blood Alley* company had run into further complications. They'd been unable to get either Peck or Bogart (who'd wanted half a million dollars) and John Wayne *had* taken Mitchum's role, after rushing in from New York. Director Wellman had fallen ill with flu and had been ordered by doctors to rest. Wayne found himself also assuming the director's chores for a short while. 'Now Wayne's directing his own acting in a film which he's producing!' observed Hedda Hopper in her column.

Although Wayne still insists he genuinely did *not* want the role, Mitchum thought it all rather odd. 'I understood Wayne had wanted the part but couldn't take it in the planning stage because of other commitments,' he said later. 'Then he found himself free after I was signed.'

By then, naturally enough, Mitchum had had more than his fill of the headlines, but whether this had anything to do with his fine performance in *Night of the Hunter* is anyone's guess. Certainly he really liked his role as a psychotic, self-educated backwoods preacher with *love* tattooed on one hand and *hate* on the other, who murders 'sinful' women to get money to build a tabernacle in the wilderness.

Charles Laughton, the distinguished actor who directed the film, wanted only Mitchum for the part. Mitchum explains what happened when Laughton telephoned him.

'Charles called me up and said, "You play a diabolical crud." "Present!" I replied. Charles said, "I'm not supposed to know about such things. I am a professional non-crud." "Charles," I said, "I will take care of that department." Then I read the book. I couldn't put it down. Then Charles wanted to lighten it all up a little. I told him, "It's okay, Charles, I'll give it a little country charm." Instead, we played the fairyland bit with the children and the owls —and damn near ruined it. Charles loathed those children. He made *me* direct them.'

Far from ruining the film, however, the Laughton-Mitchum team, combined with fine performances from Shelley Winters and Lillian Gish and a good script by James Agee, turned out a first-class macabre thriller. And Mitchum, who was as good in moments of cynical humor as in those of sadistic terror, delivered one of the finest performances of his life.

He virtually coasted through his next film, *Man with the Gun*, retitled *The Trouble Shooter* for British release, in which he played a ruthless fast gun, deserted by his wife, who is hired to clean up a lawless town. This film was one of a series made as a result of a lucrative co-production deal between United Artists and Mitchum's own production company over the next few years.

In May, 1955 Mitchum surprised Hollywood by filing suit for a million dollars damages against the scandal magazine *Confidential*, disclaiming their story that he stripped and masqueraded as a hamburger at a party. Filed by Jerry Giesler in Santa Monica Superior Court over an article entitled 'Robert M...the nude who came to dinner', Mitchum's law suit called the story 'completely and entirely false and untrue'. The article—by-lined by a Charles Jordan—alleged that Mitchum performed his strip masquerade at the Santa Monica beach home of producer Paul Gregory earlier in the year. It averred Mitchum was into his second bottle of scotch at the party, co-hosted by Charles Laughton and Gregory to celebrate *Night of the Hunter*, when he suddenly removed his clothing. Then, the magazine claimed, Mitchum grabbed a ketchup bottle, doused it over his body and demanded, 'This is a masquerade party, isn't it? Well, I'm a hamburger.'

The magazine alleged that Laughton then angrily ordered Mitchum to dress and get out and that his exit was accomplished with the aid of an unidentified girlfriend who steered him away.

This untrue story, typical of many published about stars in the fifties by the scandal sheet, made both Mitchum and his wife furious. By hiring Giesler, Mitchum proved he meant business.

Commenting on his suit, which was against the author, *Confidential*'s executive staff, and the magazine itself, Mitchum announced: 'As a member of a generous and honorable profession ... and having been awarded by my colleagues the reputation of high professional standard, I feel in return that my action in exposing the attackers of our structure is my duty.' He added that he was going to seek justice and fair play and to 'spare further loss and humiliation' to his family and friends at the hands of 'irresponsible assassins of character'. He claimed the article was published with malicious intent to defame him and bring him into public discredit and ridicule.

'Most stars prefer to ignore the whole thing rather than get tangled up in a dirty court fight,' he said. 'Personally

I don't feel that way about it. I think it's a case of fighting for your good name. You know, there is a tremendous power in the written word. People are inclined to believe what they read in magazines. They say, "If it's printed it must be true. And if it's not true, how come they are able to get away with it?" And that's the whole point. They should not be allowed to get away with it. They should not be allowed to get rich by printing lies and smut.'

Some Hollywood columnists disagreed with him. They wrote that he was unwise to bring the action because it only created more publicity for the magazine and further ballyhooed his alleged escapade.

In early June a motion to quash Mitchum's law suit was filed in Santa Monica on behalf of Robert Harrison, then president and publisher of *Confidential*. The motion was based on the grounds that the magazine was not doing and never had done business in California, that it had no property or assets there, and that it was distributed through wholesalers.

The ensuing litigation was both lengthy and complicated. Although Mitchum won no monetary damages, his action plus the later similar actions brought by other stars encouraged by his example helped put the original *Confidential* out of business. A trusted business associate of Mitchum's says, 'Bob wanted most to stop them publishing such stories, but they were clever. They had offices in New York, the magazine was printed in Rhode Island, the distribution set-up was somewhere else, so where were they legally liable? The strange thing was that in most of the stories there was a *seed* of truth. But there were enough good stories about Bob that one could write that were absolutely true, so why come out with a complete fable? Giesler found out all the different business sources and went for them. It cost the magazine a great deal of money to fight Bob's case, for they had to retain top lawyers. It cost Bob a lot of money too for Giesler, who was one of the best lawyers in the country, was also very expensive.' In fact Mitchum's law suit was one of the last cases Giesler handled before he died.

In the summer of 1955 Mitchum and Dorothy went by slow Norwegian freighter to Europe, where he was to star in *Foreign Intrigue* with Genevieve Page and Ingrid Thulin, who were making their American film débuts. Mitchum used the leisurely trip over and the later locations in Paris, Stockholm and the south of France, as a chance to give his family a European holiday.

But when they stopped off in London en route, both showed they were still angry about the *Confidential* affair. 'These wild and exaggerated stories have got to stop, and if they don't, I'll sue,' he told reporters. 'One of my sons was expelled from school because of previous notoriety, but this time I'm fighting back.'

Dorothy said, 'The backwash of these sensational stories about Bob is hurting our children. Our fourteen-year-old Jim idolizes his dad, and the other kids keep ribbing him. He's always getting into fights sticking up for Bob.'

During this trip newsmen who kept in contact with the Mitchums noticed that Robert's behavior seemed more subdued than it had been on some occasions in the past. One reporter who attended a party with Mitchum and his wife noted: 'His manners were impeccable. At the party Bob was joined by Charlie Beal, the famous colored jazz pianist with whom Mitchum sung duets. The party broke up in the early hours, and Beal invited the Mitchums to an all night jazz club.

'Robert,' reminded Dorothy softly, 'we have packing to do.'

'Tell me later if I missed anything,' said Mitchum as he obediently went off to pack.

In fact there *was* trouble at the club—between a garrulous American executive and ex-King Farouk of Egypt, sitting with a mink-wrapped American girl, who didn't want the executive's company. The noisy argument developed into a situation that Mitchum could have handled —but he was home in bed.

Foreign Intrigue turned out to be a routine drama about a press agent looking into the past of a murdered international entrepreneur who had been his employer. It was based on a successful American television series, and Mitchum did little in the film but deliver stock lines. But he did enjoy the varied locales.

'I like working in Europe except for the noise,' he said. 'These people never sleep. Even in a phlegmatic country such as Sweden, where they were building a garage next door to our hotel, they worked all night. One thing I do like though is that whatever you do, Europeans don't bother you. They leave you alone. They believe in individual liberty.'

On his return to America in October, Mitchum regaled people with stories of how the male and female members of the crew had stripped naked for a casual noon time swim together—a bit risqué in 1955.

'In Sweden the summer season only lasts two weeks. It doesn't pay to invest in a swim suit,' he joked.

Did he join them? 'No, I was hungry for lunch. Besides, the water's too cold. When it gets up to forty-five degrees the Swedes think it's like a warm bath. Those people would even swim in a martini.'

Had he perhaps been shocked? 'No, it seemed perfectly natural and wholesome,' he replied. 'I was a guest of their country, so I had to accept their customs. As a matter of fact, when we were in Stockholm the mothers were campaigning for mixed nude bathing in schools! The adults do it, so they argued it was traumatic for the children to be subjected to false prudery!'

While in New York for the première of *Man with the Gun*, Mitchum sang professionally for the first time in his career. On 23 October he aired his baritone voice in a CBS television *Stage Show* that headlined Jimmy and Tommy Dorsey, and his vocal efforts were enthusiastically received—so much so that he began to look around, albeit casually, for some songs he might put together for a long playing record.

Mitchum then went down to Mexico to make *Bandido*, under his coproduction deal with United Artists. In it he tongue-in-cheeked his way through his role as a renegade gun-runner supplying arms to both sides in the Mexican rebellion of 1916. The film was reasonably successful, but like several made at this time, it did little to enhance his career.

13

A rival to Harry Belafonte?

After making *Bandido*, Mitchum returned to Hollywood and for some months faded completely from the news columns. This was rare enough for him to be asked in mid-May why he was apparently lying low. Had he reformed?

'The heat's off,' Mitchum grinned. 'They've got other people to write about now. Grace Kelly for one. And then there's this guy Marlon Brando. How I welcomed *him* onto the scene—I knew he'd get a lot of heat!'

After he had made a long car trip back East with his family, rumors began to circulate that Mitchum might be leaving Hollywood. He denied this but admitted that he and Dorothy had been looking for a real working farm, possibly in the Carolinas, where the family could spend their summers.

'I've always wanted a place like that,' he said. 'We've looked at many but haven't yet found what we want. I would like to get the kids away for part of each year, let them see there are parts of this country where a guy can be somebody without a heated swimming pool.

'But I can't completely disassociate them from Hollywood because I'm not going to disassociate myself. To actually *live* elsewhere full time and work here would be very expensive. I could never afford it. All I can do these days is stay even with my taxes and live the year through.'

Mitchum's next film was *Fire down Below*, in which he co-starred with Jack Lemmon and Rita Hayworth, who was making her return to films after an absence of several years. During the making of it Mitchum proved he could still occasionally cut loose. Dorothy revealed a year later in an interview that Mitchum's secretary had asked her to fly out to her husband in the West Indies after he'd taken off on a temporary bout of boisterous socializing. Dorothy caught a plane and joined Robert and evidently proved to be a calming influence because he didn't get into any trouble on that occasion. In the film Mitchum and Lemmon played the owners of a small smuggling boat who help fugitive Hayworth elude a deportation order from the West Indies, but Mitchum was not as effective as the other two stars.

In late 1956 Mitchum was in the Caribbean to co-star with Deborah Kerr in *Heaven knows Mr Allison*, a film about a Marine stranded on a desert island with a nervous nun. Its director was that hard task master John Huston. Although on this occasion Mitchum took Dorothy with him for some of the time, his peculiar gift for attracting trouble again emerged.

During the filming, the world's newspapers printed stories of how Mitchum had flattened two American sailors in a bar brawl on the island of Tobago and had thus become involved with the US Navy Shore Patrol. This incident took place after Huston had engaged an assault landing craft manned by tough Marines to help in some of the scenes and had invited the men to a big dance and party to meet Mitchum and Kerr. Mitchum, who knew only too well the effect his antagonistic screen image had upon some muscular males, stayed away from the party, intending to spend a peaceful evening at his hotel with Dorothy. As they sat there quietly sipping coffee, three sailors walked in. What happened next was recorded by Bernard McElwaine in Britain's *Sunday Pictorial*:

'One of the sailors, a medium-sized character, joined Bob and Dot without waiting to be asked and started a long conversation. Then one of the other two got up, walked over to Mitchum's table and snapped out to his colleague, "Shut up." This pleasantry was accompanied by a punch that laid him out. Mrs Mitchum at once applied first aid to the victim. And an astonished Robert Mitchum said he was surprised that a big mariner would hit a smaller one. Whereupon the big one said, "Well, suppose I hit you?"

'Bob said, "Okay, suppose you do." The sailor hung a large punch on Mitchum's jaw. Bob returned the compliment and the sailor vanished through some glass doors. The third and still untouched sea rover then took it upon himself to join in the fray. Tables, chairs and all the furniture grew into a pile of rubble until sailor number three was subdued. Then the original seaman, the one Mitchum had defended in the first place, recovered consciousness and attacked his benefactor.

'The police arrived and the naval police too. The furniture was disentangled and the missing sailor was salvaged from the shrubbery. The two unconscious mariners were revived. Mitchum went slowly back to his table and finished his coffee. Proof, if any were needed, that Mitchum is more than a celluloid superman.'

Apart from this incident—not Mitchum's fault—the film location itself proved to be a tough one for a variety of reasons. Deborah Kerr was playing a nun who had not yet taken her final vows, and in those days a strict watch had to be kept on moral detail. A representative of the American Legion of Decency attended the shooting to ensure that no one in the audiences would be offended by any scenes. Whenever Mitchum had the slightest contact with Deborah, even a brushed elbow, the Legion observer held a conference on the scene.

Mitchum also had to endure some of the hardest action sequences of his life. 'I had one scene in which I had to fight a huge 350 pound turtle,' he recalls. 'John Huston outlined the action and said, "Is it going to kill you?

Think you'll break a leg?" I had a noose around the turtle and the rope tied to my waist. Those creatures fight you by bashing you against the coral boulders but I told John I'd cut loose if things got too rough.'

Mitchum didn't cut loose, but he took all the pounding the turtle could give him. He remembers the film today mostly for the hard stunts Huston demanded of him.

'I thought at times, "This guy is going to kill you yet!" I took an awful lot of punishment, getting bashed against rocks, trudging through quicksand. I was lucky to come out of it alive. A few people may think I'm a big, brave stalwart hero. Fact is I'm as chicken as the next guy.' In fact Mitchum possesses more courage and physical stamina than most movie stars, and even stunt men have refused to take part in dangerous stunts he has pulled off.

Mitchum predicted at the time that *Heaven knows, Mr Allison* would be 'one of the classically best films ever made'. While it wasn't quite that, it certainly ranks as one of the star's better movies. After it was over Mitchum paid tribute to his co-star. 'Deborah is a much better actress than her opportunities have provided,' he said. 'As a receptive artist she is the best receptacle I've encountered. Before she becomes a fat gray-haired lady, she should do comedy. She is total in her talent—a brilliant, wonderful gal.' Asked what Deborah Kerr had thought of him, Mitchum replied, 'Oh, she thought I was a large ambulant so and so.' She didn't, of course. After that film she repeatedly told anyone who would listen that Mitchum was one of the most sensitive and intuitively brilliant actors with whom she had ever worked.

Certainly Kerr's generous charm and natural femininity got through to Mitchum. Laura Nightingale, a wardrobe girl on the film, says: 'I remember a scene Deborah was playing with Bob. In rehearsal she gestured toward her feet. Bob didn't say a word. He seemed to know instinctively that her feet hurt from the sharp rock she had to stand on.

'He just kneeled down, unlaced her white sneakers, removed them and massaged her feet. It was lovely and compassionate the way he did it. No show, no affection, just all feeling. Then he put her sneakers back on and said kind of brusquely the way he does to hide his tenderness, "Gotta keep you alive for the next scene." Then he walked away. Deborah was so touched she cried.'

Indeed, Mitchum was now showing a greater compassion in his life generally not just toward his colleagues.

Basil Fenton-Smith, a sound engineer, once told Hollywood writer Lloyd Shearer that Mitchum fooled most people. 'You expect him to be a wild, careless man-of-steel, adventurous and flip. But in truth he has a heart as tender as a woman's ought to be and frequently isn't. I remember on that film [*Heaven knows, Mr Allison*] a native boy was hurt by a falling coconut, and one of the special effects men fainted on the set. Both were taken to hospital. Bob was the only member of the cast thoughtful enough to visit them.'

Further proof of Mitchum's growing benignity came when Huston ordered him to put up a real fight on the beach with Irving Allen, a native giant whom Huston hoped to promote as a professional heavyweight. Mitchum, some fifty pounds lighter, poked gently at the powerful Allen for three rounds then pushed him down for a 'knockout'.

'He was just a big lovable guy who couldn't fight worth a lick, so why should I make myself look good by pounding him?' said Mitchum. He was apparently right, Allen's boxing career never got off the ground.

The director and Mitchum became good friends while on location, and Huston, who later wanted Mitchum to star in *The Misfits* with Marilyn Monroe, said, 'He is a rarity among actors, hard working, noncomplaining, amazingly perceptive, one of the most shockingly underrated stars in the business.'

In his next film Mitchum also was extremely effective. In *The Enemy Below* he was cast as the captain of a US destroyer engaged in a cunning sea duel with a German submarine commander, played by Curt Jurgens.

In early 1957 Mitchum embarked on what has been a spasmodic secondary career as a singer. Fascinated by the art of calypso singing during his bouts of filming in the West Indies, he had occasionally sung and strummed his guitar during off camera breaks and many crewmen had suggested he ought to take it up professionally. One day Mitchum was in the Polo Lounge of the Beverly Hills Hotel when a recording executive walked in and asked him what he was doing that was new?

For answer, Mitchum launched into a brief calypso ditty that he'd composed himself. The result of this accidental meeting was a recording session from which Mitchum emerged with a five-year contract with Capitol Records. His first disc, issued in March, 1957, contained titles like 'What is this Generation?' and 'Mamma look a Boo Boo'. This last song was given big exploitation in direct opposition to the recording of it made by Harry Belafonte, and Mitchum sang it when he appeared as a vocalist in the Ed Sullivan Show that same month.

Mitchum's musical talent first really came to the fore when he made the film *Thunder Road*. Not only was this lively picture about free-minded Tennessee 'moonshiners' based upon Mitchum's own original story, but he wrote and recorded its theme song 'The Ballad of Thunder Road', and his record became a hit. Five years later the disc was still in the Top 100 records in the monthly poll of *Cash Box*, the music trade magazine.

When he first heard of Mitchum's musical success, Frank

Sinatra paid a rare compliment. 'Robert Mitchum knows more about music from Bach to Brubeck than any other man I've known,' he said.

The embarrassed Mitchum's self-mockery was swift: 'Just shows how much Frank Sinatra knows about music!' he quipped.

Thunder Road itself proved to be a popular film, and it was notable too because Mitchum's elder son, Jim, made his movie début in it—as his father's younger brother. Many critics and columnists drew attention to the extraordinarily close physical resemblance between the two. Jim was sixteen years old, 6 foot 2 inches tall and still at high school. His father was determined that film success would not go to his head. Said Jim, 'Pop says I have to go straight back to school when the picture's finished.'

While they were shooting on location, Mitchum was startled one day when a group of Blackfoot Indians from nearby Lanes, South Carolina, arrived to visit him, claiming that they were distant relatives from Mitchum's Blackfoot grandmother's side of the family. Naturally Mitchum entertained them royally.

'They were among the most frightening people I'd ever met,' Mitchum once said. 'They were pure blooded Blackfoot, wild looking men who, if you gave 'em too many drinks, would tear down the motel.'

Mitchum's entry into the popular music world came as no shock to those who knew him well. His friends had long since known of his interest in music from the time he'd composed the oratorio which Orson Welles produced at the Hollywood Bowl in 1939. Throughout the years his co-stars had frequently been amazed to hear Mitchum whistling or humming obscure passages from classical music while he pointed out their similarity to several Academy Award winning musical scores for which they had been 'milked'.

His talent as a writer was also burgeoning, and in the fifties and early sixties Mitchum occasionally had poems and short stories published in esoteric magazines, and sometimes in national magazines. One article that appeared in *This Week* in the early sixties was about his stepfather.

In the summer of 1957 it was announced that Mitchum was likely to play Colonel Dean E. Hess in *Battle Hymn*, the true-life film story of the colonel's life. Hess, a quietly spoken former clergyman before he became a fighter pilot, flew three hundred missions in World War II and Korea, helped develop the Korean Air Force and saved the lives of thousands of Korean orphans. To show 'that a person can still be a Christian, even in warfare', Hess had written his autobiography. The book had sold well and Universal International had secured the colonel's agreement to film it.

The film company wanted to star Mitchum in the leading role, but Hess gave the idea the thumbs down. A happily married man with three children, Hess was quoted as saying, 'I couldn't allow an actor who had been jailed for taking drugs to play me on the screen.' He personally vetted the private lives of actors in the film and said he was satisfied with Rock Hudson for the role. Mitchum's comments on this have not been recorded, but Hess's refusal seems somewhat unfair since it appears that Mitchum was being judged purely on his newspaper reputation. Hess clearly did not know that Mitchum's narcotics charge had been stricken from the records in January, 1951, or if he did, he had felt the fact was not sufficiently well known.

Instead, Mitchum made *The Hunters* for Twentieth Century-Fox in which, ironically, he played a World War II fighter ace seeking new laurels as a jet pilot over war-torn Korea.

After a rest at home during which he and his wife resumed their search—largely led by Dorothy—for a farm in the countryside back east, Mitchum flew to Athens in the summer of 1958 to be directed by Robert Aldrich, in *The Angry Hills*. In this rather routine story of wartime intrigue, he played a war corespondent covering the Nazi invasion of Greece who has to deliver the names of guerrilla patriots to British Intelligence.

From his remarks later Mitchum indicated he didn't regard the role as one of much importance. 'Originally they wanted Alan Ladd for the part,' he wryly told the *Sunday Express*'s Roderick Mann. 'But when they got to his desert home to see him he'd just crawled out of his swimming pool and he was all shrunken up like a dish washer's hand. You know what a little guy he is? Well, when he got out of the pool he was so small they could hardly see him, and they decided he wouldn't do for the big war correspondent. So what happened? Some idiot said, "Ask Mitchum to play it. That bum will do anything if he's got five minutes free." Well, I had five minutes free. So I did it.'

He said he was troubled on the film by an old complaint —insomnia. 'I'm not getting enough sleep. Come to think of it, I haven't had a good sleep since I was in prison. That cost me a lot of money and my reputation—but I did get plenty of sleep!'

Mitchum was also angry when the film company gave him a pair of American prison-made shoes to wear in the film. 'They were bought in an Athens shoe shop but I recognized the brand,' he said. 'They were made in our prisons and sent to Europe as gifts for the poor. Like so many other things, these have been sidetracked and are being sold in the shops.'

When asked about his role, he described it in whimsical terms. 'I play a mute war correspondent who gets to free-load on the Greek peasants. He has trouble with the goats. There are goats all over the place in Greece and this war corr., he's fighting it out among the goats and the heat. I don't know if he's a hero or a villain. I'll be clearer on that when the writer gets back!'

Mitchum's next film was a western, *The Wonderful Country*, a beautifully photographed but somewhat routine film in which he played a Mexican dictator's hired gun whose return to America to buy arms is complicated by a broken leg, an alluring Army wife (Julie London), mistrustful Texas Rangers and warlike Indians. Mitchum gave his role a suitably rugged interpretation.

He found himself once again in the news when, on 1 June, 1959, Hollywood agent Paul Wilkins filed suit in the Superior Court seeking to collect five percent of Mitchum's earnings since 17 June, 1947. In his suit Wilkins claimed that he had taken over Mitchum's career as his agent when the actor was still a local aircraft worker doing little-theater roles. Then when Mitchum achieved success, Wilkins claimed, Mitchum sought to abrogate their 1946 contract. As a result in 1947 they compromised their dispute and Wilkins agreed to take only five percent of Mitchum's future earnings. He alleged that Mitchum had since notified him that he believed he had 'no liability' under the 1947 agreement. The agent now asked the court to define his rights.

In fact it was not a personal dispute and the matter was finally amicably resolved between Wilkins and Mitchum's new agents, the influential William Morris company. This kind of business dispute was a common problem in Hollywood when a formerly unknown actor became a big star and his contract was taken over by a big international company who had more power and better international facilities to handle his career than the smaller one-man agency with whom the actor had started.

Looking back over Mitchum's career at this point, except for occasional films like *G.I. Joe, Not as a Stranger, Night of the Hunter* or *Heaven knows, Mr Allison,* it's not easy to see any clearly defined maturing in his work, despite his highly individual laconic approach. But in *Home from the Hill* there occurred a noticeable enrichment in his acting style.

Originally written for Clark Gable and Bette Davis, the story was about a rich Texan, a reformed roué who is estranged from his cool, beautiful wife (Eleanor Parker), alienated from his bastard son and suspected of seduction by an angry father. Mitchum delivered a sensitive, moving performance under delicate control and certainly proved himself something more than merely an excellent replacement for 'King' Gable.

Significantly perhaps, this new sensitivity seemed to reflect an increasing maturity in Mitchum's own personal life. From the late fifties onwards, he began to care more and more for the spiritual welfare of his family. A man who had been used to shock headlines throughout his life, Mitchum now became more concerned about the image he was creating and the effect it might be having on his children. He began to work harder to keep the spotlight turned away from himself.

Both he and Dorothy had been genuinely furious with the *Confidential* story and they were also particularly upset when a Bel Air private school called younger son Chris into the office one day and told him his 'presence was no longer desirable' at their institution.

'There was no reason. Nothing. Just get your stuff and go home,' Mitchum was quoted as saying afterwards. 'Mind you, that boy made good grades and had never been in trouble. But they had seen headlines that morning where his old man had been in trouble [about some matter years earlier] so they took it out on the boy.'

Other things happened too. Once Trina came home from

her school in tears because the mother of one of her friends said her girl couldn't play with Mitchum's daughter any more.

'This woman I knew,' said Mitchum. 'She was having an affair with a producer friend of mine whose wife was her best friend. Real nice.'

Yet for all his endeavors it seemed that Mitchum just couldn't stay out of the papers. 'And ninety percent of what was printed about me was either distorted and taken out of context or completely untrue. I'm not trying to cop out and say I was Mr Innocent. But I would have thought they would have had enough to write about without making stuff up.'

The Mitchum concern at this point was not merely with the effects of Robert's own reputation, however. Dorothy had long felt the frenetic over-stimulations of the whole Hollywood way of life was not the best atmosphere in which to continue to bring up their children. She didn't want them to be overly influenced by the 'Beverly Hills set of values', and *she* above all wanted to leave.

So, in 1959 the Mitchums made a momentous decision. They left Hollywood and moved to a peaceful three hundred acre farm nearly three thousand miles away above Chesapeake Bay on the eastern shore of Maryland—a farm which Dorothy herself had discovered on a drive back east. It was a risky decision because Mitchum was at the height of his fame, and 1959 was well before the days when top stars dared live wherever they liked, letting movie offers seek them out. The feeling was that one had to be 'seen around' to get constant offers of choice parts. But there was one additional reason for the move—Mitchum had always basically preferred country life himself, and he also had a yearning to rear quarter horses and run a farm.

Jim, who was eighteen and already on his way to begin an actor, stayed behind in Hollywood. His uncanny resemblance to Robert was proving to be a problem too, as people were comparing them.

'One day,' remembers Mitchum, 'we took a buddy of Jim's to the beach and the three of us just sat around talking—about women, acting, hunting, stuff like that, and sure I wanted to make a good impression on the boy because he was Jim's pal. But when he left he turned to Jim and said, "I used to really envy you, having Robert Mitchum as a father. But I don't anymore. How can you *ever* follow an act like that?"'

This hit Mitchum hard. He saw the look on his son's face and knew if Jim was ever to make it on his own in Hollywood, it would be better if he himself was out of the way. At the time, too, Chris was fifteen, in the throes of an education that was to take him to universities in nearby Pennsylvania and later Arizona, and Trina was only seven. So *all* the children would benefit by their leaving the Hollywood atmosphere.

If it made his wife and children happy, Mitchum felt he had little to lose and a lot to gain by leaving. He had never really been a part of the Hollywood social scene anyway. Also, to him, the one thing about stardom and his own experiences was that he as a person had been able to improve himself. He now wanted his children to have an even better chance—in a secure, peaceful and stable setting.

14

The husband and father. 'I'm not safe to be let loose!'

Perhaps the most surprising thing about Robert Mitchum is that, despite his flamboyant image, he is the only top star in the world who has been happily married so long to his childhood sweetheart. For thirty-two years dark-haired Dorothy Spence, the girl he first met in Delaware when he was sixteen and still had the chain gang shackle marks on his ankles, has been the staunch, loving wife in the background of his life.

It is not for nothing that the Mitchums' marriage has endured for so long in a milieu where no other first marriage of any star of equal caliber has survived at all. They've had quarrels in the past, and twice they've been separated for short periods, but there has never been any talk of divorce. And today their three children are well-adjusted youngsters who count their parents among their best friends.

Mitchum never talks sentimentally of his marriage. Ask him about it and he says, 'Well, it sure has been difficult for Dorothy at times. I'd say adaptability has been her greatest quality.' Then he smiles at memories. 'Look, our marriage has lasted because we adopted the course of least resistance. Dorothy used to throw me out of the house—regularly. Finally, I said, "Look honey, I can't pack anymore. If anybody's going to go, *you're* going to have to go because I'm not going any place." So that was the end of that. She's never mentioned it since!'

But surely it wasn't *really* like that? He must be very fond of his wife?

'Of course I am but sometimes she used to come unglued and couldn't abide it any longer, and Out! Then I just got tired of packing and unpacking and said I wouldn't go any more ... But women dwell and dwell upon things that happened, don't they? They say, "Well back in 1902 you did ..." They have their own little axes to grind I suppose and something you did years back can loom very large to them long after you've forgotten it. But ... I find I can survive it okay. It's not too rough!'

Mitchum of course needs and loves his wife dearly. She has always been a stabilizing influence on his life. Friends still remember one treasured occasion when Dorothy halted a minor bar brawl by hitting Mitchum with her shoe and shouting, 'Stop! You're beginning to enjoy it!' It was Dorothy who hastened to Mitchum's side after his 1948 arrest, calmed him down when he was cutting loose in the West Indies, and it was Dorothy who broke up that memorable punch-up with his brother John.

In 1947, when Mitchum was on his way up, he told Louella Parsons when she asked him about a rumored separation: 'We'll never part. The trouble is I'm married to a girl who comes from Delaware, and she's been very well brought up and is the soul of propriety. Sometimes she can't understand the hobo instincts in me, and my wish to pal up with people she doesn't think should be my friends. But I was in love with her for years after I first met her. There has never been anybody but Dorothy in my whole life.'

And in the long years since his feelings have not basically changed.

Although he sometimes likes to use his wife as a conversational butt in the way comedians do, the truth is Dorothy has long since tamed the wild man at home. No matter what the provocation today, Mitchum doesn't cut up rough when Dorothy is around.

Mitchum sometimes says Dorothy's patient and stable nature has helped civilize him and stop him from 'going native'. But Dorothy feels he has really civilized himself over the years. As she once said, 'Some people meeting Bob ask me whether there are two Mitchums in the man—the tough one and the kindly one. I don't think there are two, although I know it's a paradox when I say that Bob is the most married bachelor in Hollywood. He is a family man but he likes to take off by himself sometimes—or with our two boys—and just fish or camp out in the country.'

Dorothy says she's the type who suffers silently. 'I smoulder, maybe for several months, and then I really let go—which can be pretty cruel to the other person.' One thing she has never tried to do is *change* her husband. 'That,' she admits, 'would be a rather dangerous undertaking! But we have been married to each other since we were children and in a way we've had to learn about the world and each other and to grow up together during our marriage.

'I don't presume I can give him *everything* he needs perhaps but I need him, just as every woman needs her man, to make her feel loved and attractive.'

Dorothy attributes much of Mitchum's success to his sheer professionalism. 'He says he just works for the money,' she smiles. 'But he has never tried to better himself by playing studio politics or "making up" to people with power. He just got where he is by hard work. Until he formed his own company, I used to take every penny he earned. He never even saw it. Now it goes straight to his company with the result he's one of the few stars in Hollywood with no debts. He's been all paid up for years.'

She confirms that Mitchum learns his dialogue without effort. 'He didn't have much formal education but he soaks up information wherever he goes and can remember it,' she says. 'When we were first in Paris filming for a month or so he learned to speak Parisian French perfectly. It was the same with Italian—he just picked it up. The same with scripts. He can just look through a page of lines and remember it.'

When talking about fatherhood, Mitchum drops his tough, sardonic mask. He admits his own childhood memories affected his attitudes to bringing up his own children. It's hard for him to discuss them without referring to his own wild youth.

'They are pretty individualistic but I figured if they were well fed and given the choice of good educations, which they've had, and certain provisions were made financially, they'd be able to choose what they wanted to do and what suited each of them most.

'The only thing I ever tried to impress on the two boys was that maybe they could learn from me. "If you look real close at me," I said, "and look at the scars, you'll see there's a hard way and an easy way." They listened to that I think. They *needn't* have it the hard way.'

This approach fits Mitchum's philosophy, which he once capsulated by saying, 'The only thing I've ever really learned is that Easy Does It.'

Back in the late Fifties when Jim was starting out as an actor, Mitchum said, "One trouble is, young Jim is a hard ways character like me and maybe he has got to learn for himself, like me. Look at him. He's nine feet tall, beautiful—and with every chance in the world to be an ass. Maybe he knows that and has got beyond that point now. Because let's face it, the most endearing thing about stardom and life and experience is that I've been able to improve.' Such statements reveal something of the true man behind the roughneck mask.

Both Jim and Christopher Mitchum are successful actors

today, and both are happily married. Jim has a son Josh, and Chris has a daughter and a son, Carrie and Robbie. At first Jim did find problems in his career because his extraordinary likeness to Mitchum led to inevitable if rather unfair comparisons. When he came over to Britain to film *The Victors* in the early sixties, he said, 'I've inherited quite a reputation to live up to. People expect me to be just like the old man. But I hope on my own ability to be identified as James Mitchum and not Robert Mitchum.'

Christopher, whose slim build, golden hair, and large blue eyes conceal much of his resemblance to his father, has currently been in great demand for co-starring roles. He studied literature at Trinity College, Dublin, and graduated with a BA from the University of Arizona. Although he enjoys acting, he has more serious aspirations to be a writer.

Both young men speak of their father with fondness and respect today. Says Jim 'His own father died when he was a baby so he worried a great deal about spending time with his children when we were young. He played games with us and read us stories. Of course, later on when I grew older and my sister was born, he started making films internationally and traveling away from home for long periods and when I was eleven or twelve I'd spend my summers in summer camps. But we sort of found each other again in later years.

'He is a good father and he's a very tenacious man. He is very strongly American, has been to Vietnam twice and has strong feelings in that area. He has strong feelings about what we as a family represent. We are part Indian and that's part of our development too, and the American ideal of the rugged individual which is depicted by men like John Wayne, Gary Cooper and by my father, is a very real thing. He certainly represents that.'

Recently Chris, who says the money he's earning from movies is giving him time to polish his literary skills, has talked revealingly about his father.

'My dad made it the hard way and he's a multi-millionaire,' Chris said. 'Now he says he wants to retire and live it up, and of course he's entitled to. He wants to buy a ranch in New Mexico and a place in the Bahamas, race his quarter horses, get about on a fifty-foot boat and cruise the Mediterranean, the Caribbean and the South Seas. I've tried to talk him out of retiring though. I want him to take a year off and then, if he doesn't want to act any more, start writing and producing pictures. He could do it. He both wrote and produced *Thunder Road* and everybody remembers that picture. It made him a mint before he ever got in the really big money as an actor. But he says he wants to take it easy and enjoy himself for the rest of his life. And he's got it coming, I guess.'

Whatever the ultimate outcome of his own career, Chris says he's following a piece of advice his father once gave him. 'Whatever you become,' Mitchum once told him, 'be the best.'

In a Hollywood radio interview in 1971 when asked about the inevitable comparisons between sons and fathers in the film world, Chris answered: 'Fortunately, that hasn't happened with me except that some people say I look like my father. But with my brother Jim, he looks a great deal more like my father because he has dark hair and he's a little beefier than I am. And he has done pictures where in the reviews they'll say, "He *looks* like Robert Mitchum. However..." And they start knocking off points because he's not *exactly* like Robert Mitchum. They seem to think because of this he's therefore a not very good actor or something. The reviewers have some strange equation there.'

Of course in any family with two red-blooded young

sons and a tough, self-made father, life can't be expected to be one long simple idyll. And in the same radio interview young Chris revealed that there were some aspects about his father of which he didn't totally approve.

'Well, there are some things I don't like about him, of course,' Chris said.

'As a person?'

'As a person, yes.'

'What?'

'I don't want to get into all that.'

'No?'

'No, but we ... er ... we're different people, and I look at him as an adult to an adult, not as father to son and there are many things I admire a great deal about him and many things ... er ... not many, but *some* things I'm not particularly fond of.'

'You mean philosophies and things such as that?'

'No, not philosophies but certain character traits and stuff. For example, I have been with him when I've seen him get a little bit violent and hostile, and I'm not really into that whole thing. Violence solves nothing.'

'Well, your father was of a different generation. He was of a generation where violence and hostility represented manhood...'

'Well, also the way he was raised. I mean, like he was on the rails when he was thirteen or fourteen years old. He hit the Savannah chain gang and the whole route, plus being a professional fighter for a while...' Chris laughs. 'He *can* do it too. He can pull it off.'

'Has he used an iron hand on you, maybe?'

'No, not at all. It's just, like I say, there are just certain aspects that conflict with my character.'

For several years in the early sixties the Mitchum family lived a quiet and peaceful life at Belmont Farm in Talbot County, Maryland. Baltimore and Washington were over

seventy miles away and the nearest small town was Easton
—twelve miles by land and about five minutes by water in
their small, fast cruiser. It was above all to Dorothy a haven
of privacy—a rare commodity these days—and one which
Mitchum himself was beginning to value more and more
as the years went by. He only left the place when making
films, and he even renamed his film company Talbot Productions after his new home county.

The farm house itself was a hundred years old, large
but not too large, and furnished comfortably and inform-
ally without a 'decorated' look or any touches that smacked
of either the movie world or New York sophistication.
When friends visited, they found Mitchum mixing the
drinks, his wife cooking lunch. There were no pretentious
greetings, no effusive, unnecessary questions. Their few
visiting friends were welcomed, given good food, strong
drinks and basic but interesting conversation.

Mitchum tried his best to make the farm self-supporting.
'We have about three hundred acres and they are tilled by
contract,' he said. 'The farmers come in, plant, cultivate
and harvest. I've got barley, corn, alfalfa, white-faced Here-
fords and quarter horses. I had Dale Robertson buy the
horses for me and it took him a year and a half to find the
right ones.'

Once he took a black mare to stud in Yukon, Oklahoma,
himself. On the way back after the mare had performed
her duty with the stallion, she broke away and it took
Mitchum and his wrangler employees an hour to get her
back into the truck. 'I think she was trying to head back!'
he laughed.

Mitchum denied being a gentleman farmer and said that
farming hadn't presented him with any major problems. 'I
never bother with chickens or pigs,' he said. 'I always buy
eggs from a resident farmer who has chickens on his place.'

Within four years he had a sizable stable of a dozen

quarter horses, mostly brood mares. And he also bought a racing quarter horse stallion and another working quarter horse stallion. 'I don't race the horses myself,' he said. 'I just breed them for other people to race. I'm not really in the racing business.'

Above all he had complete privacy. 'The people there are insular and suspicious of strangers,' he said. 'They let you alone. When I'm there I can just sit around if I wish and watch the weeds grow. Apart from the farm the only other privacy I ever found was in jail or when I was driving across country alone. When I was doing that I'd stop sometimes wherever I saw water and go fishing. I like fishing. It is man's ancient and honorable excuse for doing nothing, you see. It allows meditation. You put your hook on the line and drop it into the water. Whether or not a fish takes it doesn't really matter. You can just day dream —and that's one of my favorite pursuits!'

The Mitchum farm fronted onto a river and its verandah reached down almost to their little private harbor, in which lay their cruiser and a fast speedboat.

'The countryside is so flat you can see people coming from a mile away. And if strangers come at us from the land side, I leap into the speedboat and disappear up the river. The only alternative to that is that I have half a mile of front lane and a big gate and an Alsatian dog. If a car gets through the gate I let out the dog and he won't let the people out of the car. After a while they get bored and go away—or die of carbon monoxide!'

Life down on the farm provided Mitchum with some of the most relaxed moments of his life. He experimented occasionally with his writing and he wrote poems.

Trina adored the horses. 'She was a regular little mother to them,' Mitchum remembers. 'In fact she just about took them over. And Chris loved the farm too. Even after he went off to college he loved the summers there. Dorothy complained every time a bee stung her on the behind, but she dug it too.'

Some ten years later, in 1971, Mitchum was asked by American writer Joan Dew Schmitt about the effect his star career had had upon his wife and children. She suggested that they all had to live in the shadow of Robert Mitchum, movie star.

'True, but so do I,' he replied. 'I live in his shadow too. Everybody knows me but I don't know anybody. I'm married to a billboard ten feet high. Robert Mitchum. I don't know who they're talking about or talking to. He's someone totally foreign to me. I have such a thing about it that if I need something from a store, I'll do without it for days just to avoid going to a place where they'll stare at me. When I do go, the people are very nice. But beforehand, I'll say to myself, "I can't go through that." It's the initial process of recognition that gets me. I guess it's because I don't know him. And I don't know what he's supposed to do or say.'

What if his wife had a career of her own?

'It wouldn't bother me, if it made her happy.'

Is he the kind of man who requires a great deal of attention around the house?

'A *great* deal!' he answered.

Mitchum's marriage has been a long one by any standards, more so by those of Hollywood. If for any reason he suddenly found himself single again, would he remarry?

Mitchum's response was immediate. 'No! I'd have to keep moving, keep traveling, keep myself busy. I don't think I could make it on my own now. Everything would wind up a compromise. Or I'd wind up in prison. I'm not safe to be let loose, you know.'

15

Quiet life on the farm—and a sock in the eye in Ireland

Although he enjoyed his privacy and the idyllic open air life of the farm, Mitchum was increasingly torn away from it to make films abroad. And when he came to Britain in the summer of 1959 to shoot A *Terrible Beauty* (called *The Night Fighters* in the United States) in Ireland, the star disclosed a rather embarrassing incident that had occurred on his leaving America. He'd had to register with the police.

'As an ex-convict I now have to sign out every time I leave the country,' he said. 'A lot of people don't do it but my lawyer has advised me to sign the form. Otherwise some goon might put the finger on me and I'd have to spend the rest of my days on Ellis Island or wherever it is they dump you now. But when I walked in to sign, I think the immigration people were more embarrassed than I was.'

It seemed that life on the Maryland farm was having a beneficent effect on Mitchum's spirit, for it was while he was making this film that there came further proof of his growing tolerance towards his fellow man.

One night in early August Mitchum was having a quiet drink with some friends—who included co-actor Richard Harris—in a Dublin bar. Suddenly an upholsterer's apprentice cornered him, clutched at his lapels, nagged him for an autograph, then annoyed him even more by calling him Kirk Douglas.

Mitchum said, 'Let me get my drink first.'

But the man slapped down a piece of paper and said, 'I insist you give me your autograph.' Mitchum wrote something uncomplimentary on the paper and signed it Kirk Douglas.

Minutes later the man came steaming back saying, 'Hey, this was for a lady.'

'I'd rather hoped it was for you,' Mitchum replied. Next thing he knew he'd been punched in the face. With praiseworthy self control, Mitchum didn't hit back at the apprentice, a much smaller man. Instead he pointed his finger and said, 'That's not very hospitable. And take my advice. If you can't do better than that don't try it again. You couldn't even crush an egg.'

Richard Harris said, 'The man had three friends with him. He hit Mitchum full in the face when he wasn't looking. Mitch could have killed him but he just shrugged it off like he does in film fights. He was wonderful.'

Three Irishmen sitting near Mitchum asked him if he had been offended by the man. They said if he had they'd take the legs off the tables and beat the daylights out of the fellow. But Mitchum asked them to cool down—and it remained a private matter. Just as he didn't retaliate himself, he didn't want the men to exact physical revenge either. 'You never win with that sort of thing,' he said, to many people's surprise.

Later the apprentice told the Dublin press that Mitchum had insulted motherhood, patriotism and the Irish flag. The row subsided when the Dublin police dismissed the apprentice as an undesirable person. A studio spokesman had the last word. 'Just like in western films, somebody always wants to be faster on the draw. Someone is always looking for trouble with film tough guys.'

In *The Night Fighters* Mitchum co-starred with Anne Heywood and played a tough but idealistic poet drawn into a fanatical branch of the IRA who hope to start a rebellion to unite all Ireland when Europe is fighting the Nazis in World War II. The film was reasonably successful but it did little for Mitchum. He thought there were too many clichés in the script.

'I was offered one script but when I got to Ireland I was landed with another,' he recalled later. 'What was I to do? Pay off all the actors and take the loss? [He was co-producer] Or do it? I did it and now my obligation to Raymond Stross [producer] is discharged. There is still an elemental force in the story. But it's like looking for a diamond that's been covered in sewage. You know it's there but, man, does it smell!'

At this time Mitchum and Dorothy decided to take a flat in London for a while as Mitchum was due to start *The Grass is Greener* in London with Cary Grant. After a period of living in Park Lane they took a modest flat in Eccleston Mews, where a daily housekeeper attended to their needs; all that farm life made Park Lane seem far too sophisticated. 'Even at home we don't have a bunch of servants,' Mitchum explained. 'I don't want some stranger hanging around looking over my shoulder.'

This film was a broad departure from the norm for Mitchum, a sophisticated comedy. He played an oil millionaire who, on a sightseeing tour of Countess Deborah Kerr's estate, talks her into spending a weekend with him in London.

'At least I don't have to grow a beard, fall off horses or carry people round on my back,' he joked. 'That's a hell of a change for me. I don't have much to say, which is lucky as I can't remember what little I *do* have to say. I've got a girl at the side of the set who tells me when to say, "Why?" or, "Really?" whenever Cary Grant comes to the end of a speech.'

As he walked to his dressing room at the end of one scene, a wardrobe man said, 'I'll take these shirts and have a little starch put in them. Mr Grant likes them to look crisp on you.'

'That's right,' said Mitchum sardonically. 'Cary doesn't want any dirty people in his film. I ain't neat.'

Understandably enough, Mitchum seemed a little out of place amid the film's illusion of elegance.

But when he went to Australia to play Paddy Carmody, the wandering, freedom-loving sheep shearer in *The Sundowners*, Mitchum really came into his own and delivered a naturalistic performance which many critics believe to be his finest ever. Unwilling to settle down, addicted to gambling and the bottle, Carmody lugs his wife (Deborah Kerr again) and small son everywhere with him as he goes from job to job. The film depicted his wife's attempts to tame him by love and understanding and persuade him to buy a farm of their own and thus build up a life with real roots.

Strangely enough, Carmody is not one of Mitchum's favorite roles and he once said he only signed to make it, never having read the script, because he knew Deborah Kerr was going to be in it. When he was told she would like first billing, although he was entitled to refuse, Mitchum replied, 'By all means. And you can design a twenty-four-foot sign of me bowing to her if you like.'

He remembers the picture's location scenes in Australia as being the hottest and dirtiest of his life.

'You can't imagine how hot it was, how dry and dusty. I was only clean twice during the entire shooting,' he said. 'Sometimes I thought the picture was going on so long it would be another twenty years before I could shave, cut my hair, have a bath and wash away the stink of sheep.'

Fred Zinnemann, who directed *The Sundowners*, said, 'When Mitchum had to shear sheep he almost wept for fear he would lacerate the animals' skins and that they would bleed to death.'

During the big shearing scene in which he was beaten by an eighty-year-old man, Mitchum complained: 'I have been shearing sheep as wide as this table and as tall as a pony. I don't know where the wool stops and the meat begins! I tell you one thing, I'll never complain about the price of wool again. I may never even *wear* wool again!'

Mitchum was none too complimentary when asked about his impressions of Australia. 'It's the easiest country in the world to get into and the hardest to get out of,' he said. 'They have an aggressive hospitality and they deify steak, eggs, and beer. I arrived in Sydney at 3:00 A.M. and there was a host of people meeting the plane. I'd hardly gotten on the ground when they asked, "Do you like our beer?"'

Mitchum was back in England in February, 1960, finishing interior shots on the film when his elder sister Julie married a jewelry company executive. Unable to attend, he telephoned Julie from London and wished her well. But his two younger children were at the wedding—Trina as flower girl and Chris as an usher.

Despite Mitchum's blunt comments about the filming, when *The Sundowners* was first previewed in Hollywood, the movie-hardened audience stood up at the end and gave Mitchum and the film a standing ovation. Congratulated later, Mitchum looked embarrassed. 'All I did was feed Deborah Kerr some lines,' he said. 'She took it from there. She's really the one who can act.'

In 1968 when Mitchum was asked on television about working with Miss Kerr he said, 'I haven't worked with her as often as I'd like to.' Told that she had said he was a hundred times better actor than he himself believed, Mitchum grinned shyly. 'Oh no. She's an adultress! She's very kind. I adore her. We have such rapport professionally we could phone it in. We can anticipate that much.'

In 1960 the US National Board of Review of The Motion

Picture Committee on Exceptional Films voted Mitchum the best actor of the year for his performances in *Home from the Hill* and *The Sundowners*.

Certainly Mitchum's stock as an actor zoomed higher than it had ever been, and several big studios offered him open-ended contracts whose terms he could virtually draw up himself. Indeed the financial set up of Talbot Productions had become somewhat complicated. Mitchum was receiving over $400,000 for each film, plus ten per cent of the gross. 'But Talbot cut me down to a $100,000 and they take the rest,' he said. Since Mitchum was the *head* of Talbot he was clearly getting more than enough to get by!

When asked about this, however, Mitchum deftly turned the conversation. 'Now I have my own production company I at least own what's left of my soul,' he cracked. 'I work all the time because I've got a wife and three kids to support and obligations to meet and taxes to pay. But I'm not much of an actor. I'm in demand because I don't waste the producers' money. I'm too middle class for that. I've got all the middle class virtues. That's why I laugh when people call me a rebel. I'm no rebel. So I once went to jail on a marijuana rap. Ever since I've been so damn middle class it hurts. Also lucky. Just look at my record, son. Look at the racing form and study my past performances, and you've got to come to the conclusion that I'm the luckiest sonofagun ever born.'

In this period Mitchum was rejecting from fifty to a hundred scripts a year. As we have seen, he even turned down working with a top director and his friend, John Huston, who wanted him for *The Misfits*, which later Huston directed with Marilyn Monroe and Clark Gable.

Mitchum didn't refuse the part, as was suggested at the time, because he had already worked—and waited—for the temperamental Marilyn Monroe. 'There were two reasons,' he told Lloyd Shearer. 'One, I was sure the script I read wouldn't play and I was right—it had to be re-written by Arthur Miller and Huston. Two, I was afraid Huston would kill me! That guy demands more of his actors than any other director I ever worked with.'

Instead, Mitchum returned to Britain in the winter of 1960 to make a broad comedy *The Last Time I Saw Archie*. In it he played a con-man private in a misfit outfit the army is trying to forget who charms everyone into believing he's a top general assigned to apprehend a beautiful Japanese spy (France Nuyen).

'I liked the role and I liked the picture,' said Mitchum. 'And why not? I got $400,000 for working four weeks and had a week off between Christmas and the New Year to go home to the farm.'

The director of this film was Jack Webb (star of television's 'Dragnet' series) who also co-starred in it with Mitchum. Asked how he found working with Webb, Mitchum answered, 'Once you're committed you have to submit to a style. And Jack's technique in direction is something—nobody ever gets to finish a sentence. It's a perilous prospect to play around in comedy—all situation comedy—because you're trespassing on the area of farce and that can spell doom. But he works. Man, how he works!'

After a short spell back at the farm with his wife and children, Mitchum journeyed down to Georgia for *Cape Fear*, his first trip back to Georgia since being in the Savannah chain gang nearly thirty years earlier. American writer Bill Davidson recorded what happened:

'Mitchum charmed society ladies at teas and cocktail parties and held court on the porch of the DeSoto Hotel daily for a throng of admirers, who listened with delight to his stories. But to a deputy sheriff assigned to guard the movie location, he snarled "Lay off me. I escaped from your

Chatham County chain gang in 1933, and I still owe you some time—but you're not going to get me back."

'Then he handed the deputy sheriff twenty dollars to buy lunch for himself and his fellow deputies. The show of generosity after the snarl was typical of Mitchum.'

Naturally, the Savannah papers made a big story of the star's return to the scene of his former humiliation. 'They ran a big picture of me like a ferret with a number across it: "Joe, the Wounded Tennis Player Returns" sort of thing,' Mitchum remembers. 'And at one of the parties a real sassy magnolia belle tried to take a rise out of me because of the chain gang episode and wanted me to know she knew all about it. "How'd you like it—back in Savannah?" she said. "Lady," I told her, "ah likes it anywhere ah can git it," imitating her accent. They almost locked me away in the chain gang again!'

In *Cape Fear* Mitchum played an ex-convict who plots sadistic revenge against the wife and daughter of the attorney (Gregory Peck) whose testimony sent him to jail. Playing this sexual psychopath, Mitchum turned in a performance of nerve-tingling menace. One critic wrote, 'I never realized how good he was until I saw him up against an actor like Peck.'

During the filming Mitchum's tender side once more emerged. In an unusual and difficult rape scene, he went out of his way to be gentle with newcomer Barrie Chase who was playing her first dramatic role. Director J. Lee Thompson gave Mitchum much of the credit for Miss Chase's extraordinarily fine performance.

While he was making the film the Maryland Theater Owners' Association voted Mitchum their annual Personality of the Year award for being their biggest box office draw and for 'adding prestige to the cinema'. The star was unable to collect the award himself, but his son Jim flew up to accept it on his behalf.

Nineteen sixty-one was a good year for all the acting Mitchums. In May Jim signed a seven-year contract with options at Twentieth Century-Fox, even though Fox had no specific role for Jim at the time. Until they did, he turned to singing and made a single record with a good swinging beat which enjoyed a small success. Later the same year Mitchum's brother John won the role of Goering to Richard Basehart's Führer in the film *Hitler*.

Mitchum spent the remainder of the summer back at his farm, supervising his horses, reading some of the scripts that thudded on to his doormat, and relaxing generally. Any hopes by those around him, though, that he might get through the year without incident were doomed to failure. In the fall he flew to France to play a cameo role as Brigadier General Norman Cota in Darryl F. Zanuck's film reconstruction of the D-Day landings in Normandy, *The Longest Day*. And he soon found himself back in the headlines.

On 12 November the United Press news agency released a story in world newspapers that Mitchum had complained that some of the GI's borrowed from the American Army in Germany had been afraid to board a landing craft in foul seas during a big action scene. 'It was raining, the wind was blowing and the sea was rough and these troops were afraid to board the landing craft to go to sea. I had to hop aboard first myself with some other actors and stunt-men before they gave in,' the story quoted Mitchum as saying.

It added that the army's excuse was that the bad seas required last minute substitution of landing craft for the smaller 'ducks' that were to have been used. The first landing craft, including Mitchum and thirty soldiers, was 'loaded expeditiously and with no delay noticeable on anybody's part'. In loading the second craft, the ramp had jammed and another vessel had to be brought up. There *was* a delay in the second boat's loading but through no fault of the soldiers involved.

Mitchum was further quoted as saying that he'd seen two top officers watch the operation from the beach. 'Unfortunately they got cold as we were wading in the icy water and asked for a good fire to get warm.' He said the last straw had been a man who kept firing a blank rifle into his back to make him jump: 'And when I needed him to give me a boost up this steep cliff I discovered the guy had decided to get himself "killed" and was lying on the beach.'

As the furore this story caused broke about the unit's ears, Mitchum, who *had* made a pungent remark about the inefficiency of the film's production staff, which had him prematurely at sea while soldiers were still trying to board a landing craft, denied making these statements. Next day he said, 'I have the highest respect and admiration for the soldiers. To quote me as saying the men were afraid is bordering on the ridiculous. I became good friends with these men during our work, and this story is insulting to me and the men.'

Then Zanuck himself got into the act, saying he was greatly surprised by the statements attributed to Mitchum. 'They were supposed to have been made at a lunch at which I was present,' he said. 'Since I was never present at such a lunch and never heard Bob make any such statements, I discredit the whole story.' He then went on to praise the officers and soldiers involved. Zanuck, of course, had no wish to upset the Pentagon, who could easily, if felt the army's image was being damaged, have withdrawn the two hundred and fifty troops from the film.

In interviews on 13 November Mitchum made a further denial. 'The statements attributed to me in my interview with the UP are false and a complete distortion of what I did say to UP reporters.' Of the soldiers, he added, 'They behaved beautifully.' He said if it had not been for the help of the young soldiers, aged eighteen to twenty, he—'over forty but I felt like seventy'—would not have made it wading ashore in rough seas from the landing craft. He added to this most un-Mitchum like statement that he had been given every chance to protect himself, that he was furnished with a heated trailer and other accommodations not available to the others, and that since he was playing a general, he did not have to carry anything.

No sooner had this row subsided from the headlines than Mitchum received the alarming news on 15 November that his mother Anne and his aged step-father Hugh Cunningham-Morris, then eighty-three, had been seriously injured in a traffic accident. They were returning from a holiday in Las Vegas in a sports car given them by Mitchum when they collided with a hay truck near Palmdale, California.

Both Mrs Cunningham-Morris, who had been driving, and her husband were thrown bodily from the car. Patrolman J. E. Tunnin summoned an ambulance which took the elderly couple, both unconscious, to the Antelope Valley Hospital in Lancaster. The driver of the hay truck, Louis F. Mora of La Puenta, was unhurt.

Mitchum heard the news while filming, and he immediately caught a plane and flew to Lancaster to join his brother John who had arrived from Hollywood. Both men were anticipating the worst, for their mother was still unconscious and they felt that, at eighty-three, their step-father could have little chance of recovery. It seemed likely that the extraordinary old man must have come to the end of his road.

But here is what happened as John Mitchum remembers it :

'We both got to the hospital and there is the old man, unconscious, swathed in bandages, blood seeping from all of them. He had been found a hundred feet from the point of impact and he had hit the gravel hard. The doctors told us "Your mother, well, she will pull out of it. But the old man is fading fast." Just then those old British eyes opened up and he asked "How did you two get here?"

' "Well, Dad," I replied. "It was on the radio and here we are."

' "I suppose it will be in all the papers then?" he asked.

'I said, "Dad, you've got to promise me something." He was lying there full of blood and both Bob and I felt awfully helpless. But I said, "When you get out of this you've got to come to my house and have a big glass of brandy." And he replied, "Only one!" We knew then he would pull through okay and he did, just as mother did.'

Later as the policeman told the Mitchums what had happened at the accident scene, he prefaced his remarks by asking what was Mr Cunningham-Morris's favorite television show.

John told him it was 'Highway Patrol'—a top television series, in which Broderick Crawford played police chief Dan Mathews.

'That figures!' laughed the patrolman. 'When I got there, I never saw your father at all because I found your mother first and he was a hundred feet away. He had been catapulted out of the window. When I did see him I went over thinking he was dead. But the old man looked up at me, saw the Highway Patrol uniform, and said, "Where's Dan Mathews?"

'I said, "Old timer, he just couldn't make it this time."

'He just gasped, "Ten Four!" and passed out!'

Despite their parents' serious condition, both Mitchums roared with laughter at this story. It was so typical of their indestructible stepfather.

After ensuring that his parents were receiving the best possible care, Mitchum, whose further absence would have caused costly complications on *The Longest Day*, flew back to France to complete his role. He found the row about his alleged remarks about the soldiers to be still simmering.

On 18 November, Darryl F. Zanuck told columnist Art Buchwald that Mitchum was the most popular star on the location and had endeared himself to every GI there. 'He might knock a general but he'd never knock a GI,' Zanuck said. 'I'm pretty sore about it.' The UP reporter was also pretty sore about it and told the press that he stood by his interview.

Mitchum had the last word: 'The worst thing is people will believe I said all those things. Americans believe if something appears in print it must be true, as opposed to the British who read something and throw it away because they know it isn't true.' He said what had happened was that the actors had boarded the craft two hours early and the sea was getting rough and soon they had been berating themselves for getting into the craft before it was necessary.

Despite this contretemps, Mitchum proved in the film to be thoroughly convincing in his cameo role as Brigadier General Cota, who had led the 29th Infantry Division up a cliff on the beach on 6 June, 1944.

16

*Critic bashing, with elephants and the Masai
in Africa, and farm life begins to pall*

When Mitchum was asked to star in the new Robert Wise
film *Two for the Seesaw* for United Artists, he repeatedly
refused the role. It looked like being one of those deadly
walking-about-and-talking lounge suit parts. He felt that
the role of an indecisive Omaha lawyer estranged from his
wife who becomes involved with a New York bohemian
who fancies herself as a dancer would be more suitably
played by Gregory Peck or William Holden.

But when he heard that Shirley MacLaine would be the
co-star, he accepted the role, saying, 'She is the most fantastic thing in movies today.'

In one sense Mitchum's initial hesitation appears to have
been right because romantic indecision is not a quality he
projects well. But he worked hard at the role, knowing he
was following the excellent stage interpretations of it by
Henry Fonda, Dana Andrews and Hal March, and the
film was a success. It certainly proved that he and
Shirley MacLaine had formidable chemistry as a screen
team.

Mitchum smarted later, however, under the evaluations
of his performance made by some critics, and he launched
into a rare but apt criticism of critics in general.

'The toughest chore in show business is trying to please
them when an actor appears in a film of a stage play or
book. No matter what you do it's as wrong as a sow's ear
in a silk purse factory, especially to New York critics,' he
said. 'They are guilty of intellectual snobbery. With them

nothing can be done in Hollywood or anywhere as well as in their home town, it seems.

'If you play it the same way as on stage they say the mediums are different and you should have played it with a fresh approach. If you play it with a fresh approach they accuse you of painting a rose red, especially if the stage actor received a few awards.

'If you stay in a single room as in the stage play, they roast you brown for not utilizing the vast scope of the screen for movement. If you change the setting to include numerous location backgrounds, they say "There goes Hollywood again, trying to perfect perfection." And if you try to give it a new twist they accuse you of doing it with a dagger.

'If you leave out certain scenes, they snort that those were the most important ones in the whole play, and if you don't leave out any, they yawn that the whole thing is too long and could stand editing. If some of the dialogue is cut, they yell that the movie is a watered-down version, and if none of it is cut, they yell it's too talky. You get four stars from one and a raspberry from another. One digs you with appreciation, the other with a spade.'

Actors around the world would no doubt applaud Mitchum for taking this brave stand, but he adds, 'There are times when I'm sure a critic is absolutely right. But I'm not sure which critic is right and which one is wrong on any given review. It's only human to go along with one who raves about an "acting gem" rather than with the one who holds his nose. But when it comes to a film made from a stage play or book, your chances can be described in just two classic words—*im-possible*.'

Before he went to Warner Brothers to make *Rampage*, with Elsa Martinelli and Jack Hawkins, Mitchum displayed a similarly honest *sangfroid*.

'What's it about? It's a lot of dancing girls, banjo playing and bull,' he said. 'There are these two guys on the make for this broad, see, but there's a man-eating tiger in the way, so one of them has to kill it or something ... all that jazz.' And Mitchum was right. In the film he played a wild game guide who takes a famous hunter and his mistress on a safari in Malaya. But it was acceptable hokum.

In the winter of 1962 Mitchum put himself briefly back under the direction of John Huston in *The List of Adrian Messenger*, a highly entertaining 'gimmick' mystery in which several famous stars played brief cameo roles in disguise. He tells an amusing story of what happened when Huston signed him for one of the parts: 'He said, "Kid, it's silly for you to be paid cash for this picture. We can get you a painting in Europe for 75,000 dollars that'll be worth 150,000 dollars in the States. Then you can lend it to a museum and that way the money's deductible."

'Well, that may be all right, but it was much too complicated for me. I took the money.'

After a spell back on the farm, Mitchum sailed to England on the *Queen Mary* in the spring of 1963 to make *Man in the Middle*. He took the boat because he wanted to relax alone and because he wanted to take his own car along. 'Most of the time I stayed in my room, ate there and only went out to dinner three times,' he disclosed. 'I read a lot and loved it. It's the first real solitude I've had in years. I spent some time with my guitar and wrote some letters I later tore up.' He added that he'd managed to keep to himself by hanging a quarantine sign on his cabin door!

In the film, Mitchum played an Army major assigned to to defend an American lieutenant who has murdered a British sergeant. During the studio shooting at Elstree, Mitchum led a quiet life, living in a small farm cottage near the studio, where Dorothy, Chris and Tina visited and stayed with him for a while. He avoided nightclubs and the West End. 'After all those tough pictures, there's a general impression when I'm out that I'm up to no good,' he said a trifle sadly. One night he did take Dorothy out— to a piano recital in London. 'When I walked in everyone turned round, rather archly, as if to say, "What's this bum doing here?"' he recalls.

He liked his role in the film, but after some location scenes in India he told Hedda Hopper that it hadn't been a 'fun' picture because he'd had to work too hard. 'There was a military trial that had to be precise and fair. They needed a delinquent British psychiatrist who had been sent away because the British had been screaming for his blood but who returns to testify. When they asked me who they could get to play the part, I told them Trevor Howard. Trevor always said he'd never work with me, but his part was written so well he couldn't turn it down.

'Every scene I played with him he stole from under my nose. But that's okay with me when it's right for the picture, and in my opinion it was right. If there's one thing I'd like to teach young actors, it's this: worry only about whether or not the picture as a whole is good and whether or not your performance in any small way is contributing to its being good. Only the amateur worries about whether he looks right and is getting a big enough share of the lens.

'I think my part as Barney Adams was intriguing because he faces a real dilemma only he can solve. Whichever course he chooses—justice or loyalty—in his defense of a self-confessed murderer, will bring him personal unhappiness. It's the sort of decision lots of people have had to face during a war.'

Mitchum and Trevor Howard became firm friends while making the picture, and Howard occasionally visited the Mitchums at their rented cottage near Elstree.

When the film ended Mitchum flew back to his Maryland farm but could only spend a couple of days there—to look at a dozen new quarter horses—before he had to dash down to Hollywood to make *What a Way to Go!* with Shirley MacLaine. En route west he stopped off in New Mexico to see the All American $285,000 Quarter Horse Futurity Handicap. His plane touched down at Los Angeles airport at 3:00 A.M., and five hours later Mitchum reported, sleepy-eyed but as punctual as ever, for his new picture at Twentieth Century-Fox.

'I'm actually working for nothing after taxes because I've made too many films this year,' he complained, tongue in cheek, 'but I was with [director] Lee Thompson in *Cape Fear* and couldn't turn down the chance to work with him and Shirley again.'

In *What a Way to Go!* Mitchum played Miss MacLaine's third husband, the richest man in the world, and he wore crazy outfits that spoofed the ultra high style of the new men's fashions. In one scene at a swimming pool his bathing suit was a gold lamé diaper held together by two huge gold safety pins. Equally wacky were the outfits he wore for water skiing, tennis, golf and skeet shooting.

'They are what *not* to wear no matter where you are or how rich you are. No one in his right mind would be caught dead in them,' Mitchum said, to the consternation of the studio publicists. 'The film is a far-out, crazy comedy. In one of the dream sequences I bed down with a girl in a champagne glass. I also have a run-in with a big bad bull, which is more like the things I'm used to doing in pictures.'

Mitchum revealed that at first the Mirisch brothers were going to make the film and Sinatra was to be its star. 'They also wanted Liz Taylor but couldn't get her. Sinatra wanted $500,000 for two weeks' work. Then, when the picture got to Twentieth, Zanuck wasn't interested in Sinatra or his terms. So when Zanuck wouldn't settle for Sinatra the six men in the picture were contingent on one man. Shirley said, "What's wrong with Bob Mitchum?" They said, "Sold." '

When the film was over, Mitchum returned to his Maryland farm. In 1964 he flew out to Africa on a really long rugged location for *Mr Moses*, a film in which he spent a good deal of time in muddy rivers and on an elephant's back. 'I never really became friends with that elephant,' Mitchum later recalled. 'My only concern was to *look* like I was a friend, but it wasn't really my type. Elephants can suddenly run off through the thorn trees trumpeting and squealing when they're frightened and can be very dangerous. They can get very confused and I had to watch myself with that one. It had to work hard and long, doing things to which it wasn't accustomed.'

Mitchum's role was that of an itinerant diamond smuggler and con-man who is tossed into a river by enraged Africans after his magic muscle tonic hasn't worked. Found drifting downstream, he is hailed by the chief of a new tribe as the true 'Moses' who will lead them from their flooded lands to a new and better home. He has to go along with this new plan or be betrayed to the government agents.

At first the unit, Mitchum and his co-star Carroll Baker, stayed at a hotel in Lemura some thirty miles from Nairobi and commuted sixty miles to and from the location each day. Mitchum soon got tired of this, so he moved in with a Masai tribe and lived in their village in a beaten-up old trailer.

'I loved it,' he remembers. 'The tribal huts were made of straw and cow dung and the natives subsisted largely on a diet of milk and blood from their cows. But I ate at the camp where we had safari caterers and did very well.

'Those natives are honest folk—never steal anything

except one another's wives, but that's okay under their code. They hunt with their spears, can hit a dime at fifty paces, and the men do no work at all—just sleep, eat, and make love.

'But if we think these people are primitive we had better take a good look at ourselves. Think of their free lives, then you tell me—who's civilized, them or us?'

The Masai liked Mitchum as much as he liked them, and he was offered several of their wives during his stay.

Asked how he'd got along with Carroll Baker, Mitchum replied, 'She's a lovely girl, but I hardly got to know her. She lived back in town with the rest of the cast and crew while I stayed in the trailer. When she was at the location at nights, she was usually off washing her hair or writing letters to columnists. But we had no trouble working together.' He paused, then added, 'I don't write notes to columnists any more. I wrote one to a woman columnist back in 1955. My note seemed to give her typewriter arsenic poisoning, so I decided, "Forget it, Charlie."'

When visiting, Hedda Hopper reminded Mitchum that Carroll Baker was then being hailed as the new 'sex goddess' and did *he* think she was, he answered, 'There's got to be someone for everyone! How would I know?'

Baker herself said, 'I was afraid of Mitchum before I met him. I never quite got over my apprehension. I was always waiting for him to sock someone in the nose, but he didn't. It's strange how a reputation for violence precedes him.'

After finishing his suitably rugged performance Mitchum returned to his farm for a few months, but in April, 1965, he again surprised Hollywood by agreeing to go on a long publicity junket to promote *Mr Moses* in New York, Chicago, Houston, Boston, Pittsburgh, Denver and other major cities. He arrived for the première in film town at the time the Academy Award presentations were being held, completely oblivious of the fact. 'I don't pay much attention to that stuff,' he said.

He told columnists he thought *Mr Moses* was a 'pretty good picture' and that he was going on the inter-city junket because he'd been asked. 'No one ever asked me before,' he said. 'They just took it for granted I wouldn't go.' Dorothy was with him at this time, taking a break from life at the farm, and the Mitchum's celebrated twenty-five years of married life with a big night out in Hollywood.

Mitchum was asked if he now missed the movie town life. 'People always ask me that,' he said. 'What Hollywood life do they mean? I never traveled with the mob. I've only been to one movie star's home, Kirk Douglas's, and that was for all of ten minutes. All actors are freaks, and I guess I'm a freak's freak. When I walked into a restaurant here, people held their breath—waiting for me to walk up and sock someone. In Maryland I'm not an actor. I'm just another farmer, and I like it that way. I've got nothing against Hollywood—and when I lived here no one asked me what I had against Maryland. But why not live there? I don't care where I live as long as we have a roof.'

Then he said something which revealed that all might not be well with life up on the farm. He added 'Dottie's looking round Laguna now, so we may be living there next. Every time a wasp or a bee flies by she complains about the farm!'

The truth was that after nearly six years the initial charm of the farm's remoteness was beginning to pall for Dorothy, and when Mitchum had finished his promotional tour for *Mr Moses*, the couple took an apartment in Malibu for a while. It was then that Mitchum began to speak of the farm in less complimentary terms.

'My most costly mistake in farming was in buying the place,' he grinned one day. 'I thought I'd like to own a farm so I bought it, but nobody told me about the blinding snowstorms in winter or the wasps and mosquitoes in summer. I really do love it there most of the time, the privacy, having my own waterfront and so forth. I thought this is the great fun in life, going fishing, maybe doing a little writing between films, doing nothing. If people come to visit with me, fine, just coming there would be a sign of true friendship. So fewer people came, and my doing nothing has become just that. Much of the time I don't even crank the boat and go fishing. I just goof. Sit there staring at the stars, until Reva calls me from Hollywood for a new film somewhere.'

It was Dorothy who first made up her mind that they ought to leave Maryland. With Chris away at university most of the time and with Trina well past her thirteenth birthday and therefore in need of more sophisticated schooling and stimulating friends of her own age, Dorothy felt sure the time had come to move on. Life had never been easy on the farm for her, with the nearest store twelve miles away and with Robert frequently away on distant film locations. After so many years in such a wild and deserted spot, the outdoor country life was beginning to drag for her, especially since she was spending long periods of time on her own.

Mitchum, however, was by no means anxious to leave. He'd grown to love his untroubled interludes at Maryland, to know that no matter how tough a movie location had been, he had his peaceful home to return to, a place where he could be completely his own man.

Years later he recalled how Dorothy began to complain about being stranded alone with the animals while he was always off on some glamorous movie. 'Glamorous movies!' he snorts. 'I was usually in Mexico sliding my backside down some mountain or getting my skin burnt to a crisp on some location in a place like Death Valley.

And as for the beautiful girls I was supposed to work with
—John Wayne, Dean Martin, Kirk Douglas. These are
beautiful dames? Anyway, they always got the girl. I got
the horse!'

Mitchum took a year off from filming during this
period. He wanted to go to Vietnam to help bolster the
morale of American troops out there, as a few other stars
were also doing.

Little did he know when he set off on his first trip to
Vietnam at the end of 1965 that he would virtually be
without a roof over his head on his return.

17

'I don't care where I live as long as the roof
doesn't leak.'

Before Mitchum left on his trip as an official observer
to visit the troops fighting in Vietnam, he and Dorothy
were arguing seriously about whether they should leave
their farm and return to Hollywood.

He recalls them in his usual caustic style:

'After six years my old lady just didn't like living out
there any more—what with me being away so often.
Every time a wasp flew by or a bee stung her on the behind,
she'd look at me accusingly as if I had engineered it. So in
the end I said, sort of jokingly, "Okay, sell the joint."
She'd say, "What's this bill for $417 for spraying the alf-
alfa?" I'd say "That's just what it is, a bill for $417 for
spraying the alfalfa." She'd say, "We just went through
that." And I'd say, "Listen honey, don't bug me. Sell it.
If it bothers you that much, forget it." She said, "But where
would we live?" I said, "Who cares? Paris, Tokyo, Rome,
Omaha ... I don't give a darn as long as the roof doesn't
leak. Don't moan at me. Prove it. Just don't bug
me."'

And Dorothy took Robert at his word. While her husband was away on his three month trip to Vietnam, she
thought deeply. Finally she telephoned Reva Fredrick,
Mitchum's secretary, to ask if Reva thought Mitchum had
meant what he said about her selling the place. Reva confirmed that he probably did. Whereupon Dorothy quickly
advertised the farm for sale and within a matter of weeks
clinched a deal.

The first Mitchum knew about it was when he was on his way back from Vietnam. He stopped over in Honolulu and telephoned Dorothy to let her know all was well.

'I expected tears of rejoicing that I was coming back in one piece,' he recalls. 'But all Dorothy said was, "You know, I sold the place."'

Mitchum, who'd forgotten all about their argument, said, 'What place?'

Dorothy replied, 'Our place. Belmont Farm.'

Mitchum was completely speechless. 'I just didn't know what to say,' he remembers. 'She told me she had sold everything—the cows, the farm, the house and all. Everything but the horses. When I recovered, I said "Great, where do we go from here?" And she said "Honey, you asked for it. It's your move now." That's what it was, of course. So I called Reva, still from Honolulu, and told her about it.'

Miss Fredrick knew all about it, naturally, and knew exactly what to do. She had a list of new pictures from which Mitchum could choose, thus saving him the trouble of moving his belongings personally. He finally went to make The Way West with Kirk Douglas while Dorothy supervised the move from the Maryland farm to Cole Porter's old house in Hollywood, in which the composer had lived some twenty-three years. When he saw this house, Mitchum thought it was dreary, and after a while the couple moved into actress Ruth Roman's house before buying their present home in Bel Air.

Mitchum thoroughly enjoyed his work on The Way West, one of the best westerns made in recent years, and during the location scenes in Oregon he bunked in with the wranglers while co-stars Kirk Douglas and Richard Widmark rented houses in Christmas Valley.

One day Mitchum was walking across the set when he saw his younger brother coming toward him.

'How the hell did you get here? Who let you in?' he asked.

'Hey,' said John with a grin, who had a character role in the movie, 'I have the right, you know. I pay my ten per-cent too!' This unscheduled reunion of the brothers led to some highjinks and impromptu musical evenings, and one of these helped Mitchum to revive his lagging side-career as a singer.

'Bob called me on the phone one day and asked me to visit him,' recalls John. 'I went over and he had this record which had been put out by Charlie Walker, a cow-boy singer from Bakersfield. He played it and one of the songs was "Little Old Wine Drinker". He asked me what I thought of the song and I said it was fine. "Why don't you record it?" he asked me. I said, "Why don't *you* record it?" And right then we got our guitars out and went through it together. That was the cue, and night after night we would party and play. We threw a won-derful drunk for Lola Albright's birthday party, and "Little Old Wine Drinker" was our favorite song.'

After the film Mitchum returned to Hollywood, still thinking about the song from time to time. One day he met Dean Martin and told him, 'I've got a great song for you.' Dean listened to it and said, 'It's not really the kind of song I want to do.' So Mitchum went over to Nash-ville and recorded an album for Monument Records, writ-ing two of the songs on it himself. Naturally he included 'Little Old Wine Drinker', and it became his biggest hit record since 'Thunder Road'.

'Bob has a very keen ear for songs,' says John Mitchum. 'He knows what's good instantly. He also recorded some Dean Martin standards but we both fell in love with "Wine Drinker" and I usually include it when I do an occa-sional nightclub engagement myself.'

Dean Martin must have kicked himself for not following Mitchum's advice, for the ironic upshot was that he recorded the song himself later—and also enjoyed success with it.

When *The Way West* was released many months later, critics declared it to be a rare western. Some even said it could have benefited by being *longer*. Kirk Douglas gave a strong performance as the tough, visionary, disciplinarian boss of a wagon train who is mutinied against by the traveling pioneers. He forces a Negro servant to beat him after his son's death and tries unsuccessfully to seduce Lola Albright. Richard Widmark as a new pioneer driven to the wilderness he's never seen was also excellent. But of them all Mitchum seemed to have fared the best, for as the wagon train's reluctant guide who is slowly going blind, he added subtle innuendoes of compassionate humanity and humor to his rather more sympathetic role.

Mitchum's next western was *El Dorado,* in which he was ideally cast with John Wayne. The acting chemistry between the two men helped to make the film an enormous success. Mitchum was just right as a jowly, paunchy, drunken sheriff beset by gastric troubles who is enraged at being laughed at by the townsfolk. Wayne, hired as a fast gun by a wealthy rancher trying to steal valuable water rights due to the homesteaders, finally goes on the side of right and not only helps Mitchum restore justice but to recover his manhood. Although *El Dorado* was a fine 'spoof' on most westerns, its bizarre violence was right, the drama was right, and Mitchum's flare for humor came through perfectly.

John Mitchum also played a small role. He was the bartender who reaches for his gun when Mitchum first decides to get tough—and gets bar splinters in his hands from Mitchum's bullet for his pains.

In early 1967 Mitchum made his second trip back to Vietnam on another morale boosting tour of the troops fighting in isolated places. Unlike some stars, he has made very little of his good will missions, but in truth they took a great deal out of him. After his first trip his doctor told him he couldn't be cleared for another for at least a year.

He traveled by helicopter and truck to many outlandish spots and saw firsthand what the fighting men were going through. 'You know what the gooks do out there?' he said on his return. 'They bomb our boys everywhere, even in their outhouses. Get the Yankee dog right where he lives. The Yanks are always building outhouses, and the Cong are always shooting them down.'

He found one problem was that the men always expected him to drink with them as heavily as his public reputation demanded. 'One day we were out there in the boondocks and I must have consumed fourteen or sixteen cans of beer and the greater part of a bottle of whiskey, just being sociable. I could hardly drink orange juice with them, could I? And that was at lunch. Then they took me back to base in a helicopter and everyone said again, "Come on, Bob, have a drink." "No way," I said. "No way. I'm a Mormon bishop." "Sure, Bob, we know, but just have another ..."' He sometimes spent fifteen hours a day working, so he could get to visit small units miles from the main centers because the men in them wanted to meet him.

On 3 March he made a phone call to Dorothy and learned he had become a grandfather for the third time. His son and daughter-in-law, Cindy, who had already had a daughter Carrie, had just welcomed their son Robbie into the world.

When Mitchum arrived back in America from Vietnam he was not in the best of health; he had barely slept for the last three weeks. But in his hotel room while in transit to Hollywood, he began pulling scraps of paper from his pocket. Then he made phone calls to parents of soldiers all over America, assuring them that their sons were all right. Many couples were startled to pick up the phone and hear, 'This is Robert Mitchum and I just got back from Vietnam. I shared a cold beer with Charlie on Hill 17 and he's doing fine.' He would talk a little more then pull out another piece of paper and dial again. To Mitchum the men in Vietnam were among the few honest, down-to-earth young men left. 'It's just about the only place where there isn't any bull,' he once said.

To writer Tim Tyler, of *Time* magazine, Mitchum delivered some random thoughts on society and war at this time. 'If society isn't careful, this is what people come to be for, to be pushed this way and that,' he said. 'Ignorance is just to be made money out of, by the smart guys ... If there were no more pestilence and war, many would be out of work ... There's no more happy cobbler. Today he has to *own* the shoe factory ... Yet when you think you've arrived, nothing has really happened. The realization comes too late, when you realize life *is* the purpose of life and that when you give you're not losing anything ... Every time you breathe it's a new life ... I think it would be good to be an architect—the building endures, and the word endures ... "Sink or swim, I have at least had my dream." Was that from Byron?' Tyler asked him why then he didn't stretch himself, write seriously, try the stage or something new. But Mitchum didn't answer.

From the point of view of work, it seemed that the Mitchums' move back to Hollywood had been a good idea. From the spring of 1967 and for most of the next two years he entered upon his most intensive period of filming since the early forties, but then he was the leading name or among the two or three top stars of all his films. 'Dorothy was right at that stage in our lives,' Mitchum admits. 'As much as I had loved the farm at Maryland, we needed to spend more time back in the city because of work.'

The search for a new home did not prove easy. One day the Mitchums found a beautiful house with large grounds, but the owners wanted between six and seven hundred thousand dollars for it. Mitchum turned it down, only to hear his daughter Trina say, 'But, Daddy, we're not exactly paupers.'

Eventually they found their new home in Bel Air; as usual Dorothy handled most of the details of the move. It is a comparatively modest establishment for a man of Mitchum's wealth, for although it is an elegant ivy-covered house with a big den for himself and a swimming pool in the patio, it only has four bedrooms. Within a few months of moving into it, Mitchum had found himself another ranch—this time a smaller, seventy-six acre, spread much nearer to Hollywood, in Atascadero, California.

'Well,' Mitchum excuses himself. 'I had to have somewhere to put my twenty-six quarter horses. Until we found the ranch I had them all over the place, some even at the Beverly Hills hotel. I couldn't keep them there—not and show a profit at least. Also, they might have brought about a rapid change of clientele! Besides, I can now actually breed them more successfully. I couldn't really breed out at Maryland because every time I got a filly to be sired, Trina would dissolve into tears! So I had to wait. But the new farm really does make out; we show a profit.'

In May 1967 Mitchum flew to Italy to star in *Anzio* (British title: *The Battle for Anzio*), in which he played a fictitious American journalist who lands at Anzio during World War II with the army of General Mark Clark. In the film, when the Americans dig in at the beach fearing a trap, Mitchum and his friends decided to reconnoiter. To their astonishment they drive to Rome without seeing a single German. It is historical fact that some six thousand American soldiers paid with their lives at Anzio, and the book on which the film was based claimed the hesitancy of the American army to advance gave the German Command time to make a stand.

'I consider the picture to be violently anti-American,' Mitchum said shortly after his arrival. 'Or rather, it was.' At his request the script was being changed slightly. Apparently the days when he would parrot any lines given to him were coming to an end. Director Edward Dmytryk did not quite agree with Mitchum, however. 'We are being factually correct,' he asserted.

In a talk with writer Fred Robbins at the time, Mitchum said, 'It is inconceivable to me that an army would think of making a landing in force and number anywhere without the proper use of available intelligence. They didn't and fell into all sorts of holes and traps. Good Lord, they should have known what the terrain was like at Anzio. They could have asked anyone. There were lots of co-operative Italians who were tired of the Germans and they could have furnished the Allies with the information they needed. But for some reason or other, a commander looked upon them as informers and was sort of morally against it. As a result, he killed a lot of men.'

When *Anzio* came out, a critic for one influential Hollywood trade paper wrote: 'Fact masquerading as fiction, an antiwar indictment, a routine journal of individual heroism, the tragic miscalculation of generals and one man's encounter with the futility of war. A routine war drama with heavy handed jabs at the military command there. Mitchum plays a newspaperman struggling to get back to his HQ with information of the placement of the German Caesar line. Finally forced to take up a gun to survive after being initiated into killing, he manages to suggest more than the script provides. Small solace for a bum trip.'

Mitchum next flew to Spain to make *Villa Rides*, a fictitious story about part of the bandit career of Mexico's folk hero Pancho Villa, with Yul Brynner in the title role.

Mitchum played a gun-running American pilot who is captured by the bandit, reprieved by him from sentence of death, then later joins forces with him to help his guerrillas capture a heavily fortified town. Dorothy and Trina joined him for a two week holiday but had to leave for home after that so that Dorothy could supervise Trina's enrollment at Westlake School for Girls.

Villa Rides turned out to be a hard-headed, soft-hearted, entertaining film with the emphasis heavily on explosive action and violent death.

After Christmas and New Year's Day at home Mitchum flew down to Durango in Mexico in early 1968 to play a murderous preacher who carries a pistol in a hollowed-out Bible in *Five Card Stud*. His co-star was Dean Martin, and during the dusty location shooting one of Mitchum's traits was shown clearly. While Martin had a professional entourage of a makeup man, hairdresser, and permanent companion-secretary with him, Mitchum had no one. He always uses whatever technical staff the film companies care to provide. When Mitchum says, 'I never had or needed an entourage—I'm a loner,' you can believe it.

One day while he was in Mexico, director Joseph Losey, actress Elizabeth Taylor and some others involved in preparing a film called *Secret Ceremony*, were sitting in London discussing who they could get as Miss Taylor's co-star. They didn't want an actor whose accent was so heavily English that it would disadvantageously spotlight Miss Taylor's. On the other hand they didn't want a pronounced American accent either. Miss Taylor, who knew of his talent with accents, suggested Mitchum. Losey got on the phone and called him in Mexico. Could he do a certain kind of English accent? 'Hell, yes,' replied Mitchum. 'What do you want—north country, Cockney, Lancashire?'

Losey said no, they wanted a sort of transatlantic *in-*

different English accent. Mitchum tried a few out on the phone, and was asked to play the role.

Before agreeing to take the part, however, he explained that he was already contracted to make another film in the summer. Losey finally came up with what must be one of the shortest deals for a starring role ever made.

'I was only held contractually for ten days on *Secret Ceremony*,' Mitchum remembers. 'They did some weird things with that script too. They were in trouble when I got there, and I don't think I improved the situation any!'

He may have been right. In the first week of June, *Time* magazine came out with a frolicsome little story which ran this way: 'A sultry night at Holland's sea coast spa of Noordwijk and the guests at Hotel Huis ter Duin were finishing a late supper when in dropped Mia Farrow, 23, fagged out after a day on the set of a gay little flick called *Secret Ceremony*. From then on the facts are hard to come by but according to witnesses, co-star Robert Mitchum, 50, bounded to his feet and smothered Mia with a kiss—so all-consuming that Mia allowed her dangling cigarette to burn a hole in the suit of a somewhat wobbly diner. "I don't like that," he protested, staggering to his feet and menacing poor Mia. Neither did Mitchum, who plastered a plate of salad on the Dutchman's face. In return, the gentleman heaved a salad at Mia. Before the waiters broke up the festivities, the air was full of cucumbers and tomato slices. Custard pie, anyone?'

Mitchum has not commented on this report, but he does tell an odd story about the filming: 'Apparently after my ten days were finished they took two scenes I was in and recast them with Elizabeth Taylor,' he says. 'You know that bathtub scene? In the script I was in the bathtub with Mia—that scene where's she's rubbing Elizabeth's back, licking her back. In the script that was *my* back.' He gives a slow grin. 'All the same, *Secret Ceremony* was good at the box office. Just after we made it lesbianism came in. Maybe that's *why* they reshot the bathtub scene. I'm no damned good as a lesbian. I'll play anything else but not that! Of course, lesbianism has been around a long time, if not in films. But Losey's heart must be gladdened by the success of *Secret Ceremony*. Maybe not. I doubt if anything gladdens old Joe's heart. I think he has dyspepsia.

'We were shooting in that hideous house the whole time,' he continues. 'Joe has an architectural fetish. Sometimes you think he'd be happy to clear the actors out altogether and just photograph the rooms. He never says a word. Not one word. He walks into a room and engineers and choreographs and then the actors go through it. Then he prints it and that's that.'

Mitchum had worked in four major films in just over a year—a considerable output of sustained effort. While he showed no signs of physical tiredness, he did begin to exhibit impatience when things went wrong on his next two pictures.

After only a short break he flew out to Tucson, Arizona, to star in *Young Billy Young* and he lost little time in joking about his return to his familiar casting as a vengeful hired gun.

'Every time the same damned role. I'm wearing the same hat and the same boots I wore in *Five Card Stud*,' he groaned.

At the end of one scene when director Burt Kennedy yelled, 'Cut!' Mitchum astonished a bunch of tourists who'd gathered to watch him in action by exploding into a wild, furious, and devastatingly accurate imitation of a stereotypical homosexual dance.

Ask by Tim Tyler why he stayed in the movie business if he no longer liked it, Mitchum replied. 'Because I don't like calluses.' When Tyler asked him about the money and fame, Mitchum grimaced. 'Hah, money—The Man takes all that in taxes. Fame? I live in a cage. Some day somebody's going to feed me a poisoned peanut. I can't have peace any more. If you want to be rich and famous, go and rob a bank without a mask or shoot a man like Martin Luther King. Who needs fame? I just clock in and clock out and that's about the extent of it.'

He paused a moment, then added, 'You know, Stanislavsky wrote a book about the Method, and he admitted he did it for the money. And so now everybody follows him and he laughs. Talent is like having an ear for pitch. You either have it or you don't; you can't develop it.'

'But can't you improve?' asked Tyler.

'Well, I suppose it keeps some kids off the streets,' he grinned. 'But where are the real artists, the Da Vincis, the Botticellis? Today it's four-barrel carburetors and that's it.'

In the film Mitchum played a gunman who comes to town and becomes a deputy so he can settle an old feud with a villain who years earlier had killed his son in a jail break. The local corrupt law officer thwarts Mitchum and tries to alarm the town by predicting that this confrontation will bring trouble to the community. Despite Mitchum's colorful complaints, his performance was true to life and an additional bonus came with his singing of the title song, written by Shelly Manne and Ernie Sheldon.

No sooner had Mitchum completed this role than he had to dash without a rest to New Mexico to fulfil a contractual agreement to star in *The Good Guys and the Bad Guys*. Although his impatience with delays increased, largely because of the back-breaking schedule he'd set himself, he still managed to retain his sense of humor, but the members of the crew found themselves going about their work to a caustic verbal barrage from Mitchum. After two months of shooting, the unit was having trouble getting a scene on a train right. 'Why don't we quit and try something else?' he demanded. 'Like another movie.'

At one point when something else went wrong, Mitchum demanded in a loud voice, 'How in hell did I get into this picture anyway? I kept reading in the papers that I was going to do it, but when they sent me the script I just tossed it on the heap with the rest of them. But somehow, one Monday morning, here I was. How the hell do these things happen to a man?'

Nevertheless Mitchum enjoyed his role in the film and contributed many innovations and ideas of his own. Deaf to the western tradition that good men wear white hats and bad men black hats, Mitchum wore a brown one. 'In case I feel like being a little wicked,' he cracked.

When *The Good Guys and the Bad Guys* came out it proved to be a fine western, every bit as good as *El Dorado*. In it Mitchum and George Kennedy were the good guys. They played two aging men who have been pushed aside by the younger men—youngsters who lack the style, pride, and sense of honor that Mitchum and Kennedy share. The two men unite to obstruct the young men's robbery of the town bank. Mitchum's too infrequently exploited gift for comedy came to the fore, and he delivered one of the liveliest and best performances he had given for quite a while.

When filming was over, Mitchum was tired. He had just completed two of the hardest and most intensive years of filming since he'd been a hungry young newcomer back in the early forties. He returned to spend the rest of the winter at his Atascadero ranch, and he told his friends that he intended to retire.

18

*'If you'll just do this wretched little film of
ours, we'll pay your funeral expenses'*

As Robert Mitchum, enjoying his new found 'retirement',
walked into his house one afternoon in early 1969, his
wife said, 'Robert Bolt just called you. I told him you'd
call him back.'

'You told him wrong,' said Mitchum, walking on into
the lounge and dropping down onto a large divan.

He had met Bolt before, at the London opening night of
the author's play *A Man for All Seasons*, and he knew
what the call was about. Director David Lean and Bolt, two
of the world's finest film makers after *Lawrence of Arabia*
and *Dr Zhivago*, wanted *him* to star in their third film
together, *Ryan's Daughter*.

Mitchum had already read the script, had thought it
lyrical and one of the finest he'd ever been offered. But
he'd turned it down, mostly because of its enormously long
shooting schedule. 'I didn't figure I could keep myself glued
together long enough. And besides, right then I was intending to give up work altogether.'

But Robert Bolt called again. He knew Mitchum's reputation of old, that on receiving a script the actor always
first looked through it to see how many days off he got.

'Look,' Bolt told Mitchum in his ultra English voice.
'Is it the protracted *tenure* of the schedule that you find
off putting, because ... er ... you can have a fortnight or
three weeks at a time on your own ...'

Mitchum said 'No, it's not that at all.'

Asked Bolt 'Then why are you ... er ...'

'Actually, I had planned suicide.'

Bolt paused. 'I can't understand what you ...'

'I *planned suicide!*'

'Er ... there seems to be a fault on this line.'

Mitchum said '*I plan to kill myself, and that's eliminated all further discussions and questions.*'

There was a further pause, but Bolt proved equal to the occasion. He said, 'Oh, yes ... I see ... er ... Well, if you would just do this wretched little film of ours and *then* do yourself in, I'd be happy to stand the expenses of your burial!'

Mitchum was momentarily stunned by this, then he said, 'I'm flattered, cajoled, and seduced. Yes, yes, yes.'

Now it was Bolt's turn to be surprised again. In a disbelieving voice, he said 'Really, do you *mean* that?'

'I'm *telling* you that.'

'Can I tell David in the morning?'

'You can tell the queen if you like,' replied Mitchum.

Bolt recovered quickly. 'Now then, sir,' he said. 'I mean, the queen, after all!'

Mitchum explodes as he recalls this phone call that inveigled him into *Ryan's Daughter*. 'The son of a bitch! I'd just finished a film and I needed time to sit around and lick my wounds. I have to get myself *up* for these things. When I asked him why he didn't get someone else, he said they'd been through all the actors and still wanted me. I didn't quite know how he meant that. But then he suggested I could be useful to them. *Useful!* Well, it's always nice to be needed—and to be wrapped in the warm cloak of the big movie budget.'

In June later that year, Mitchum and his secretary, Reva Fredrick, who holds his power of attorney, sat in the conference room of Mitchum's film company, Talbot Productions. Reva was taking care of the drinks, and she showed Mitchum a map of Europe. She pushed several papers in front of him to sign as he complained about having to go to Ireland, but he forgot to sign one of them.

'What is it?' he asked as she pushed it back to him.

'Oh, it means you can get back $100,000 at seven percent, that's all.'

'Why should I give a crud?'

'You're terrible,' said Reva. 'You don't even know where your bank is.' She told Mitchum he would have to pick up his new Porsche Targa in Stuttgart. She also pointed out the town of Dingle on the map of Ireland. 'The ferries are all marked clearly,' she said.

Mitchum laughed sardonically. 'They really don't know when they're going to finish this bloody picture?'

Reva lifted her eyebrows. 'You want me to tell you the truth or make you feel good?'

In fact Mitchum left early for Ireland so he could pick up the lilting Irish accent afresh. And though shooting took nearly a year—the longest film he'd ever made—he stayed 'glued together' long enough in his unusual role as a bespectacled, impotent schoolmaster to deliver the kind of performance that has made him one of the finest screen actors alive.

As the weeks dragged by and the bad weather delayed filming time and time again, Mitchum grumbled. But he stuck with it, and his work was always professional. One reporter visited him in Dingle after three months shooting and found him lying down in his trailer bunk with a large wide-brimmed floppy hat over his face. The interview began with the hat still there. After a few minutes the reporter, who couldn't understand a word Mitchum was saying, said, 'Well, that's the first time I ever interviewed anyone who *really* talked through his hat!'

Immediately Mitchum jumped up to talk with a loud laugh. 'Yeah, it's a big change for me, this part,' he agreed.

'At least I don't have to grow a beard, fall down and break my ass, or fall off horses and get all skinned up. And I don't get the shit kicked out of me.'

He heaved a short sigh. 'Until I got to Dingle my life was all downhill and shady. But this is now the most joyless period of my life—except for working at Lockheed and being in the army. I've put away more scotch since I got here than I've put away in my whole goddamned life.'

Mitchum may have *started* drinking heavily, as he says, but as time wore on the crew noticed Mitchum was in fact drinking very little. This may have been due to lack of anywhere interesting to go at nights or with an increased absorption in his difficult role, but when Mitchum was asked about it he said he'd stopped drinking out of 'sheer boredom'. And it was the same for his old colleague hell raiser, Trevor Howard, he said. They were both too bored to raise any hell.

On the film an old problem recurred. How should they dress a man of Mitchum's powerful physique, especially with his unusual walk, with its exaggerated hip and shoulder movements?

'We've had to reshoot many of the scenes because David decided he didn't like my wardrobe,' Mitchum revealed after a few weeks. 'He said, "I didn't realize you were so large." Then Johnny Briggs, the wardrobe man, told him, "You must know, you have seen some of his films. You must realize how large he is. There's nothing we can do about his shoulders."

'But I had told David all this in the beginning,' Mitchum added. 'I said that if he made the jacket tight I'd just look like I was bulging out of it. So they left it loose and then I just looked bulky, like a retired policeman. No matter what they do, from the back I'm going to look like a Bulgarian wrestler. So it took them a million dollars and three months to get it right. You see, I've made films before under these circumstances, and I know what my problems are. Years ago they told me, "If we take the slack out of your jacket, you'll look like an Italian Charles Atlas, big shouldered and wasp waisted." In the end they had to pad up poor old Trevor Howard so as to make me look normal in proportion!'

Mitchum admits he has a 'freak physique' but denies that it's part of his stock in trade or that it's been lucky for him. 'I can never buy readymade clothes,' he smiles.

By late August visiting American writers were returning home with stories that Mitchum was talking more and more about retirement. During some vital beach scenes between himself and Sarah Miles, who played his young wife, the clouds obscured the sun after two days of bright weather, and the rain poured down for several days. Mitchum complained bitterly of the wasted time. 'Ireland makes the rain a national monument, so the tourist season lasts twelve months a year,' he said. 'After the first ten days of this film we were already seven days behind. So here I sit, practicing my accent.' He stared at the lowering black clouds and the heaving grey sea and went on. 'The tide comes in so fast here that if you take your shoes a hundred yards up the beach they might not be there if you turn your back.'

Asked about David Lean's working methods by one newsman, Mitchum said, 'He shoots the film; then he re-shoots it. Then he looks at it all and shoots it again. The rehearsals take the budget. This film will cost well over $10 million before we're through': it cost a total of $14 million. Once in October after more delays, Mitchum voiced his impatience with the director's detailed and lengthy quest for perfection in an unorthodox manner. David Lean walked off the set but came back a short while later and the contretemps was smoothed over.

Then on one occasion Sarah Miles, who is Robert Bolt's

wife, showed she'd had enough of Mitchum's comments. She rounded on him, saying he must have known when he signed on for a David Lean picture that it would take a long time and that anyway, no one could help the weather. She used a couple of highly salubrious words of profanity too. Mitchum, to his credit, grinned and apologized to her. He likes people who stick up to him.

Ryan's Daughter told the story of a romantic triangle that unfolds amid the buried passions of simple folk and the violence of nature via a certain series of alienations and misunderstandings. It contained the essence of classical melodrama, was told with enormous purity of style and was beautifully photographed. The characters were archetypes, like those in a Greek tragedy, but clearly identifiable because of the contemporary setting and situation. Mitchum gave a sensitive performance as a sexually reticent schoolmaster returning from a trip to Dublin to whom Miss Miles pours out her idealistic conception of love. United in marriage, the pair never reach a full sexual-spiritual union—he is twenty years her senior, and she is immature. The arrival of shell-shocked Christopher Jones to take over the occupying British garrison starts an illicit affair. The village folk become scandalized by the affair and believe that Miss Miles is an informer against local revolutionaries. She is stripped and shorn. At the end the couple leave the village, presumably to start life anew. Fine portrayals by Trevor Howard, John Mills (who won an Oscar for the best supporting actor as the village idiot), and Leo McKern backed up the two principals.

Although the British critics were somewhat less than enthusiastic, their American counterparts were full of high praise. Several of them singled out Mitchum's performance. 'Robert Mitchum in his finest performance for many years,' said Judith Crist of the *New York* magazine. Wrote another: 'Sarah Miles' Rosie is as incredibly brilliant as

Trevor Howard's peasant priest, and perhaps most incredible of all is Robert Mitchum's impotent schoolmaster.'

When his work on the film had finished and David Lean had begun the long task of editing it down to its final 206 minutes, Mitchum returned to Hollywood. He recuperated at his ranch at Atascadero, driving the two hundred miles between it and Hollywood alone in his new Porsche. Once, after meeting a Californian sharecropper in a small village where he stopped to buy gas on the way, he spent three days with the man's family. They hadn't been to a film for many years and didn't know who he was. 'They wouldn't have given a damn if they had known,' says Mitchum. 'Besides, who am I?'

A year after those difficult beach scenes Mitchum was still talking about the expense of *Ryan's Daughter*. 'They are probably still up there now, chasing some parasol down a beach, waiting for the wind to blow right and an old crew man to pull the strings correctly,' he said drily.

During the summer of 1970, when young Christopher Mitchum was making *Rio Lobo*, with John Wayne, he said that his father was talking seriously about retiring from the screen. One day Mitchum had told him: 'I figure to live maybe twenty years longer. I might spend everything I've got. What would you think of that?'

To which Chris had replied, 'Go ahead. It's your money. Jim and I can make out on our own.'

John Wayne, however, dispelled the rumors about Mitchum's retirement. 'Bob says that every time he finishes a hard picture,' he laughed.

But Chris stuck to his guns. 'He really means it,' he maintained. 'He's even talking about closing his production company.'

In late June, 1970, it seemed that the stories about Mitchum's retirement might have been premature, for Dorothy told columnist Earl Wilson: 'He says he's retired, but it may just be how he feels for the moment. He's too young to retire, and I hope he finds something else to do. I think he's just tired.'

In mid-November, as rumors began to circulate around Hollywood that Mitchum would be nominated for an Oscar for his performance—he wasn't—Mitchum gave in to MGM's request that he go on a long publicity promotion tour of major American cities for *Ryan's Daughter*, along with David Lean and the other principals. He enjoyed every moment of the junket, visiting many of the towns in which he'd been a rail-riding hobo in his youth.

His 'retirement' lasted only eight more months. The announcements of it certainly hadn't stopped scripts from thudding onto the doormat of his executive offices on Sunset Boulevard. Reva Fredrick says, 'He meant it about retirement as much as any life-long actor can mean it, but after being home a while there's nothing much else to do. He doesn't fish much these days, and he never hunts. In fact he only went deer hunting once in his life, and he didn't shoot any himself. He couldn't shoot a deer or anything else!'

So in the summer of 1971 Mitchum climbed back into harness once more after MGM had sent him the script of *Going Home*. The story is about a man who murders his wife and then, after leaving jail, attempts to re-establish a filial relationship with his son, whose life has been deeply affected by witnessing his mother's death. Mitchum says he took the role because there were 'interesting parallels' in his own life, but he won't elaborate. Instead he just jokes: 'I took one look at my 1971 taxes and decided I'd better get back to work.'

Going Home provided another unusual role for Mitchum, for the movie was full of psychological overtones and required him to portray many facets and moods—

brawling, repentant, loving, self-doubting, and sensitive. But while on location at Wildwood, New Jersey, and at the small harbor of McKeesport, in Pennsylvania, Mitchum proved that at fifty-four he'd lost none of his rebellious or imprudent qualities. During a rare weekend off at Cape May, he hired a fifty-seven foot cruiser and took his wife out for a quiet trip at sea. It was the only way he could escape the huge crowd of tourists and rubber neckers who'd flocked to the area when they'd heard the controversial star was at work there.

When they were a few hundred yards out, Mitchum turned to look back at the gawking matrons, the giggling girls, and the noisy youths who had been bothering him and said:

'Aren't they the greatest ad for birth control you've ever seen?'

And as is usual on his films, the local legends sprang up and became exaggerated. Reva Fredrick remembers one such occasion:

'We were shooting in the streets down at McKeesport and a dog suddenly ran away from some kids and bit a man, acting like it was going to bite everyone. A cop came over to see if it had had its rabies' shot and the dog promptly attacked the cop. The cop pulled out his pistol and shot the dog dead with one bullet. He had little choice as he had to protect the public. So, the dog was dead. The kid was crying. The mother, who happened to be colored, was screaming, "Pig!" at the cop and suddenly it was a pretty nasty situation. But the cop had been right because he didn't know if the dog had been given a rabies' shot—it was acting mad and he didn't want it to escape until he knew if the bitten guy needed treatment.

'But by the time night came and we were having dinner, you wouldn't believe the different versions of this simple story that were going round. One woman came up to us and said, "I understand Mr Mitchum really screamed and yelled at that cop and was going to hit him. Good for him." Everyone outside the group believed this too.

'Heck, he wasn't even there! He was in Connecticut at the time because he had five days off.'

After shooting was over, Mitchum returned to Hollywood and within a few days was in his office discussing future projects. He was a little gloomy about his next role —as a would-be priest torn between conscience and violent revolution in the Mexico of the 1920s—in the MGM film *The Wrath of God*. Most of the location shooting was around the small village of Laluz, eight thousand feet up in the Sierra Madre mountains and some six hundred miles north of Mexico City, in the early winter of 1972.

Mitchum, who was suffering from a damaged shoulder, thought that he would be ready for this, his eighty-fourth film, after a few weeks break at his ranch. He moved his left arm and winced.

'Hell, I think I've busted something,' he said. 'The doc's going to X-ray it.'

Had he injured himself doing a stunt?

'Hell no, they couldn't pay me enough to do a stunt as dangerous as that,' he replied. 'I was going up the steps of our apartment to go to bed. I went to vault the last one, grabbed for the porch rail but it came off in my hand.

'I did a one and a half somersault backward—from two stories up. I thought I'd break my neck, but I managed to save that. I landed hard on my shoulder and I heard the whole heavenly chorus. I thought my back was busted. I couldn't breathe. Heck, it stopped my watch and no fall ever did that before. I lay there fifty-five minutes till finally someone came and hauled me to my feet. When I crawled upstairs again Dorothy had gone to sleep and didn't hear my knocking. So I just lay there in a huddled, shattered heap.'

He laughed ironically. 'Do you know what my old lady did when she finally woke up? She made me take her out to dinner!'

19

The Actor

The only person in the film world who puts Mitchum down as an actor is Mitchum himself. And when he played the gentle, diffident, spectacled schoolmaster in *Ryan's Daughter* Mitchum reluctantly admitted it was a different role. Then he delivered his own view of himself as an actor.

'Usually, you know, I make a film called *Pounded to Death by Gorillas*. They open up with a long shot of me standing and then a huge gorilla looms up behind and hits me on top of the head. Boom, and I crumple. Boom, Boom. I keep falling down and getting up again. Then they cut to a little girl skipping through fields of daisies and finally she comes to this house and a voice says "Who's there?" As the writers haven't got that figured out yet, they cut back to me. Boom, Boom, that gorilla is still knocking me down. And I'm still getting up again. Finally the gorilla collapses on top of me, exhausted. Then the little girl comes in and says "He's around here some place, I just know." Finally, she peels away the gorilla and there lies our hero —me. So she hauls me to my feet, puts her arms round me, looks straight into the camera and says "I don't care what you think—*I like him*." So you know he's got to be a hell of a man.'

That is a funny script. Why doesn't he film it?

'I have,' he replies. 'I've been playing it all my life. It's easier than writing, you see. Every time the writers run out of words, they just kick the shit out of Mitchum. A tried and true formula.'

Would he rather play the gorilla for a change?

'No. The gorilla doesn't get the girl.'

The public, who often see him as a swaggering, sleepy-eyed character who just ambles through his movies, might agree with Mitchum's cynical self-assessment. But the top men in Hollywood know better. Directors, writers and even other actors have long admired the force and surprising nuances Mitchum can bring to even the most boring flat, cardboard role. In truth he is a top pro who never shows egotistical temperament, who is never late on the set and even after a hard night out always knows his lines. As David Lean once said, 'I've seen him in lousy parts which he did well, and in good parts which he did marvelously. In *Ryan's Daughter* I cast him completely against type and he delighted us all.'

Mitchum's insouciant dismissals of his own talents are not the words of a man who knows he has 'made it' and can afford to be over modest. Right from the start, when few actors would have taken such chances with their future careers, Mitchum denigrated himself as a performer. Back in the late fifties he said:

'I've got a baritone voice, broken nose, stand six feet high and can change a tyre without having a stand-in. Hell, I *look* as though I've changed five million tyres. So men say that bum's just a goddamn mechanic. If *he* can get to be a movie star, *I* can be king.'

His was always a deeply unconscious effort to remain an ordinary guy.

In 1958, when asked what parts he liked to play, he said, 'Just passive parts. I can't stand strenuous activity. Just mute passivity. People say I play myself in every part. I don't know. I just stand and do what I'm told. I point in the direction they tell me to. If they ask me what I think, I tell them and it only provokes arguments. So I don't like to be asked. I like to be told.

'The truth is I'm not really attached to acting, although

I could have gotten attached if they hadn't forced me to go on making the same pictures over and over again. It isn't your fault if you make bad pictures—all that is required of you if you are a so-called film star is to stand there and register so much meat. But you survive bad pictures. Look at Rin Tin Tin. Bad pictures had no ill effects on him so far as I know.' He added that he liked to make good pictures but that he didn't believe in originality for the mere sake of originality, only if it enhanced the story.

It was also early in his career that he realized that neither he nor any other actor could save a really bad film. 'Nobody can, except perhaps freaks like Brigitte Bardot,' he said in 1958. 'And even she will have to do a good picture sometime!'

Clearly there was no point in being big-headed in Mitchum's philosophy. As he told Roderick Mann, 'Many actors set too much stock on being characters. I remember when one of your British chums arrived in Hollywood. The studio spent $5,000 redecorating his dressing room. It had everything—a bar, built in shower, the lot. The actor came in, took one look round and said, "You don't expect me to stay in a dump like this, do you?" You see, he'd been told that was the best way to impress Hollywood. The same thing happened with another British actor. When he first came to Hollywood he went on strike because there was a delay in getting a 22-carat gold name plate on his dressing room door. Can you imagine?'

In May 1960 Mitchum further elaborated this theme to writer Robert Robinson. 'Some stars create an image of themselves and they're mortally afraid of that image slipping out of its frame. But I don't care. If I get fat I'll just have to play fat roles. I'll just ask them if they have any parts for a fat man.

'Most of the stars know about all these images they create, they know which is their best side, how to light themselves, all that jazz. I don't know anything. I never looked through a camera but once and that made me sick. I never see rushes and I don't see my films. I'm easily bored. Well, maybe I'll go to an opening of one of my films, if the opening occurs in some town where I'm vacationing. But if I go that means I'm working—and I can send 'em my hotel bill.'

Mitchum *does* remember going to one film back in Hollywood years ago, however. It was called *The Duchess of Idaho* and it starred Esther Williams. 'But halfway through I walked out and demanded my money back because I didn't like it. What's more, they gave it to me. They didn't want some bum hanging around in the foyer saying how lousy the picture was.'

In Britain after making *The Grass is Greener*, with Cary Grant, he dismissed the latest crop of Hollywood stars when talking to Donald Zec. 'Some of 'em are pretty good actors,' he said, 'but most of 'em wear high collars and hairdos and look like they've been nowhere and seen nobody. Of course, there are the others, the handsome young boy type who figure they still have to give out with that college boy smile [he demonstrated the smile] when they're pushing sixty.' But he didn't mention anyone by name.

Asked about acting schools and the Method, Mitchum replied, 'These Method guys—they've done nothing. They *invent* experiences. I tell you, there's no substitute for the real thing. Today every fruit figures he's got to be an actor. So he gets a diploma. But how many have you ever heard of? There are the peekers and the doers.' And the impression one has when talking to Mitchum is that almost everybody else is a peeker.

He once said that what he minded most about filming was the enormous amount of his personal *time* it took up. He'd far rather be working with his horses down on his farm. 'It's the actual attendance in films that bothers me,'

he says. 'If you could just phone it in, *indicate* your attitude, I'd be happy. But I have to work because I have to
write checks. I have to cover my chagrin and embarrassment at not being born a Persian prince. I tell people I'm
really born to the purple, but then they show up at the
studio and see some assistant director saying "Come on,
you crumb." It's all pretty embarrassing.'

Much of the criticism directed at Mitchum stems from
the fact that he makes it all look so simple, that people
don't think he's working. 'Well, if they want to sit up
all night and scratch themselves about it, fine. I've no
observations to make about it,' he replies. 'I'm not concerned with other people's interpretations.'

But is acting to him really as easy as he makes it look?

'Sure,' he responds quickly. 'It's even *easier* than it
looks, unfortunately. They don't pay you to invent in this
business, just to follow the script and the formula, the
familiar pattern.'

How then does he achieve his professionalism and the
lack of temperament for which he's renowned?

'It's just a total lack of energy. I have learned to guard
my enthusiasm.'

Once Mitchum was asked about the hordes of young
men and women who crowd into Hollywood today hoping
for acting careers in even greater numbers than they did
in the old days, and he delivered his customary whimsical
explanation:

'Every seventeen-year-old girl feels some uneasiness and
she figures it must be *art*. She tries the cello but it gives her
trouble on buses and bangs her knee when she plays. So
she tries ballet and sprains an ankle. She takes up painting
and screws that up too. So she says she must be an actress
and that's easier, you don't need any equipment. So one
night at a beach party with a summer stock company she
meets a director. Afterward she's greatly relieved and says,

"Ah, *that's* what it was." Next thing she's got a contract and they've got to put her in position for every shot and show her where the lights are. She figures she's on her way, poor kid.'

Mitchum takes a dim view of the current trend in movies towards total, and frequently petty, realism. 'Slice of life pictures,' he calls them. 'They are an hour and seventy minutes about some guy's headache but they find a lot of empathy with the public. Guys say "Gee, I know just how he felt." As for flaming European geniuses—you know (director) Fred Zinnemann's definition of an Ingmar Bergman picture? That's where twenty-five friends go out and shoot a movie. Me, I am surrounded by a hundred enemies.'

A few years ago Mitchum was asked if he was as interested in the artistic rewards of filming as much as the financial. Yet again his reply was iconoclastic. 'No, I am the breadwinner for my wife and kids. That is why I make pictures. To say you're in the business for artistic rewards is sham. It's a nursery tale. I hate to repeat it, but the actor's original purpose was to keep the audience turned to the front while the pickpockets went to work from behind. I think, to some extent, this is still true.'

All this is fine controversial stuff, of course, and is typical Mitchum self-denigration. But his view of himself isn't shared by other top pros at all. It's hard indeed to find a director with a bad word to say about him. Apart from William Wellman's remark 'There's something about Mitchum that just thrills me to death,' there is the elaborate tribute paid to him by top actor Charles Laughton shortly before he died. Laughton, who directed Mitchum in one of his best performances in *Night of the Hunter* in the mid fifties, told writer Helen Lawrenson:

'Bob is one of the best actors in the world. In addition he can imitate any accent there is. At his Maryland farm once he put on a bewildering performance for me; he talked in about twenty different Irish accents and they were all perfect. You'd have thought he'd spent his life in the streets and pubs of Ireland. I started telling him that I was about to make *Advise and Consent* and complaining I'd have to play the role of a Senator with a southern accent. "Bob, it's as if you had to play a Cockney," I said. He answered me in a perfect Cockney accent, starting off with, "You bull-necked son of a bitch, what makes you think I can't play a Cockney." He has a great talent. He'd make the best Macbeth of any actor living.

'All his tough talk is a blind, you know. He is a literate, gracious, kind man with wonderful manners and he speaks beautifully—when he wants to. He's a very tender man and a great gentleman. You know, he's really terribly shy. I can tell you one thing; he won't thank you for destroying the image he's built up as a defence. He's one of my favourite people in the whole world. I can't praise him too much.'

Coming from a man like Laughton this was an extraordinary eulogy. Maybe director Stanley Kramer's feelings run along similar lines for after directing him in *Not as a Stranger*, Kramer presented Mitchum with a leather script cover in which he'd written: 'To Bob—who possesses within himself the unfortunate ability to be whatever he wishes.'

Reminded once of such tributes and that director John Huston felt he would make an ideal King Lear, Mitchum was asked why he just coasted along in Great White Trapper type roles.

'That's just the point,' he answered. 'These pictures ... I can do them and then walk away and just forget about them. It's all finished and I never have to see them. I usually never do see them—and I'm not *involved*. Furthermore, I don't let anybody down. I don't want that responsibility. I don't *want* that deep involvement.'

What is most surprising in the face of Mitchum's apparent indifference is the fact that his popularity is increasing, especially among young people. In 1967 Bob Hull, the *Los Angeles Herald Examiner's* television and radio editor, writing about the declining popularity of feature movies on the television ratings, revealed that Mitchum was 'In' with the teenage crowd and on many campuses had replaced Humphrey Bogart as a cult figure. Today Mitchum's popularity with young and old alike is undeniable. Perhaps youngsters identify with his rebellious spirit yet can also perceive that his track record proves he is a hard-working talented man despite his complete lack of pretension.

There are, of course, those occasions when Mitchum astounds the people working with him by his sheer professionalism, like the time when he arrived on the set of *The Angry Hills* and found he had eight pages of solid new dialogue to film. Many actors would have fallen sick or betrayed anger but he read them through a few times and remembered every word. 'That's my job,' he replied tersely when a crew member praised him. 'And when you know what the author had in mind, it's easy enough.'

If you really press him hard, refuse to accept his normally cursory explanations, he will eventually admit: 'Oh, if you're trusted with the cash box, you must bring *some* honest effort into it. My job is making pictures, but for me it's really an economic expedient. I actually started out to be a sex fiend, but I couldn't pass the physical. And I don't like getting up early or having people point me out. But I'm not bored. If I'm to go through the general humiliations of the profession, I ought at least to try to contribute something new and exciting if I can. I'm not sure how I do what I do. But anyone is welcome to try. I mean, the store is open to anyone to buy the same materials Picasso uses.'

And that's about as far as he will go.

It's a curious fact that nearly every top woman star who has acted with Mitchum cannot wait to work with him again. After *Two for the Seesaw* and *What a Way to Go!* he is certainly Shirley MacLaine's favorite co-worker. Elizabeth Taylor, with whom he made *Secret Ceremony*, says, 'He is one of the five best actors alive.'

When Deborah Kerr met Mitchum on the set of *Heaven Knows, Mr Allison* and rather timidly asked him how he was feeling, he treated her to his *Beaten to Death by Gorillas* story. She says she loved him from that moment on. 'As an actor he is superb. However you read a line he has anticipated it. It's like a fine marriage. The director, John Huston, had never worked with him either. He was truly in love with Mitch. I finally found out his secret. He is a fantastically sensitive, decent human being.'

For all that, it's doubtful that Mitchum will ever change the face he shows to the outside world. In many ways his boast that he never changed anything but his underwear since first arriving in Hollywood is true. Praise by critics disturbs him. 'I often regret my good reviews because there is no point in doing something that I know to be inferior and then I find I have come off best in the film. Wouldn't you find that worrying?

'I have sometimes caught myself putting on an act, saying to myself, "Look at me. I am giving a great acting performance." On these occasions I pull myself back sharply.'

The last assessments of Mitchum as an actor can be left to two men.

Says director Fred Zinnemann, 'He is one of the finest instinctive actors in the business, almost in the same class as Spencer Tracy.'

The most unlikely tribute of all, perhaps, comes from a rival. George Hamilton, who played Mitchum's son in *Home from the Hill*, says:

'I've grown to learn and to respect a man in his position because it's not easy to be a star and to be kind to somebody, as he was to me. He took time to help me with my part, never tried to steal or take a scene from me. I don't think there's any way I *could* have stolen a scene from him, but nevertheless he tried to do nothing but help. That's very different from most actors.

'He's a bit embarrassed about being the great actor he is. He covers it up. I remember once we went to some friends' house for dinner. They were very kind to us, gave us a great time, and Bob didn't know how to say thank you.

'Their little girl had hurt her arm on a swing at the back of the house, so next day Bob wrote a note to the child saying "I want to compliment you on your choice of parents. I think you did a marvelous job of choosing them. It was a very intelligent, wise choice." I think that shows his humor, his intelligence, warmth, and his natural timidity—which I don't think people realize he has. He is one of the kindest, nicest men I've ever met.'

Finally, what does Mitchum himself think would have happened to him if he hadn't become an actor?

'I'd probably have ended my days in the same poorhouse where I will anyhow,' he replies.

At least, it *sounded* like 'poorhouse'.

20

On women and sex

Robert Mitchum's personal appeal and his ability to get along well with women have certainly contributed to his success. It would be an oversimplification, however, to presume that all the top women stars who are prepared to work with him again at any time feel that way merely because he is a talented actor. The film world is full of that species.

His attraction is basically that of the complete man who brings out the most feminine qualities in a woman. Around Mitchum women seem only too eager to forget their feelings about equality. Men admire Mitchum out of respect for his genuine masculinity. Women like him for more than his mere sex appeal, they feel that they can *trust* him.

When asked about this some years back, Mitchum mused, 'I suppose they really can. I admire women basically. I never go around picking up actresses and waitresses or drive around looking for lonely wives at bus stops. I've never made a pass at a woman I've worked with in my life. I figure, simply, that roughly fifty percent of the population are women and I appreciate the fact. Receive them warmly, treat them courteously, and they love you for it.'

Mitchum recently surprised writer Joan Dew Schmitt by agreeing with her that it might be a good idea if many of the world's problems were handed over to women to solve.

'Perhaps many of them would then reach a socio-economic sophistication many of them don't have now,' he

236

said. 'Of course, a lot of men don't have much of this either. But in a way, some women who are seeing the world for the first time, as it were, are like children. They preach about problems they know nothing about. Take Southeast Asia. "Let's get out," they say. Great. Wonderful idea. But it's like saying "Let's get out or cancer." First you must find the *cause*, and that involves getting into generations of Asian culture and politics. I think women would learn a lot if they had to make the decisions. And who knows? Maybe women would come up with answers. But it wouldn't be as simple as they think now.'

'Would you not feel personally threatened if women were running the world?' he was asked.

'Hell no. I like women.' He laughed, then went on in more personal vein.

'Even now I don't always know when a woman is leaping at me. I don't have a moral reaction when I meet a woman who comes on strong, though. It's just that I get stuck for an answer a lot of times.'

He told a story of how when he was in Paris he visited Françoise Sagan with his secretary. Sitting in the writer's flat was a French girl with eyes as innocent as a Girl Scout's. The girl patted the place by her side and motioned for him to come over.

'I sat down and the *first* words out of her mouth were "While you are here, you have ze time to make love to me?" I mean, what *do* you say? Peter Viertel [Deborah Kerr's husband] was standing there too, and he thought it was funny and he kept saying "Go on, Robert. Answer her." So I looked at my watch and I said "Well, how long does it take? Should I get out a calendar or what?"'

At first Mitchum's views on sex seem conservative. 'Sex loses its mystery, its beauty, and value when it's reduced to the commonplace,' he says. He enunciates this view during a discussion on today's new sexual freedoms but just as one thinks he's finally wound up with traditional views after all, he goes on to deliver a shattering argument about how modern attitudes to sex could be one factor in bringing about the downfall of the West. Basically his argument, hard to follow because he expresses his thoughts elliptically, is that the permissive sex era could be used by Leftist political opportunists in much the same way that 'free for all' capitalism was exploited by the old Marx-Lenin-Engels philosophies and later Chairman Mao's manifestos to 'help bring about the moral and economic devaluation of the West'.

Mitchum doesn't hold much truck with women who blindly follow the dictates of fashion. Way back in 1953 when he was making *White Witch Doctor* in Africa, he presaged the 'hang free' look of today's modern girl. At the time he said 'Not long ago I said I believed the average woman should never wear a girdle. That comment created a bit of a stir. But I'll stick by my convictions. I believe a well-proportioned woman is an object of great beauty. I feel that the lines nature gave us are the ones we should show. This doesn't happen when a woman who has read too many fashion articles decides what she needs to make her appear stylish is to put on a tight fitting item that is designed to take away from her femininity and give her the contours in a certain part of her anatomy of a boy. I always had an intense dislike for anything that detracts from the feminine qualities of a woman, and I look upon a girdle as such a device. I believe women aren't quite as sharp as they'd have us think, because most women, whether they say so or not, are dressing not for themselves but for the attentions of the opposite sex. And when they distort nature's lines, they are defeating their purpose. I don't see why you should not be able to recognize a person from the back as well as from the front. But how are you going to accomplish this when through the use of some constricting device, all women manage to look exactly alike when viewed in physiological retrospect?'

Tongue-in-cheek though this argument undoubtedly is, it does illustrate Mitchum's fundamental approach to the opposite sex.

It was also in Africa, some ten years later while he was making *Mr Moses*, that Mitchum encountered a group of women whom he feels were the most feminine he ever met in his life—some wives of the Masai tribe.

'I was down there making this film in which I had been given five wives—a dreamy idea!' he recalls. 'One day there was this ceremony for which the women shaved their heads, greased themselves up with fat, anointed themselves with cow urine, had their ears stretched down to here, had misshapen feet and wore rings to distort their legs— and then had a tooth knocked out as part of the ritual. Yet they were the most electrically feminine women—I mean you could *feel* it—that I'd ever come across.

'They projected femininity in a fantastic way although by our standards they were far from beautiful. In the ritual they danced forward to touch their heads to your breast and then they danced back, and it was uncommonly feminine. It's difficult to explain, but there was something suppliant and at the same time compliant about their behavior that got right under your guard.'

But how does Mitchum feel about women on the purely personal level? While he was making *Ryan's Daughter* in Ireland, there were long breaks between shooting, and once he was in an unusually talkative mood. He said:

'Really, I suppose I get on better with women than with men,' he said. 'I'm more at ease with them, enjoy their company more. Maybe that has something to do with what *you* call my success with women. I don't know. Or it could have something to do with the kind of life I've led. Maybe some of them feel it was sort of romantic to be a hobo and ride freight trains and get chased by the railroad cops and even find yourself on a chain gang. With that kind of background maybe some of them figure I'm big and tough and am doing this sex challenge thing, so who am I to disabuse them? Anyhow, maybe that's the preconceived idea. Then, when they meet me, I'm not what they expected. I mean, I don't rough 'em up or anything like that. I'm not a wild man after all. Maybe it puzzles them.

'I suppose some women reason I'd be able to protect them. That's a basic feminine drive, wanting protection. For me, though, real femininity hasn't much to do with looks and that sort of thing. It's a recognition by a woman of a *man's role*.

'But I do take women seriously, talk to them seriously. Maybe they think I'm flattering them, but I'm not. I don't have any resentment of brains and ability in women. I don't resent any social eminence they may reach—or even their social superiority. I've always regarded them as equal human beings. That's been my experience.

'But I wouldn't want to spread any idea that I've been a great success with women in real life. I've never gone out and tried to take my opportunities with them. Why? Basically because I've always been afraid of being rejected!

'Oh sure, plenty of women have told me how they felt about me, said they really had a thing for me, and hinted that we could have had a ball. But they said it *afterward*. "Honey, why didn't you tell me?" I might say. "Wish you'd told me before." That's all you can say, isn't it? But how can you be sure at the time? A man can make a big ass of himself if he reckons all he has to do is flex a muscle and the nearest woman will fall into his arms. Oh, I know the argument that a man's supposed to *know* when a woman's attracted. But I guess although I'm all for feminine equality, I'm not too attracted by the woman who makes it *obvious*. I'm attracted by the really feminine woman and I don't appreciate women who feel they have to get out and challenge a man, to stand on the same ground, to prove they're equal.

'They are equal all right, but their role is a complementary one to a man's. They have a different function in life —both biologically and socially. But if they get the idea they've got to dominate or yell the house down to prove something, then they're cheating. Baby, they're not cheating me—the minute they shed their femininity they're cheating themselves.'

21

The Man

One never really *interviews* Robert Mitchum. Somehow he always conveys the impression it's an accident that you and he should be in the same room together. If the questions show the interviewer subscribes to the popular theory that he is just a big, tough, sleepy-eyed ex-hobo who got lucky in movies, Mitchum will fend him off with tall stories, sardonic one line answers or four letter words. But it's done in such a way that the interviewer leaves feeling *he* is the fool, not Mitchum.

'I learnt early in life that by telling a story far more colorfully than the truth, one's truth would be let alone,' he once said. 'I like to be let alone.'

The colorful, violent, and extroverted front most people see is not only a protective device but the opposite of what Mitchum really is. However, he feels no need to prove himself to anyone. He never tries to impress with the overwhelming narcissistic charm that many top actors employ, nor does he talk 'in depth' about his work, or his approach to a particular role. Most of the time you're talking to Mitchum it's hard to believe he *is* an actor.

Probing him has always been hard work. His thoughts run off at tangents, seeming, despite the richness of his language and imagery, to go nowhere in particular. If you don't understand him first time, it's tough luck, for he never repeats himself or explains. Nothing will stop him if he wants to talk but on the other hand, if he doesn't nothing will induce him to converse. He never resorts to the usual conversational clichés about the weather, or clothes,

242

or says things like 'How well you're looking today'. Silence doesn't bother Mitchum in the way it bothers most people, a vestige perhaps of his Blackfoot Indian ancestry.

In a perceptive magazine article about Mitchum, Helen Lawrenson wrote in *Esquire*: 'Through an astonishing strength of will and intellect and character, he has chosen to keep his mind, his attitudes, inviolate from the usually inevitable corruption of money and fame and adulation.' This is perfectly true. Mitchum is a loner, never has an entourage around him as most stars do. He remains a man who lives by his own standards, as indeed he has done since the start.

Asked about the movie world of Hollywood by Miss Lawrenson in the early sixties, Mitchum replied 'It's a dull, aching euphoria ... There is all this asinine waste of money. They decide they want to use a shot of a harvesting machine. So three guys go tearing round the country, stay at expensive hotels, get stoned, spend days taking color tests of the machine. Then they decide it won't work ... This whole place has no relation to real life, to real people. Oh, there are real people here, but they're in oil refineries and the factories, not in movieland. This is Atlantis.'

At about the same period Mitchum told American writer Lloyd Shearer: 'I'm an actor only because I don't know any other job at which I can make so much dough. Let's face it, being a movie star doesn't call for skill. One of the greatest and most popular actors who ever lived was Rin Tin Tin, a dog.

'I'm ashamed of being an actor because people accord you the respect and fame and attention you don't merit. The other month I was on a plane flying back to Maryland where I've got my home, raise horses, and keep away from the crowds. And some guy sits down next to me. He's an executive with some steel company. And he says "My wife and I were discussing you only the other night." "Well sir," I said. "All I can tell you is that my wife and I sure weren't discussing *you*, and you're a bigger man than I am."

'Then I get letters from all sorts of people. Recently a lady who teaches blind children wrote me. Blind children attend movies, you know, and this teacher wrote "My pupils believe that when you say something on the screen, whatever it is, it must be true. Your voice has the ring of honesty and sincerity in it."

'Stuff like that bothers the hell out of me. It's embarrassing because I'm only a survivor of the Stone Age of American middle class culture. I'm no hero or paragon.'

Like several top stars over the last thirty years who play tough, violent parts on screen, Mitchum has had his share of trouble from men, usually in bars, who want to prove themselves. It's true enough that, when he was young, Mitchum was a brawler like few others—especially when provoked beyond endurance. Once when he was prodded by a persistent interviewer into talking about fighting, Mitchum is recorded as saying 'The only man in this town I wouldn't want to tangle with is Frank Sinatra. I might knock him down, but he'd keep getting up 'til one of us got killed!'

Later maturity, however, has made Mitchum a fairly tolerant man—as was evinced by his nonretaliation when hit by the small Irishman in the Dublin bar in 1959. The truth is that Mitchum, who is basically shy, was always privately troubled when this kind of incident occurred.

'My problem is that I look right in dirty clothes,' he said during the late fifties. 'Therefore I get dirty parts—and people think I'm a regular bar brawler. The guys want to sock me to prove they can. I'm tired of this tough guy tab. All I really want is a quiet life.

'Hell, half my trouble is that people expect me to behave as I do on the screen. It can get pretty damn dangerous when some guy comes up and cracks you over the head with a bar stool just to see how tough you are. I was standing in some joint in New York once when a guy comes up and hits me. Wap, just like that. I just turned to him and said "Why?" I'm interested in people's motives. Know what this guy said? He said he just had an impulse to hit me.' On that occasion Mitchum saw red. He took the man out into the alley, held his legs against his body and stuffed him into a garbage can.

Shortly after the incident with the three husky sailors in Tobago in 1956, Mitchum was asked how it was he had this seemingly irresistible attraction to a brawl. He replied gravely, 'self-defense'. And, of course, it usually was just that.

Today, however, such incidents have become rare. As he said on television in 1968: 'Occasionally a guy slaps the bar and waves his arms about but very rarely now. I think people are more stable today than they're credited with being. If they get obstreperous now, I just try to reason with them.'

Reports of brawls during his earlier life were, of course, only one aspect of the problem of Mitchum's public image. In the mid fifties, when he was becoming more conscious of the effect his hell-raiser image was having on his children, Mitchum explained another aspect—undue attention by the press, and distortion of the facts.

'Look, somebody I know gets drunk in Paris and wrecks his car, and nobody says a word. Somebody else wrecks a young girl's life and has to give her $150,000 and pay the hospital bills and you don't hear a thing about it. Me, I shout in an alley and get ninety days, and it's all over the newspapers!'

As he once told Joan Dew Schmitt: 'No matter where I live, whatever I do gets into the papers. I had to face the fact that my precious privacy was gone years ago.' He gave an example of press distortion:

'I was stopping at a second-rate hotel in Manhattan. It had deteriorated since my previous visit and had become a sort of convention hangout—the kind of hotel where the rooms smell. I ran into an English journalist and his photographer companion in the hotel restaurant and invited them up to my room for a drink. During conversation he asked me what I thought of London? "I love it," I said. "It's one of my favorite cities in the world."

'"But what *don't* you like about it?"

'I said "There's nothing I don't like about it."

'"But if you could change something about it, what would it be?" He was persistent and I was getting bored, so I said "If I could change something I'd make the airport closer to the city."

'When I got a clipping of the story, this guy had written:

'"I finally tracked down cinema star Robert Mitchum. He is staying incognito in a luxurious suite at the elegant so and so hotel. 'What do you think of London?' I enquired of Mr Mitchum. 'I think they ought to move it closer to the airport,' the burly Yank replied."

'I don't know why they go to so much trouble to make up things about me,' Mitchum finished. 'I should have thought I've done enough that they could write the truth.'

The difference Mitchum made here is a subtle one. He wasn't fool enough to kid himself that controversial publicity was necessarily bad for an actor like himself—not that he has ever deliberately done anything good or bad to *court* publicity. But as long as the truth was adhered to he was, and is, prepared to live with it. Just as he's prepared to live with the publication of any controversial *remarks* he makes. The fact is many of the observations Mitchum makes in public are uttered for their shock value. He once admitted he subscribed to the policy of the late Humphrey Bogart, who said 'I don't care what it is, kid. Just be agin it!' But colorful though Mitchum's remarks have been and still are, he makes certain they affect no one but himself. And when analysed it can be seen that none of them is ever really vicious or malicious.

Early in his career Mitchum was doing an interview in New York and the conversation turned to a tough period during his hoboing days—which his studio were trying to keep quiet. The publicity girl suddenly kicked Mitchum under the table to shut him up and said 'Actually, Bob had a very delicate condition and physical structure in childhood, and his parents sent him to a private boarding school high in the West Virginia mountains.'

Mitchum said, simply, 'Come off it. The cops were looking for me then.'

Mitchum possesses the most caustic wit in the film world, and as he said before, he often uses it to hide the real truth about himself. He does like to shock and he has a better turn of phrase than many of the writers who script his films. Some examples:

'People think I have an interesting walk—like John Wayne. Hell man, I'm just trying to hold my gut in.'

To a man who asked how his family took his hell-raising image: 'They take it all right—put it in the bank.'

To a girl who asked him about his drinking: 'I drink as a preparation for death. When the great day comes I will be completely inured. It will be just one more hangover.'

To another: 'I have to be able to drink. I find the only way I can get rid of people is to outdrink them. It takes thirty-six hours or more sometimes, and it nearly kills me. But in the end they go.'

To a man trying to test him on international affairs: 'Listen, I've read only one newspaper in three years. I figure if things get really tough, they'll sound the siren.'

When mobbed by fans when filming in Athens in 1958:
'I don't know why people collect film stars' signatures—
unless it's because they're free. In most places one goes to
they can't even read.'

To a middle-aged spinster who stopped him to say she'd
seen and loved all his films. A kindly smile and: 'Oh lady,
save your money.'

To a man who asked him how he kept so fit? 'I breathe
in and out all the time. And once in a while I grudgingly
lift something—like a chair.'

In 1955 when returning from a film in France: 'You
look down the Champs Elysées and find that a pretty girl is
one of two things—a prostitute or an American tourist.'

When filming in Italy: 'I ask "What's the next shot?"
and I get a plate of spaghetti. I ask "What are we doing
tomorrow?" and I get another plate of spaghetti. I asked a
cashier what time she got off work, and she gave me spaghetti. Then we went down to Sorrento—a harbor. So we
got spaghetti and barnacles.'

About the movie world: 'People think we go to bed with
every leading lady and they go to the cinema subcon-
sciously hoping they're going to catch us at it. I talked to
Frank Sinatra about this once and he said "Don't let it
worry you. They jerk off. We buy yachts."'

It must be remembered that all such remarks, plus the
hundreds of others that Mitchum has uttered over the
years, are straight off the cuff. And yet they are much
funnier than those made by most professional comedians
who suddenly find themselves without a well-rehearsed
script.

All this, of course, is surface Mitchum. And even in his
wit there is often a defensive quality. Today he's a little
more chary with his remarks, because often they're misunderstood or taken seriously, which gives them a meaning
he didn't intend.

Recently he said 'I take great care now that I'm not offensive or misunderstood—because people have differing areas of humor. I mean, everybody thinks they're playing it straight. I put people on all the time but they go away and say "Aw, what he *really* meant was ..." And they get it wrong. I remember when we lived in Maryland some friend gave me a photograph—Adolf Hitler seated in the back of a big Mercedes touring car and standing up behind him in the back seat giving the Nazi salute was Heydrich, the former Nazi boss of Czechoslovakia, who looked rather like me. And written on it was "Mitch baby, sorry things didn't work the way I planned because we had a ball, but that's show business, Love, Dolf." I had it up in the playroom of the farm and those local people said, "He's got a picture of himself with Adolf Hitler, personally signed." They were quite upset. They didn't understand it was funny, a joke.'

Mitchum doesn't like being seen around Hollywood night spots. He rarely socializes, and the only stars ever to visit his house have been Jack Palance and the late Robert Taylor. He dislikes having to be dignified in public places, never uses the weight of his star name in private life, and hates even giving his name over the phone when booking a restaurant table. As he told Roderick Mann:

'Once in San Francisco I wanted to go to a place called The Blue Fox. They were full up, so I rang Frank Sinatra in Los Angeles and asked him to recommend another place. "Mother," he said. "The Blue Fox is the only place." "It's full," I said. "Don't be ridiculous," he said. "Just go there. It'll be all right." So I went. And of course he'd rung ahead and they'd thrown some people out to make room for me. It made me feel bad. That's not my way. I'm no good either at all the wheeling and dealing that goes on.'

Mitchum, as his wife Dorothy once confirmed, has never wheeled and dealed or curried favor with the film chiefs, even when he was young. Nevertheless, he is today a rich man and worth somewhere in the region of $10 million. His earnings from *Ryan's Daughter* alone total over a million. Apart from owning Talbot Productions into which the healthy salaries and capital from the percentages of his films are paid, Mitchum has interests in industrial properties and buildings, parking lots and a telephone answering service. Movies have allowed him to purchase other interests so that today he is not totally reliant on income from his films.

Mitchum himself takes little personal interest in these ventures, however. He leaves the administration side to a small staff, chief among whom is his woman manager-secretary Reva Fredrick, who confirms: 'He doesn't care to clutter his mind with the nonsensical stuff. It's easier for him to rely on two or three people in whom he puts his total faith. If we say to him "It's a good idea to get X, Y and Z," he says "Go on—do it." He doesn't take an active part in this diversification because that's not his particular style.'

Reva is an ultra-efficient sophisticate who can be as tough as her boss when occasion demands. She has been known to ride herd on Mitchum, to bully him. She is Mitchum's barrier between himself and the world. Anyone who wants to meet, proposition, or even telephone Mitchum must first go through Reva Fredrick. A former actress herself, she was originally a friend of Mitchum's half-sister Carol, and she knew Mitchum only casually then. In the late forties when Mitchum threw a reception for Carol's wedding, they met again. Mitchum, snowed under with paper work after the complications with his previous manager, asked Reva to do some part time secretarial chores. Eventually Reva had so much to do that she gave up her full-time job and went to work permanently for Mitchum.

The way in which Mitchum acquired Reva Fredrick's capable services—meeting her again at the reception he gave for Carol—has some faint significance, in that it gives a clue to the Mitchums' family life. Despite the ups and downs of Mitchum's own life, he and the other members of the family remain in fairly close touch, are immediately ready to hurry and help each other should the occasion arise.

Today Carol, a talented nightclub performer, has remarried and lives with her husband and five children in Skokie, Illinois, where she still occasionally performs in the local clubs and also works for the Ba-hai faith, which she has recently espoused.

Mitchum's mother and his elder sister Julie, who is married to a jewelery executive, live in Scottsdale, Arizona, where they enjoy the equable climate and have homes near each other. Hugh Cunningham-Morris, Mitchum's stepfather, who was 95 at the time of writing, lives permanently in a resthome near to where they live, as he has become totally deaf and at his age needs constant attention. He is still cheerful and able to walk, however, and his wife frequently walks over to see him.

John Mitchum smiles as he speaks of the gentlemanly qualities of his step-father. 'He's a tremendous personality. He still asks mother's permission before he lights up a cigarette. And before he went into the resthome he would insist she stayed in bed while he made breakfast. And he always put fresh flowers on her table to brighten up her day.'

Comparisons between family relatives in any field as capricious as the film world are usually odious because the fame and adulation heaped upon one member as opposed to another are not necesarily a true reflection of their respective talents. While no one would pretend that John Mitchum enjoys the same kind of unique international stardom as his brother, he does have the reputation of being one of the finest character actors in Hollywood. He played Goering to Richard Masehart's Führer in *Hitler*, has had top character roles in films such as *Chisum*, with John Wayne, *El Dorado* with Wayne and his own brother, and he played the Mormon with two wives in *Paint your Wagon*. In the first half of 1971 John had roles in no fewer than five top television shows and three movies.

The brothers remain good friends, and John is in no way envious of Robert's career. 'Frankly, I get embarrassed if anyone comes and asks for my autograph,' he says. 'I have no pressures in the world. I'm happy I can go out and people will say "Haven't I seen you someplace before?" To me it's a great compliment to be only half recognized because if I can play a show and do it convincingly and people remember it and say "Oh, I saw that but I didn't know it was *you*," I know I produced a good job. Robert is embarrassed when people make a big thing out of him being a star. And I don't hanker after that at all.'

John Mitchum's remark about his brother's *type* of stardom has a slight pertinence when one considers Mitchum's own somewhat mellow attitudes today. Talk to people who've worked with Mitchum recently and many will say that what appeals to them most is his combination of masculinity and tenderness. He has always been on the side of the under-dog, for instance. Once when a director fired a crew man, Mitchum said nothing and when the scene was over he returned to his dressing room. But when the director called for shooting to resume, he was told 'Mr Mitchum can't work without a full crew.' The director got the point, sent for the banished man, apologized to him, and filming carried on. This kind of incident is by no means rare. What impresses the lower paid ranks who work on his films is that Mitchum spends more time 'shooting the bull' with them that he does with his peers. While this genuine affection for the under-dog may be a reflection from his own past, it is still rare in a man who has reached Mitchum's stature as a star actor.

Now and again Mitchum has let his guard drop a little. 'The important things to me,' he once said quietly, 'are warmth, shelter and a bed. Many film actors surrender their lives for big white chairs with their names on. They want power, a status symbol. I need a status symbol like I need another armpit. Someone once called me a "masturbation image". Well, that's what we all are, I suppose. Up there on the screen, you're thirty feet wide, your eyeball is six feet high, but it doesn't mean that you really amount to anything or have anything important to say.' There was a slight sadness to him as he said this.

If it irks Mitchum that he's not accorded the kind of respect as an actor that 'classical actors' such as Spencer Tracy, Charles Laughton, and Marlon Brando have enjoyed, he doesn't show it. In fact, he says often he doesn't really care, and it may be true.

One of Mitchum's problems is undoubtedly that he's just too intelligent to find true expression as a movie star. And clearly he hates to feel he's *expected* to take himself seriously, especially in public. His true feelings lie too deep to be excavated ad hoc by a mere interviewer. For a man who left school at fourteen and virtually educated himself, he is extraordinarily well read, and with his prodigious memory can quote accurately from many classics, including the works of obscure American poets such as Nathalia Crane and Mary Austin. His favorite passages usually pertain to the ethical and the lonely. They come from writers as diverse as Shakespeare, Wordsworth, Jefferies, Conrad, and Thomas Wolfe.

Helen Lawrenson was once startled to hear Mitchum quoting a sonnet by Wordsworth:

'The world is too much with us; late and soon,

Getting and spending we lay waste our powers...'

On another occasion he recited this passage complete from Conrad's *Lord Jim*: 'It when we try to grapple with another man's intimate need that we perceive how incomprehensible, wavering and misty are the beings that share with us the sight of the stars and the warmth of the sun. It is as if loneliness were a hard and absolute condition of existence; the envelope of flesh and blood on which our eyes are fixed melts before the outstretched hand, and there remains only the capricious, unconsolable and elusive spirit that no eye can follow, no hand grasp.'

Far from just being able to quote passages such as these —and there are many more—Mitchum will, in the right company, go on to cerebrate on all Conrad's work as well as that of his other favorite writers, and often with such flair, imagination, and insight that he has astounded writers working temporarily in Hollywood on a quick big cash film deal.

Another of his remembered quotations comes from Wolfe's *Look Homeward, Angel*: 'Which of us has known his brother? Which of us has looked into his father's heart? Which of us is not forever a stranger and alone?'

One doesn't presume to read Mitchum's mind, but it's worth remembering that these were the sorts of passages Mitchum admired as a youngster. And in their choice alone there is a reflection of at least one side of his thinking.

His musical knowledge is also considerable. Colleagues have sometimes been surprised to hear Mitchum whistling arias from operas—and then explaining which modern tunes were constructed from them.

One can dredge up snippets of conversations with him from notebooks, all recorded in the last few years:

'As a young man you were a wanderer, so you know something of loneliness. Do you believe a man must master loneliness before he can really know himself?'

He stares at the floor, then says 'All the contradictions in life help supply that, I think, at one age or another. It depends upon the ability of the individual to mature. No, I'm not sure loneliness is necessary. There is no set order or way. Loneliness enhances insight, certainly. Whether one can turn that insight into something positive is something else ... it depends how much time you can afford to waste perhaps. Insight can also make you wastefully hedonistic if you apply it wrongly.'

On the modern permissive era onslaught on the old concepts of marriage:

'Until there's an effective international system of birth control and the legal-moral factor of marriage reaches any new clearly defined level, I think there will evolve a contract of some sort between persons. Up till now marriage has been almost overwhelmingly involved in religion. All major religions are guides to moral health, and to living efficiency. Unfortunately the Church became an institution of power—it's either pay up or go to hell. But almost by necessity there must be a contract of union between two persons. Otherwise the State is stuck with all the book keeping on children and rights and wealth, which will have its abuses—in the incidence of strife, disagreement, in the divorce courts—for the State's lawyers will jump smartly and sharply in; to cut it up, in their different fashions, according to the legal system. This would only mean more bureaucratic interference with the individual.'

On the trivializing influences of much of television and advertising:

'There is thought conditioning on television and in advertising, but it's really trivia. It's got to be all hokey hasn't it? The faster they kid the people, the faster the public catch on. And many young people, for instance, are mostly way ahead of many of those who control television and mass media. So are the negroes—for social change and real

255

equality if not more. If ever television gets over its Clairol syndrome it might help people realize that it is possible to devote as much time to art as to war. Meantime, it is where it rightfully belongs—in the hands of children.

'I agree it's hard for young people to be truly individual today; they are pressured from all sides. But the trivia in mass media separates the men from the boys. A large portion of the people accept and believe this trivia perhaps—and you have a nation largely composed of granny gooses. But you'll have that anyway, just as you get uncreative spoilers and throwbacks in any race or nation.

'The United States is the most materially developed nation in the world, and it has projected itself in time. There is a group of people in their twenties today to whom any marked significant break-through is meaningless, just like the next chapter in a television show. No more than that.'

Mitchum pauses a moment then goes on. 'Not long ago man broke the sound barrier. A great break-through. Then the nuclear fission barrier. Then the space barrier ... Whatever happened to those funny little things like radio which used to thrill us with wonder? It's *all* communications today and it has resulted in a general symposium of thinking hasn't it?

'You can bang information, messages, ideas and news off the satellites today and everyone knows what is happening at the same time. They all see it and hear the same words about it together. It's bound at first to lead to a similar thinking, generally. It doesn't mean it will have to stay that way, nor that what is communicated won't have more value in the future. But at least we're getting an advanced peasantry, aren't we?

'I suppose what we really have to keep pressing for in the individual is true awareness to what is *really* going on. For education and communication of the fine proved values and the true facts. It's the only hope really for ignorance leads to prejudice on all levels. So the youngsters who are wipe-outs—I don't call them cop-outs—the wipe-outs really become aware of what life today is really all about. Rebellion for its own sake only is meaningless. Look at some of this rebellious minority. Their faces show *nothing*. Nada be thy name. Nada, nada. I'm not your son. I'm not your daughter. I'm *me*. I'm nothing. Now may I be old? ... If only they knew what they were talking about and advocating, had some real experience of life.

'Maybe it is an overpublicized minority who behave this way, but it's not only youth who agitate publicly without any real knowledge of life. There are other groups who have purpose and want to achieve their goals with violence. One hope is that they always finally seem to lose individuality and order. And when they eventually *do* learn, they often become very conservative, almost all of them, even the violent groups. What they're doing most of the time is jerking, jerking at our jackets and saying "Look, look at me!" And that's really all. And yet—if you can get some of these youngsters together and really talk to them, many of them will listen.'

It's rare that Mitchum ever opens up like this—and of course one doesn't pretend that these stray quotes delivered impromptu in answers to sudden questions are truly representative of his thinking—but when he's on form Mitchum can put on a dazzling display of verbal pyrotechnics which reveal a remarkably large field of consciousness. And when he does so one gains a momentary glance of the deep thinking man behind the seeming indifference, the normal flip and laconic speech.

Not so long ago the students at the Yale Law School invited him to speak. They ran four of his films over a Saturday and Sunday. It was an honor because they had never invited an actor before. But Mitchum didn't attempt to lecture. He merely talked about making the films and answered questions.

Perhaps this lack of pretension, this reluctance to put himself into a position where he is responsible and deeply involved, where he could conceivably let someone down, is a weak point in his make up. That is, if one judges him as a potential crusader who could communicate some of the lessons learnt in an extraordinary and well rounded life to the younger generation. But why should one? He entertains millions. He is one of the few actors left whose name alone can bring audiences into the cinema. He has more than merely survived and for him maybe that's enough.

Like many basically shy people, Mitchum once took refuge in voracious reading and in writing. Certainly the few of his poems that have leaked out reveal unusual beauty and delicacy—yet he will occasionally spoil them with a four letter word. It's as if he dislikes the presumption of a railroad man's son writing poetry.

Characteristically, Mitchum dismisses such attempts, calling them 'fragments ... private nothings'. He squirms with embarrassment when any of them are published, but bearing in mind they were written when he was younger, they do show a little more of the man.

'What we need above all,' he says, 'are good teachers and good writers. I always wanted to be a writer myself but I guess I'm too lazy—and for me it's too revealing. Besides, it's a little too late.

'Actually, I'm a Utopian anarchist—which means nothing. You know, the intellectuals take over and the government crumbles. I'm a less than convincing dilettante, much less an intellectual. I go to the store for a loaf of bread and come back with a quart of milk. So I act. To compensate for this indignity they put roses in the dressing room on the first day of shooting.'

He smiles wryly and adds: 'I suppose I followed the

course of least resistance really. There are things I should have done and things I'd like to do but I don't have time for them now. And if I don't have time for all of them, then I won't regret not having time for any of them. I'd like to get back to writing some day perhaps ... I don't want to write my autobiography because I feel it would have little value.

'Sometimes I think I ought to go back and try to do at least one thing well. But again, indolence will probably cause me to hesitate about finding a place to start. Part of that indolence perhaps is due to shyness because I'm a natural hermit. I've been in a constant motion of escape all my life. I never really found the right corner to hide in.'

Robert Mitchum is probably the most complex character in the entire international film world. He has always seemed to be engaged in a perpetual battle with himself. It has produced a fascinating iconoclast. Whether the sensitive, worldly-wise and cultured side of his nature will eventually outshine the primordial face he prefers to show the world, only the future will tell. But perhaps a verse he wrote years ago may even today be taken as at least a partial confession:

> With my shamed sad
> hope
> In my tell tale eyes
> And the fleet fears
> trapped within my
> breast
> There is no last mercy
> There are no last lies
> For my sweet dumb
> dreaming is confessed.

Appendix

FILMOGRAPHY

1 HOPPY SERVES A WRIT. United Artists. 1943. William Boyd, Andy Clyde, Jay Kirby, Victor Jory, George Reeves, Jan Christy. (Dir.: George Archainbaud.)

2 THE LEATHER BURNERS. United Artists. 1943. William Boyd, Andy Clyde, Jay Kirby, Victor Jory, George Givot, Shelly Spencer. (Dir.: Joseph E. Henabery.)

3 BORDER PATROL. United Artists. 1943. William Boyd, Jay Kirby, Claudia Drake, Russell Simpson, Duncan Renaldo. (Dir.: Lesley Selander.)

4 FOLLOW THE BAND. Universal. 1943. Leon Errol, Mary Beth Hughes, Eddie Quillan, Skinnay Ennis, Anne Rooney, Samuel S. Hinds. (Dir.: Jean Yarbrough.)

5 COLT COMRADES. United Artists. 1943. William Boyd, Andy Clyde, Jay Kirby, George Reeves, Gayle Lord, Earl Hodgins. (Dir.: Lesley Selander.)

6 THE HUMAN COMEDY. MGM. 1943. Mickey Rooney, James Craig, Frank Morgan, Fay Bainter, Marsha Hunt, Van Johnson, Donna Reed. (Dir.: Clarence Brown.)

7 WE'VE NEVER BEEN LICKED. (British title: TEXAS TO TOKYO.)—Wanger-Universal. 1943. Richard Quine, Noah Beery Jr, Anne Gwynne, Martha O'Driscoll, Samuel S. Hinds, Harry Davenport. (Dir.: John Rawlins.)

8 BEYOND THE LAST FRONTIER. Republic. 1943. Eddie Dew, Smiley Burnette, Lorraine Miller, Richard Clarke, Harry Woods, Ernie Adams. (Dir.: Howard Bretherton.)

9 BAR 20. United Artists. 1943. William Boyd, Andy Clyde, George Reeves, Dustin Farnum, Victor Jory, Douglas Fowley, Betty Blythe. (Dir.: Lesley Selander.)

10 DOUGHBOYS IN IRELAND. Columbia. 1943. Kenny Baker, Jeff Donnell, Lynn Merrick, Guy Bonham, Red Latham, Wamp Carlson. (Dir.: Lew Landers.)

11 CORVETTE K–225. Universal. 1943. Randolph Scott, James Brown, Ella Raines, Barry Fitzgerald, Andy Devine, Richard Lane. (Dir.: Richard Rosson.)

12 THE LONE STAR TRAIL. Universal. 1943. Johnny Mack

Brown, Tex Ritter, Fuzzy Knight, Jennifer Holt, George Eldredge, Harry Strang. (Dir.: Ray Taylor.)

13 FALSE COLOURS. United Artists. 1943. William Boyd, Andy Clyde, Jimmy Rogers, Tom Seidel, Claudia Drake, Douglas Dumbrille. (Dir.: George Archainbaud.)

14 DANCING MASTERS. 20th Century-Fox. 1943. Stan Laurel, Oliver Hardy, Trudy Marshall, Robert Bailey, Matt Briggs, Margaret Dumont. (Dir.: Mal St Clair.)

15 RIDERS OF THE DEADLINE. United Artists, 1943. William Boyd, Andy Clyde, Jimmy Rogers, Richard Crane, Frances Woodward, Tony Ward. (Dir.: Lesley Selander.)

16 GUNG HO! Wanger-Universal. 1943. Randolph Scott, Grace MacDonald, Alan Curtis, Noah Beery Jr, J. Carroll Naish, David Bruce. (Dir.: Ray Enright.)

17 JOHNNY DOESN'T LIVE HERE ANY MORE. Monogram. 1944. James Ellison, Simone Simon, William Terry, Minna Gombell, Chick Chandler, Alan Dinehart. (Dir.: Joe May.)

18 WHEN STRANGERS MARRY (also called BETRAYED). Monogram. 1944. Dean Jagger, Kim Hunter, Neil Hamilton, Lou Lubin, Milt Kibbee, Dewey Robinson. (Dir.: William Castle.)

19 THE GIRL RUSH. RKO. 1944. Wally Brown, Alan Carney, Frances Langford, Vera Vague, Paul Hurst, Patti Brill. (Dir.: Gordon Douglas.)

20 THIRTY SECONDS OVER TOKYO. MGM. 1944. Van Johnson, Robert Walker, Spencer Tracy, Phyllis Thaxter, Tim Murdock, Scott McKay. (Dir.: Mervyn LeRoy.)

21 NEVADA. RKO. 1944. Anne Jeffreys, Guinn 'Big Boy' Williams, Nancy Gates, Richard Martin, Craig Reynolds, Harry Woods. (Dir.: Ed Killy.)

22 WEST OF THE PECOS. RKO. 1945. Barbara Hale, Richard Martin, Thurston Hall, Rita Corday, Russell Hopton, Bill Williams. (Dir.: Ed Killy.)

23 G.I. JOE (also called THE STORY OF G.I. JOE). Cowan-United Artists. 1945. Burgess Meredith, Freddie Steele, Wally Cassell, Jimmy Lloyd, Jack Reilly, Bill Murphy. (Dir.: William Wellman.)

24 TILL THE END OF TIME. RKO. 1946. Dorothy McGuire, Guy Madison, Bill Williams, Tom Tully, William Gargan, Jean Porter. (Dir.: Edward Dmytryk.)

25 UNDERCURRENT. MGM. 1946. Katharine Hepburn, Robert

Taylor, Edmund Gwenn, Marjorie Main, Jayne Meadows, Clinton Sundberg. (Dir.: Vincente Minnelli.)

26 THE LOCKET. RKO. 1946. Laraine Day, Brian Aherne, Gene Raymond, Sharyn Moffet, Ricardo Cortez, Henry Stephenson. (Dir.: John Brahm.)

27 PURSUED. Warner Brothers. 1947. Teresa Wright, Judith Anderson, Dean Jagger, John Rodney, Harry Carey Jr, Clifton Young. (Dir.: Raoul Walsh.)

28 CROSSFIRE. RKO. 1947. Robert Young, Robert Ryan, Gloria Grahame, Paul Kelly, Richard Benedict, Sam Levene. (Dir.: Edward Dmytryk.)

29 DESIRE ME. MGM. 1947. Greer Garson, Richard Hart, George Zucco, Morris Ankrum, Florence Bates, Richard Humphreys. (No final director credit.)

30 OUT OF THE PAST. (British title: BUILD MY GALLOWS HIGH.) RKO. 1947. Jane Greer, Kirk Douglas, Rhonda Fleming, Richard Webb, Steve Brodie, Paul Valentine. (Dir.: Jacques Tourneur.)

31 RACHEL AND THE STRANGER. RKO. 1948. Loretta Young, William Holden, Gary Gray, Tom Tully, Sara Haden, Frank Ferguson. (Dir.: Norman Foster.)

32 BLOOD ON THE MOON. RKO. 1948. Barbara Bel Geddes, Robert Preston, Phyllis Thaxter, Walter Brennan, Frank Faylen, Tom Tully. (Dir.: Robert Wise.)

33 THE RED PONY. Republic. 1949. Myrna Loy, Louis Calhern, Sheppard Strudwick, Peter Miles, Margaret Hamilton, Patty King. (Dir.: Lewis Milestone.)

34 THE BIG STEAL. RKO. 1949. Jane Greer, William Bendix, Patric Knowles, Ramon Novarro, Don Alvarado, Pascual Garcia Pina. (Dir.: Don Siegel.)

35 HOLIDAY AFFAIR. RKO. 1949. Janet Leigh, Wendell Corey, Gordon Gebert, Griff Barnett, Esther Dale, Henry O'Neill. (Dir.: Don Hartman.)

36 WHERE DANGER LIVES. RKO. 1950. Faith Domergue, Claude Rains, Maureen O'Sullivan, Charles Kemper, Harry Shannon, Ralph Dumke. (Dir.: John Farrow.)

37 MY FORBIDDEN PAST. RKO. 1951. Ava Gardner, Melvyn Douglas, Janis Carter, Lucile Watson, Basil Ruysdael, Gordon Oliver. (Dir.: Robert Stevenson.)

38 HIS KIND OF WOMAN. RKO. 1951. Jane Russell, Vincent Price, Tim Holt, Charles McGraw, Raymond Burr, Mar-

jorie Reynolds. (Dir.: John Farrow.)

39 THE RACKET. RKO. 1951. Lizabeth Scott, Robert Ryan, William Talman, Ray Collins, Joyce MacKenzie, Robert Hutton. (Dir.: John Cromwell.)

40 MACAO. RKO. 1952. Jane Russell, William Bendix, Thomas Gomez, Gloria Grahame, Brad Dexter, Ed Ashley. (Dir.: Josef von Sternberg.)

41 ONE MINUTE TO ZERO. RKO. 1952. Ann Blyth, William Talman, Charles McGraw, Margaret Sheridan, Richard Egan, Eduard Franz. (Dir.: Tay Garnett.)

42 THE LUSTY MEN. RKO. 1952. Susan Hayward, Arthur Kennedy, Arthur Hunnicutt, Frank Faylen, Walter Coy, Carol Nugent. (Dir.: Nicholas Ray.)

43 ANGEL FACE. RKO. 1952. Jean Simmons, Mona Freeman, Herbert Marshall, Leon Ames, Barbara O'Neill, Kenneth Tobey. (Dir.: Otto Preminger.)

44 WHITE WITCH DOCTOR. 20th Century-Fox. 1953. Susan Hayward, Walter Slezak, Mashood Ajala, Jos. C. Norcisse, Elzie Emanuel, Timothy Carey. (Dir.: Henry Hathaway.)

45 SECOND CHANCE. RKO. 1953. Linda Darnell, Jack Palance, Sandro Giglio, Rodolfo Hoyes Jr, Reginald Sheffield, Margaret Brewster. (Dir.: Rudy Mate.)

46 SHE COULDN'T SAY NO. (British title: BEAUTIFUL BUT DANGEROUS.) RKO. 1954. Jean Simmons, Arthur Hunnicutt, Edgar Buchanan, Wallace Ford, Raymond Walburn, Jimmy Hunt. (Dir.: Lloyd Bacon.)

47 RIVER OF NO RETURN. 20th Century-Fox. 1954. Marilyn Monroe, Rory Calhoun, Tommy Rettig, Douglas Spencer, Ed. Hinton, Murvyn Vye. (Dir.: Otto Preminger.)

48 TRACK OF THE CAT. Warner Brothers. 1954. Teresa Wright, Tab Hunter, Diana Lynn, Beulah Bondi, Phillip Tonge, Carl Switzer. (Dir.: William Wellman.)

49 NOT AS A STRANGER. United Artists. 1955. Olivia de Havilland, Frank Sinatra, Gloria Grahame, Broderick Crawford, Charles Bickford, Myron McCormick, Lon Chaney, Jesse White, Harry Morgan, Lee Marvin. (Dir.: Stanley Kramer.)

50 THE NIGHT OF THE HUNTER. United Artists. 1955. Shelley Winters, Lillian Gish, Evelyn Varden, Peter Graves, Billy Chapin, Sally Jane Bruce. (Dir.: Charles Laughton.)

51 MAN WITH THE GUN. (British title: THE TROUBLE SHOOTER.)

United Artists. 1955. Jan Sterling, Karen Sharpe, Henry Hull, Emile Meyer, John Lupton, Barbara Lawrence. (Dir.: Richard Wilson.)

52 FOREIGN INTRIGUE. United Artists, 1956. Genevieve Page, Ingrid Thulin, Frederick O'Brady, Eugene Deckers, Ingrid Tidblad, John Padovano, Peter Copley. (Dir.: Sheldon Reynolds.)

53 BANDIDO. United Artists. 1956. Ursula Theiss, Gilbert Roland, Zachary Scott, Rodolfo Acosta, Henry Brandon, Douglas Fowley. (Dir.: Richard Fleischer.)

54 HEAVEN KNOWS, MR ALLISON. 20th Century-Fox. 1957. Deborah Kerr. (Dir.: John Huston.)

55 FIRE DOWN BELOW. Columbia. 1957. Rita Hayworth, Jack Lemmon, Herbert Lom, Bernard Lee, Bonar Colleano, Edric Conner. (Dir.: Robert Parrish.)

56 THE ENEMY BELOW. 20th Century-Fox. 1957. Curt Jurgens, Al Hedison, Theodore Bikel, Russell Collins, Kurt Kreuger, Frank Albertson. (Dir.: Dick Powell.)

57 THUNDER ROAD. United Artists. 1958. Gene Barry, Jacques Aubuchon, Keely Smith, Trevor Bardette, Sandra Knight, Jim Mitchum, Betsy Holt. (Dir.: Arthur Ripley.) Based on Mitchum's own story.

58 THE HUNTERS. 20th Century-Fox. 1958. Robert Wagner, Richard Egan, May Britt, John Gabriel, Lee Phillips, Stacy Harris. (Dir.: Dick Powell.)

59 THE ANGRY HILLS. MGM. 1959. Elisabeth Mueller, Stanley Baker, Gia Scala, Theodore Bikel, Sebastian Cabot, Peter Illing, Leslie Phillips, Donald Wolfit, Marius Goring, Jackie Lane, Kieron Moore, George Pastell. (Dir.: Robert Aldrich.)

60 THE WONDERFUL COUNTRY. United Artists. 1959. Julie London, Gary Merrill, Pedro Armendariz, Jack Oakie, Albert Dekker, Charles McGraw. (Dir.: Robert Parrish.)

61 HOME FROM THE HILL. MGM. 1960. Eleanor Parker, George Peppard, George Hamilton, Everett Sloane, Luana Patten, Anne Seymour. (Dir.: Vincente Minnelli.)

62 THE NIGHT FIGHTERS. (British title: A TERRIBLE BEAUTY.) United Artists. 1960. Anne Heywood, Dan O'Herlihy, Cyril Cusack, Richard Harris, Marianne Benet, Niall MacGinnis. (Dir.: Tay Garnett.)

63 THE GRASS IS GREENER. Universal-International. 1960.

Cary Grant, Deborah Kerr, Jean Simmons, Moray Watson. (Dir.: Stanley Donen.)

64 THE SUNDOWNERS. Warner Brothers. 1960. Deborah Kerr, Peter Ustinov, Glynis Johns, Dina Merrill, Chips Rafferty, Michael Anderson Jr, Lola Brooks, Wylie Watson, Ronald Fraser, John Meillon, Mervyn Johns, Molly Urquhart, Ewen Solon. (Dir.: Fred Zinnemann.)

65 THE LAST TIME I SAW ARCHIE. United Artists. 1961. Jack Webb, Martha Hyer, France Nuyen, Joe Flynn, James Lydon, Del Moore. (Dir.: Jack Webb.)

66 CAPE FEAR. Universal-International. 1962. Gregory Peck, Polly Bergen, Lori Martin, Martin Balsam, Jack Kruschen, Telly Savalas, Barrie Chase. (Dir.: J. Lee Thompson.)

67 THE LONGEST DAY. 20th Century-Fox. 1962. Eddie Albert, Paul Anka, Arletty, Jean-Louis Barrault, Richard Beymer, Bourvil, Richard Burton, Red Buttons, Sean Connery, Ray Danton, Irina Demich, Fabian, Mel Ferrer, Henry Fonda, Steve Forrest, Gert Froebe, Leo Genn, Henry Grace, John Gregson, Paul Hartman, Werner Hinz, Jeffrey Hunter, Curt Jurgens, Alexander Knox, Peter Lawford, Christian Marquand, Roddy McDowall, Sal Mineo, Kenneth More, Edmond O'Brien, Ron Randell, Madeleine Renard, Robert Ryan, Tommy Sands, Rod Steiger, Richard Todd, Tom Tryon, Peter Van Eyck, Robert Wagner, Stuart Whitman, John Wayne. (Dirs: Andrew Marton, Ken Annakin, Bernard Wicki.)

68 TWO FOR THE SEESAW. United Artists. 1962. Shirley Mac-Laine, Edmond Ryan, Elisabeth Fraser, Eddie Firestone, Billy Gray. (Dir.: Robert Wise.)

69 THE LIST OF ADRIAN MESSENGER. Universal-International. 1963. George C. Scott, Dana Wynter, Clive Brook, Kirk Douglas, Frank Sinatra, Burt Lancaster, Tony Curtis. (Dir.: John Huston.)

70 RAMPAGE. Warner Brothers. 1963. Elsa Martinelli, Jack Hawkins, Sabu, Cely Carrillo. (Dir.: Phil Karlson.)

71 MAN IN THE MIDDLE. 20th Century-Fox. 1964. France Nuyen, Barry Sullivan, Trevor Howard, Keenan Wynn, Sam Wanamaker, Alexander Knox, Gary Cockrell, Robert Nicholls. (Dir.: Guy Hamilton.)

72 WHAT A WAY TO GO! 20th Century-Fox. 1964. Shirley MacLaine, Paul Newman, Dean Martin, Dick Van Dyke,

Gene Kelly, Robert Cummings, Lou Nova. (Dir.: J. Lee Thompson.)

73 MR MOSES. United Artists. 1965. Carroll Baker, Alexander Knox, Ian Bannen. (Dir.: Ronald Neame.)

74 THE WAY WEST. United Artists. 1967. Kirk Douglas, Richard Widmark, Lola Albright, Michael Witney, Stubby Kaye, Sally Field. (Dir.: Andrew V. McLaglen.)

75 EL DORADO. Paramount. 1967. John Wayne, James Caan, Charlene Holt, Paul Fix, Arthur Hunnicutt, Michele Carey. (Director-Producer: Howard Hawks.)

76 ANZIO. (British title: THE BATTLE FOR ANZIO.) Columbia. 1967. Peter Falk, Earl Holliman, Mark Damon, Arthur Kennedy, Robert Ryan, Reni Santoni, Joseph Walsh, Thomas Hunter, Giancarlo Giannini, Anthony Steel. (Dir.: Edward Dmytryk.)

77 VILLA RIDES. Paramount. 1968. Yul Brynner, Charles Bronson, Grazia Buccella, Herbert Lom, Robert Viharo, Frank Wolff, Alexander Knox. (Dir.: Buzz Kulick.)

78 5 CARD STUD. Paramount. 1968. Dean Martin, Inger Stevens, Roddy McDowall, Katherine Justice, John Anderson, Ruth Springford, Yaphet Kotto. (Dir.: Henry Hathaway.)

79 SECRET CEREMONY. Universal. 1969. Elizabeth Taylor, Mia Farrow, Pamela Brown, Peggy Ashcroft. (Dir.: Joseph Losey.)

80 YOUNG BILLY YOUNG. United Artists. 1969. Angie Dickinson, Robert Walker, David Carradine, Jack Kelly, John Anderson, Deana Martin. (Dir.: Burt Kennedy.)

81 THE GOOD GUYS AND THE BAD GUYS. Warner Brothers— Seven Arts. 1969. George Kennedy, Martin Balsam, David Carradine, Tina Louise, Douglas V. Fowley, Lois Nettleton. (Dir.: Burt Kennedy.)

82 RYAN'S DAUGHTER. MGM. 1970. Trevor Howard, Christopher Jones, John Mills, Leo McKern, Sarah Miles, Barry Foster, Arthur O'Sullivan, Marie Kean. (Dir.: David Lean.)

83 GOING HOME. MGM. 1972. Brenda Vaccaro, Jan-Michael Vincent, Sylvia Miles, Lou Gilbert, Josh Mostell. (Director-Producer: Herbert B. Leonard.)

84 THE WRATH OF GOD. MGM. 1972. Victor Buono, Rita Hayworth, Paula Pritchett, Frank Langella, John Colicos. (Director-Producer: Ralph Nelson.)

Index

Albright, Lola 204
Aldrich, Robert 164
Alexander, Adolph (Dep. Dist. Atty.) 103, 104
Allen, Irving 160
Allen, Jay (Sgt) 100
Ambrose, Thomas L. (Judge) 100-102
American Legion of Decency 158
Andrews, Dana 191
Armstrong, Louis 15
Austin, Mary 27, 252

Bacall, Lauren 147
Baker, Carroll 197, 198
Baker, Norma Jean (Marilyn Monroe) 59
Bardot, Brigitte 228
Barr, Alva M. (Sgt) 89, 93, 95, 103, 127
Barrymore, John 123
Beal, Charlie 153
Behrmann, Paul 85, 87, 118-120
Belafonte, Harry 161
Belmont Farm 167, 175, 176, 179, 185, 194, 196-200, 202, 203
Berg, Phil 76, 91
Bergman, Ingmar 231

Blackfoot Indians 18, 161, 242
Bogart, Humphrey 81, 147, 148, 233, 247
Bolt, Robert 12, 215, 216, 218
Bordeaux, Nanette 102-5, 114, 127
Bourbon, Ray 54
Brando, Marlon 156, 253
Bridgeport, Connecticut 18, 19, 26, 79
Brynner, Yul 209
Buchwald, Art 191
Burr, Raymond 126

Caldwell, Walter 96, 97
Camden, Delaware 40-2
Camp Roberts, California 74
Capitol Records 161
Cassidy, Hopalong (William Boyd) 12, 66, 67
Castaic Honor Farm 112-116
Castle, William 69
Charleston, South Carolina 17
Chase, Barrie 186
Chatham County Camp, Georgia 36, 37, 186
Churchill, Winston 22
Civilian Conservation Corps 43
Cohen, Mickey 119

Coleman, George 147, 148
Colman, Ronald 81
Confidential Magazine 150-3, 166
Conrad, Joseph 27, 29, 253, 254
Cooper, Gary 72
Cooper, Grant D. (Attorney) 103
Craig, William 89
Crane, Nathalia 27, 253
Crawford, Broderick 146, 147, 190
Cunningham - Morris, Mrs Ann (Robert Mitchum's mother, on her re-marriage in 1927, after the death of Mitchum's father in 1919) 16-20, 22-4, 30, 40, 53, 60, 62, 103, 189, 190, 250, 251
Cunningham - Morris, Carol (Robert Mitchum's half sister) 23, 250
Cunningham - Morris, Hugh (Robert Mitchum's step-father) 21-5, 26-30, 48, 60, 75, 163, 189, 190, 251

Davidson, Bill 33, 121
Davis, Bette 166
Day, Laraine 79
de Havilland, Olivia 126, 147
Diaz, Rudy (Officer) 120, 121
Dmytryk, Edward 80, 82, 209
Dorsey, Jimmy and Tommy 155
Doss, Betty 120
Dougherty, James 59, 141
Douglas, Gordon 71
Douglas, Kirk 179, 180, 200, 203-5
Dover, Delaware 26, 56

Ekberg, Anita 148
Ellis Island 179
Ellis, Richard 86, 119
Evans, Vicki 92, 94, 100-2, 104, 114, 115, 119-21

Farouk, Ex-King 154
Farrow, Mia 211
Fast, Frederick 49, 50
Fears, Peggy 54
Fellows, Bob 148
Fenton-Smith, Basil 160
Film Festival, Cannes 145, 146
Fitzgerald, Charles (Chief Jailor) 112, 115
Folsom Penitentiary 116
Fonda, Henry 192
Ford, Robin 91-4, 99-104, 115, 120
Fort MacArthur 74
Fredrick, Reva (Robert Mitchum's Secretary) 92, 97, 202, 203, 216, 222, 223, 250, 251
Freund, Leo (Judge) 143, 149

Gable, Clark 166, 184
Gardner, Ava 126
Garson, Greer 80, 130
Giesler, Jerry 96, 98, 100-4, 112, 123, 151-3
Gish, Lillian 150
Gorky, Maxim 59
Grant, Cary 181, 182, 229
Greenbaum, Harry 20
Gregory, Paul 151
Grey, Zane 71

Grossman, Herbert (Prosecutor) 86

Haaren High School, New York 24
Hacker, Dr Frederick 87
Hamilton, George 234
Hardy, Oliver 68
Harris, Richard 179, 180
Harrison, Robert 152
Hathaway, Henry 133-5
Hawkins, Jack 193
Hayward, Susan 131-4
Hayworth, Rita 156, 157
Hepburn, Katharine 77, 81
Hess, Colonel Dean E. 163
Heywood, Anne 180
Hitler, Adolf 249
Holden, William 82, 192
Hollywood Women's Press Club 125
Hopper, Hedda 83, 122
Horta, Walter (Dep. Sheriff) 108
Houston, John 157-60, 184, 194, 232, 234
Howard, Trevor 195, 218, 220, 221
Hudson, Rock 163
Hughes, Howard 76, 116, 123-5
Hunter, Kim 69

Jones, Christopher 220
Jurgens, Curt 161

Kelly, Grace 156
Kennedy, Arthur 132
Kennedy, Burt 212
Kennedy, George 214
Kerouac, Jack 32

Kerr, Deborah 157-9, 181-3, 234, 237
Kramer, Stanley 144, 147
Kupcinet, Irv 102

Ladd, Alan 126, 164
Langford, Frances 71
Laughton, Charles 81, 143, 149, 150, 230, 231
Laurel, Stan 68
Lean, David 12, 215, 216, 218-221, 227
Leeds, Lila 88-94, 100, 102-108, 110, 111, 114-116, 119-121
Leigh, Janet 125
Lemmon, Jack 156, 157
LeRoy, Mervyn 68-71, 80
Lockheed Aircraft Plant 58-61, 141, 218
Long Beach Civic Theater 53
Losey, Joseph 210-212
Louis, Joe 129

MacLaine, Shirley 192, 196, 197, 234
March, Hal 192
Martin, Dean 201, 204, 210
Martinelli, Elsa 193
Marvin, Lee 146
Masai, tribes 197, 198
Mature, Victor 71
Mazurki, Mike 72
McGraw, Charles 129
McKern, Leo 220
McKesson, William K. (Judge) 114
McKinnon, J. B. (Sgt) 89, 93
Meredith, Burgess 73
Method, The 229
Miles, Sarah 219, 220
Milestone, Lewis 83

Miller, Arthur 185
Mills, John 220
Mitchum, Chris (Son) 69, 118, 132, 133, 166, 168, 172-177, 183, 194, 200, 206, 221
Mitchum, Mrs Dorothy (Wife) 57-64, 68, 75, 78, 82-87, 94, 96-99, 118, 122, 130, 132, 136, 137, 145, 146, 149, 153, 156, 157, 163, 166-171, 176-178, 181, 194, 195, 199, 200, 202, 203, 206-208, 210, 215, 221-225, 249
Mitchum, James (Father) 17, 18
Mitchum, Jim (Son) 60, 64, 69, 118, 132, 133, 162, 167, 168, 172-174, 187
Mitchum, John (Brother) 18-20, 23, 26, 27, 40-48, 78, 130, 187, 189, 190, 203-205, 251, 252
Mitchum, Julie (Sister) 17, 20, 25, 43, 47, 48, 53, 54, 60, 74, 183, 251
Mitchum, Nancy (Sister-in-law) 130
Mitchum, Trina (Daughter) 132, 166, 168, 177, 183, 194, 200, 208, 210
Monroe, Marilyn 81, 140, 141, 146, 160, 184
Monument Records 204
Murphy, Charlie 66

Nicholls, Mrs Anne 86, 119
Nightingale, Laura 159
Nuyen, France 185
Nye, Clement D. (Judge) 103-106, 108-110

Oscar, The 75, 76, 84, 144, 162, 198

Page, Genevieve 153
Palance, Jack 136, 137, 139, 140, 249
Parsons, Louella 94
Peck, Gregory 148, 149, 186, 192
Poe, Edgar Allan 60
Preminger, Otto 141, 142
Price, Vincent 126
Pyle, Ernie 72, 73

Reid, Wally 99
Rettig, Tommy 141
Reynolds, Bernard B. 128, 129
Rice, Betty 120
Richthofen, Baron von 22
Righter, Carroll 54, 55, 57
Rin Tin Tin 54, 228, 243
Rising Sun, Delaware 39, 42
Robertson, Dale 176
Rooney, Mickey 68
Ross, Frank 71
Rudin, Milton 127
Russell, Jane 126
Ryan, J. N. (Traffic Officer) 142, 143
Ryan, Robert 79, 126

Sagan, Françoise 237
Savannah, Georgia 35, 36, 175, 185, 186
Schoemann, Wanda S. 85, 86
Selznick, David O. 76, 93, 95, 99, 116
Shakespeare, William 27, 253
Shannon, Leonard 79
Shay, Jack 65
Sheridan, Margaret 130

Sherman, Harry 'Pop' 65, 68
Silva, Simone 145, 146
Simmons, Jean 133, 140
Simpson, William E. (Dist. Atty) 118, 119, 121
Sinatra, Frank 146, 161, 162, 196, 197, 244, 248, 249
Skolsky, Sidney 80
Stanislavsky, Mike 59
Stanley, H. Leo (Chief Investigator) 118, 120
Steinbeck, John 83
Sternlight, Mel 79
Stross, Raymond 181
Sullivan, Ed 161

Talbot Productions 176, 184, 216
Taylor, Elizabeth 196, 210, 211, 214
Taylor, Robert 77, 249
Thompson, Charlie 56, 57
Thompson, J. Lee 186, 196
Thulin, Ingrid 153
Tracy, Spencer 234, 253
Tunnin, J. E. (Patrol Officer) 189, 190
Tyre, Norman 96

Viertel, Peter 237
Viet Nam 201, 202, 204-207

Walcott, Jersey Joe 129
Walker, Charlie 204
Wallace, Tim 133, 134
Wayne, John 148, 149, 173, 201, 205, 221, 247, 252
Webb, Jack 185
Webber, Jerry (Attorney) 114
Welles, Orson 54, 162
Wellman, William 72, 73, 76, 144, 147-149, 231
Whitney, Eleanor (Policewoman) 91
Widmark, Richard 203, 205
Wilkins, Paul 63, 64, 66, 165
Willey A. W. 113
Williams, Guinn 'Big Boy' 72
Winters, Shelley 150
Wise, Robert 192
Wolfe, Thomas 27, 253, 254
Woodside, Delaware 18, 23, 30, 40
Wordsworth, William 27, 253

Yale Law School 257
Young, Loretta 82, 126

Zanuck, Darryl F. 135, 187, 188, 191, 196, 197
Zinneman, Fred 182, 231, 234